EPISTEMIC INJUSTICE

In this exploration of new territory between ethics and epistemology, Miranda Fricker argues that there is a distinctively epistemic type of injustice, in which someone is wronged specifically in their capacity as a knower. Justice is one of the oldest and most central themes in philosophy, but in order to reveal the ethical dimension of our epistemic practices the focus must shift to injustice. Fricker adjusts the philosophical lens so that we see through to the negative space that is *epistemic injustice*.

The book explores two different types of epistemic injustice, each driven by a form of prejudice, and from this exploration comes a positive account of two corrective ethical-intellectual virtues. The characterization of these phenomena casts light on many issues, such as social power, prejudice, virtue, and the genealogy of knowledge, and it proposes a virtue epistemological account of testimony. In this ground-breaking book, the entanglements of reason and social power are traced in a new way, to reveal the different forms of epistemic injustice and their place in the broad pattern of social injustice.

Miranda Fricker is Reader in Philosophy at Birkbeck College, University of London.

Epistemic Injustice

Power and the Ethics of Knowing

MIRANDA FRICKER

OXFORD
UNIVERSITY PRESS

OXFORD
UNIVERSITY PRESS

Great Clarendon Street, Oxford OX2 6DP
Oxford University Press is a department of the University of Oxford.
It furthers the University's objective of excellence in research, scholarship,
and education by publishing worldwide in

Oxford New York

Auckland Cape Town Dar es Salaam Hong Kong Karachi
Kuala Lumpur Madrid Melbourne Mexico City Nairobi
New Delhi Shanghai Taipei Toronto
With offices in
Argentina Austria Brazil Chile Czech Republic France Greece
Guatemala Hungary Italy Japan South Korea Poland Portugal
Singapore Switzerland Thailand Turkey Ukraine Vietnam

Oxford is a registered trade mark of Oxford University Press
in the UK and in certain other countries

Published in the United States
by Oxford University Press Inc., New York

ISBN 978-0-19-957052-2

Printed in the United Kingdom by
Lightning Source UK Ltd., Milton Keynes

For K, G, and A

Every volume of moral philosophy contains at least one chapter about justice, and many books are devoted entirely to it. But where is injustice? To be sure, sermons, ... drama, and fiction deal with little else, but art and philosophy seem to shun injustice. They take it for granted that injustice is simply the absence of justice, and that once we know what is just, we will know all we need to know. That belief may not, however, be true. One misses a great deal by looking only at justice. The sense of injustice, the difficulties of identifying the victims of injustice, and the many ways in which we all learn to live with each other's injustices tend to be ignored, as is the relation of private injustice to the public order.

Judith Shklar, *The Faces of Injustice*, 15

Preface

From time to time, ethicists may glance back to the imploded state that philosophical ethics was once in under the positivistic regime of linguistic analysis, and sigh with relief that the subject gradually rediscovered itself. It did so in significant part through a renewed attention to what we may broadly call ethical psychology—that is, to human beings' real experience of ethical value. So a moribund region of philosophy was revivified by a closer attention to lived experience. I sometimes wonder if epistemologists might soon be making a similar retrospective glance back to epistemology as conducted under the regime of conceptual analysis. One could overdo the comparison, but it seems to me that epistemology is gradually being broadened and enlivened, rather as ethics once was, by various efforts to cultivate a closer relationship to actual epistemic practices. This book is a contribution to those efforts, in that it is driven by a sense of the possibilities that open up for epistemology when we take epistemic psychology more seriously—that is, when we take our primary subject matter to be those human practices through which knowledge is gained, or indeed lost. More specifically, my interest is in epistemic practices as they are, of necessity, played out by subjects that are socially situated. This socially situated conception puts questions of social identity and power centre stage, and it is the prerequisite for the revelation of a certain ethical dimension to epistemic life—the dimension of justice and injustice. That is the territory explored in this book.

The exploration is orientated not to justice, but rather to injustice. As Judith Shklar points out, philosophy talks a lot about justice, and very little about injustice. While she is surely wrong to claim the same of art, the point about philosophy is true and deeply significant. In the humanities it is distinctive uniquely of philosophy that it is centrally concerned with rational idealizations of human beings and their activities. Philosophers are very keen to understand what it is to get things right. That's fine; but we should not stop there if we also want to understand the human practices that may only very patchily approximate the rational ideal. The focus on justice creates an impression that justice is the norm and injustice the unfortunate aberration. But, obviously, this may be quite false. It also creates the impression that we should always understand injustice negatively by way of a prior grasp of justice. But, less obviously, the route to understanding may sometimes be the reverse. My interest here is in injustice specifically in the sphere of epistemic activity, and certainly in this sphere I believe that there are areas where injustice is normal, and that the only way to reveal what is involved in epistemic justice (indeed, even to see that there is such a thing as epistemic justice) is by looking at the negative space that is epistemic injustice. This book is an exploration of that negative space.

The material was drafted during research leave from the School of Philosophy at Birkbeck College in conjunction with leave from the Arts and Humanities Research Board, and I am very grateful to both institutions for their support. Some of the basic ideas were originally conceived some years before when I held a British Academy Postdoctoral Fellowship (1997–2000), and I remain grateful to the Academy for that opportunity and privilege. What follows is for the most part published here for the first time, though some of Chapter 3 is a development of the discussion in 'Epistemic Injustice and a Role for Virtue in the Politics of Knowing', *Metaphilosophy*, 34, nos. 1/2 (Jan. 2003), 154–73; reprinted in M. Brady and D. Pritchard (eds.), *Moral and Epistemic Virtues* (Oxford: Blackwell, 2003), 139–58; and Chapters 4 and 6 each contain an echo from 'Rational Authority and Social Power: Towards a Truly Social Epistemology', *Proceedings of the Aristotelian Society*, 98, no. 2 (1998), 159–77. Material mostly from Chapter 7 is published as 'Powerlessness and Social Interpretation', *Episteme*, 3, 1–2 (2006).

I have presented various permutations of the material at research seminars held at the universities of Birmingham, Cambridge, Dundee, Hull, Leeds, Oxford, Sussex, and Warwick, at the LSE and Birkbeck College in the University of London, and at the 2006 annual conference of *Episteme*, which was held at the University of Toronto. I sincerely thank participants on these occasions for their invaluable constructive comments and questions. More particularly, I am very grateful to those colleagues and friends who have been kind enough to read and comment on draft chapters: Jen Hornsby, Susan James, Sabina Lovibond, and Kate Summerscale; and I am especially grateful to Anne Kelleher, Keith Wilson, and to two (then anonymous) readers for Oxford University Press, Chris Hookway and Rae Langton, for their enormously helpful and encouraging comments on full-length drafts. Thank you to Jean van Altena for marvellously careful work on the typescript. And finally, a heartfelt thank you to my editor, Peter Momtchiloff.

Miranda Fricker

Contents

Introduction

This book explores the idea that there is a distinctively epistemic kind of injustice. There are a number of phenomena that might be brought under the general head of epistemic injustice. Given how we normally think about justice in philosophy, the idea of epistemic injustice might first and foremost prompt thoughts about distributive unfairness in respect of epistemic goods such as information or education. In such cases we picture social agents who have an interest in various goods, some of them epistemic, and question whether everyone is getting their fair share. When epistemic injustice takes this form, there is nothing very distinctively epistemic about it, for it seems largely incidental that the good in question can be characterized as an epistemic good. By contrast, the project of this book is to home in on two forms of epistemic injustice that are distinctively epistemic in kind, theorizing them as consisting, most fundamentally, in a wrong done to someone specifically in their capacity as a knower. I call them *testimonial injustice* and *hermeneutical injustice*. Testimonial injustice occurs when prejudice causes a hearer to give a deflated level of credibility to a speaker's word; hermeneutical injustice occurs at a prior stage, when a gap in collective interpretive resources puts someone at an unfair disadvantage when it comes to making sense of their social experiences. An example of the first might be that the police do not believe you because you are black; an example of the second might be that you suffer sexual harassment in a culture that still lacks that critical concept. We might say that testimonial injustice is caused by prejudice in the economy of credibility; and that hermeneutical injustice is caused by structural prejudice in the economy of collective hermeneutical resources.

The overarching aim is to bring to light certain ethical aspects of two of our most basic everyday epistemic practices: conveying knowledge to others by telling them, and making sense of our own social experiences. Since the ethical features in question result from the operation of social power in epistemic interactions, to reveal them is also to expose a politics of epistemic practice. Ideas with a politicizing portent for how we think about our epistemic relations—ideas such as that epistemic trust might have an irrepressible connection with social power, or that social disadvantage can produce unjust epistemic disadvantage—tend not to feature in the context of Anglo-American epistemology. Perhaps they are not featured because they are presumed to be necessarily allied with the relativistic outlook of which postmodernism was the apotheosis, or perhaps simply because the theoretical framework of individualism and compulsory rational idealization that epistemology traditionally creates for itself makes it very hard to see how such questions might have a bearing on epistemology proper. Whatever the explanation, it is an impetus of this book that epistemology as it has traditionally been pursued has been impoverished by the lack of any theoretical framework conducive to revealing the ethical and political aspects of our epistemic conduct. Within the Anglo-American tradition, feminist epistemology has been rather a solitary voice as it bravely insisted on this point, though I hope to show that virtue epistemology provides a general epistemological idiom in which these issues can be fruitfully discussed.

One finds a similar blind spot in ethics, and it does seem equally a pity that ethics has not traditionally taken our epistemic conduct into its remit. In the ethics case, however, the inattention to the rights and wrongs of our epistemic lives seems more contingent and not conducive to any special diagnostic comment beyond the general observation that there has been a historical preoccupation with the second-order. One way or another, given the traditional background, this book is neither straightforwardly a work of ethics nor straightforwardly a work of epistemology; rather, it renegotiates a stretch of the border between these two regions of philosophy.

A philosophical literature that did seem, notably to many feminist philosophers, to promise a theoretical space in which to investigate the ethics and politics of our epistemic practices was that of postmodernism. A crucial attraction of postmodernist philosophical thought was that it placed reason and knowledge firmly in the context of social power. Age-old worries about the authority of reason gained a new, seemingly radicalizing theoretical context in which they could be played out in a more political key. But this turned out to be largely a vain hope, for the extremist bent in so much postmodernist writing led too often to reductionism, and the driving force behind the postmodernist spirit emerged as more a matter of disillusionment with untenable ideals of reason than any real will to bring questions of justice and injustice to bear in reason's entanglements with social power.[1] Suspicion of the category of reason *per se* and the tendency to reduce it to an operation of power actually pre-empt the very questions one needs to ask about how power is affecting our functioning as rational subjects; for it eradicates, or at least obscures, the distinction between what we have a reason to think and what mere relations of power are doing to our thinking. If one has an interest in how questions of justice might present themselves in relation to our epistemic practices, then the reductionist tendency obscures essential distinctions between, say, rejecting someone's word for good reason and rejecting it out of mere prejudice. Far from opening up theoretical space in which to explore questions of justice and power in epistemic practices, then, postmodernism effectively pre-empted such questions, and so what it had to say of an epistemological bearing did not ultimately lead in a progressive direction at all, but was if anything orientated towards conservatism.

But we must not allow there to be mere silence where there was once a postmodernist buzz, for we can surely find other, better ways of discussing reason's entanglements with social power. What form, we might ask, should such discussion take? One answer to this question is that it should take the form of asking first-order ethical questions in the context of socially situated accounts of our epistemic practices.[2] A socially situated account of a human practice is an account such that the participants are conceived not in abstraction from relations of social power (as they are in traditional epistemology, including most social epistemology) but as operating as social types who stand in relations of power to one another. This socially situated conception makes questions of power and its sometimes rational, sometimes counter-rational rhythms arise naturally as we try to account for the epistemic practice itself. Many philosophical questions may be best served by the traditional, maximally abstracted conception of the human subject, but confining oneself to that conception restricts the sorts of philosophical questions and insights one can come up with, so that the philosophical repertoire

---

[1] I have argued for these claims in 'Pluralism without Postmodernism', in M. Fricker and J. Hornsby (eds.), *The Cambridge Companion to Feminism in Philosophy* (Cambridge: Cambridge University Press, 2000).

[2] 'Socially situated': this term is widely used in feminist philosophy, but the first use that I am aware of is by Donna Haraway ('Situated Knowledges: The Science Question in Feminism and the Privilege of Partial Perspective', *Feminist Studies*, 14, no. 3 (1988), 575–99; repr. in Evelyn Fox Keller and Helen Longino (eds.), *Feminism and Science* (Oxford: Oxford University Press, 1996).

incurs a needless impoverishment. Starting from the socially situated conception, by contrast, allows us to trace some of the interdependencies of power, reason, and epistemic authority in order to reveal the ethical features of our epistemic practices that are integral to those practices. Ultimately, the point is to see how our epistemic conduct might become at once more rational and more just.

Throughout the book I make use of the concept of social power, and so my first task in Chapter 1 is to define a working conception. The conception I arrive at is fairly broad, and the core idea is that power is a socially situated capacity to control others' actions. I then introduce a subspecies of social power that I call *identity power*—a form of social power which is directly dependent upon shared social-imaginative conceptions of the social identities of those implicated in the particular operation of power. The rest of Chapter 1 is devoted to presenting the main idea of the book, in that it characterizes the primary form of epistemic injustice: *testimonial injustice*. The basic idea is that a speaker suffers a testimonial injustice just if prejudice on the hearer's part causes him to give the speaker less credibility than he would otherwise have given. Since prejudice can take different forms, there is more than one phenomenon that comes under the concept of testimonial injustice. I introduce the notion of *identity prejudice* as a label for prejudices against people *qua* social type, and this allows me to home in on the central case of testimonial injustice: the injustice that a speaker suffers in receiving deflated credibility from the hearer owing to identity prejudice on the hearer's part, as in the case where the police don't believe someone because he is black. Thus the central case of testimonial injustice can be defined (if rather telegraphically) as *identity-prejudicial credibility deficit*. This definition captures the kind of testimonial injustice that is connected with other forms of social injustice that the subject is likely to suffer, and that is what makes it the central case—it is central from the point of view of revealing the place of epistemic injustice in the broader pattern of social injustice.

Chapter 2 takes up the question of how identity prejudice gets into hearers' judgements of speakers' credibility, often despite, rather than because of, their beliefs. I suggest that such prejudices typically enter into a hearer's credibility judgement by way of the social imagination, in the form of a prejudicial stereotype—a distorted image of the social type in question. And I make an initial proposal (the full argument for which is given in Chapter 3) to the effect that a spontaneous credibility judgement is a matter of the hearer *perceiving* her interlocutor as credible to this or that degree, so that when prejudice enters in, it ordinarily does so by way of a prejudicial stereotype distorting this epistemically loaded social perception.

Any claim of injustice must rely on shared ethical intuition, but we achieve a clearer idea of why something constitutes an injustice if we can analyse the nature of the wrong inflicted. The analysis I give of the wrong done to the speaker in testimonial injustice relates it to the wrong done in epistemic injustice taken generally: any epistemic injustice wrongs someone in their capacity as a subject of knowledge, and thus in a capacity essential to human value; and the particular way in which testimonial injustice does this is that a hearer wrongs a speaker in his capacity as a giver of knowledge, as an informant. I argue that the primary harm one incurs in being wronged in this way is an intrinsic injustice. Clearly, this harm may go more or less deep in the psychology of the subject, and I explore the idea that, where it goes deep, it can cramp self-development, so that a person may be, quite literally, prevented from becoming who they are.

In Chapter 3 I situate the phenomenon of testimonial injustice in the epistemology of testimony. A non-inferentialist position is developed in a virtue epistemological frame by way of a parallel between the hearer's perception of the speaker and the moral cognitivist conception of the virtuous person as endowed with a capacity for moral perception. I argue that just as the moral subject is depicted as perceiving the world in a morally charged way, so the virtuous hearer in a testimonial exchange perceives her interlocutor in an epistemically charged way—she perceives him as credible to this or that degree. The idea of a *testimonial sensibility* is introduced as a form of rational sensitivity that is socially inculcated and trained by countless experiences of testimonial exchange, individual and collective. This real-life training instils in the virtuous hearer empirically well-grounded habits of epistemically charged social perception, and thus reliable perceptual judgements of speaker credibility. But our predicament as hearers is that even if we are personally innocent of prejudiced beliefs, still the social atmosphere in which we must judge speakers' credibility is one in which there are inevitably many stray residual prejudices that threaten to influence our credibility judgements; so the primary conception of the virtuous hearer must be that of someone who reliably succeeds in correcting for the influence of prejudice in her credibility judgements. With the general conception of a virtuous hearer in place, I go on, in Chapter 4, to present one testimonial virtue in particular: namely, the virtue of *testimonial justice*—a virtue such that the influence of identity prejudice on the hearer's credibility judgement is detected and corrected for. The genealogical origins of this virtue are then traced in Chapter 5. Using first Bernard Williams's and then Edward Craig's epistemic State of Nature stories, I argue that testimonial justice emerges in the State of Nature as an original 'virtue of truth'.[3] The structure of the virtue is then specified, and the virtue is revealed as hybrid in kind: both intellectual and ethical.

In Chapter 6 I revisit the question of the wrong that testimonial injustice inflicts, this time examining it through the lens of the State of Nature story about the origins of the concept of knowledge. I argue that we can understand the wrong in terms of *epistemic objectification*, and I explain that notion by way of a parallel with a feminist conception of sexual objectification and the associated phenomenon of 'silencing'. I then argue that it follows from Craig's practical explication of the concept of knowledge that the wrong of testimonial injustice cuts conceptually deeper than anything we had so far envisaged: a matter of exclusion from the very practice that constitutes the practical core of what it is to know.

Finally, Chapter 7 addresses the second kind of epistemic injustice that I want to explore: *hermeneutical injustice*. A central case of this sort of injustice is found in the example of a woman who suffers sexual harassment prior to the time when we had this critical concept, so that she cannot properly comprehend her own experience, let alone render it communicatively intelligible to others. I explain this sort of epistemic injustice as stemming from a gap in collective hermeneutical resources—a gap, that is, in our shared tools of social interpretation—where it is no accident that the cognitive disadvantage created by this gap impinges unequally on different social groups. Rather, the unequal disadvantage derives from the fact that members of the group that is most disadvantaged by the gap are, in some degree, *hermeneutically marginalized*—that is, they participate unequally in the practices through which social meanings are generated. This sort of marginalization can mean that our collective forms of understanding are rendered structurally prejudicial in respect of content and/or style: the social experiences of members of hermeneutically marginalized groups are left inadequately conceptualized and so ill-understood, perhaps even by the subjects themselves; and/or attempts at communication made by such

---

[3] 'Virtue of truth' is Bernard Williams's phrase; see *Truth and Truthfulness: An Essay in Genealogy* (Princeton: Princeton University Press, 2002), 11 and *passim*.

groups, where they do have an adequate grip on the content of what they aim to convey, are not heard as rational owing to their expressive style being inadequately understood. As in the discussion of testimonial injustice, I offer a characterization of the wrong done to the person involved. The nature of the primary harm caused by hermeneutical injustice is analysed as a matter of someone suffering from a *situated hermeneutical inequality*: their social situation is such that a collective hermeneutical gap prevents them in particular from making sense of an experience which it is strongly in their interests to render intelligible.

While hermeneutical injustice is not perpetrated by individuals, it will normally make itself apparent in discursive exchanges between individuals. There is therefore something to be said about what virtue is called for on the part of the hearer. She cannot be blamed for a certain initial lack of trust that she may feel towards the testimony of someone whose communicative labours are hampered by hermeneutical injustice, since some such lack of trust is epistemically justified—both speaker and hearer are labouring with the same inadequate tools. But the epistemic goal of understanding would none the less be served by an intellectual virtue of *hermeneutical justice* being incorporated into the hearer's testimonial sensibility. This virtue is such that the hearer exercises a reflexive critical sensitivity to any reduced intelligibility incurred by the speaker owing to a gap in collective hermeneutical resources. That is, he is alert to the possibility that her relative unintelligibility to him is a function of a collective hermeneutical impoverishment, and he adjusts or suspends his credibility judgement accordingly. On the face of it, this virtue is intellectual and not ethical. But I argue that the virtue reveals itself also to be an ethical virtue. Like testimonial justice, the virtue of hermeneutical justice is a hybrid.

The main aim of the book is to characterize two forms of epistemic injustice: testimonial injustice, in which someone is wronged in their capacity as a giver of knowledge; and hermeneutical injustice, in which someone is wronged in their capacity as a subject of social understanding. I think that there is a lot to be gained philosophically by concentrating on the normality of injustice, and one of the gains might be that we achieve a better grasp of what is required in practice to operate in a way that works against it. This hope is what inspires the discussion of the two corrective ethical-intellectual virtues, virtues which stand to improve our lives as both subjects and objects of knowledge. There is a limit, of course, to what virtues on the part of individuals can achieve when the root cause of epistemic injustice is structures of unequal power and the systemic prejudices they generate. Eradicating these injustices would ultimately take not just more virtuous hearers, but collective social political change—in matters of epistemic injustice, the ethical is political. Still, this simply underlines the fact that testimonial and hermeneutical injustice must first be explored as ethical problems, for that is what they most fundamentally are. In terms of our philosophical understanding of these phenomena, the political depends upon the ethical.

1

Testimonial Injustice

In Anthony Minghella's screenplay of *The Talented Mr Ripley*, Herbert Greenleaf uses a familiar put-down to silence Marge Sherwood, the young woman who [but for the sinister disappearance of his son, Dickie, was soon to have become his daughter-in-law: 'Marge, there's female intuition, and then there are facts.]¹ Greenleaf is responding to Marge's expressed suspicion that Tom Ripley—a supposed friend of Dickie and Marge, who has curried much favour with Greenleaf senior—is in fact Dickie's murderer. It is easy to see that Greenleaf's silencing of Marge here involves an exercise of power, and of gender power in particular. But what do we mean by power? And how does gender power relate to the general notion of social power? In order to paint a portrait of testimonial injustice and to home in on its distinctive central case, we need to answer these questions about the nature of social power in general and the particular kind of social power (of which gender power is one instance) that I shall call *identity power*.

1.1 POWER

Let us begin from what I take to be the strongly intuitive idea that social power is a capacity we have as social agents to influence how things go in the social world. A first point to make is that power can operate *actively* or *passively*. Consider, for example, the power that a traffic warden has over drivers, which consists in the fact that she can fine them for a parking offence. Sometimes this power operates actively, as it does when she actually imposes a fine. But it is crucial that it also operates passively, as it does whenever her ability to impose such a fine influences a person's parking behaviour. There is a relation of dependence between active and

¹ Anthony Minghella, *The Talented Mr Ripley—Based on Patricia Highsmith's Novel* (London: Methuen, 2000), 130.

passive modes of power, for its passive operation will tend to dwindle with the dwindling of its active operation: unless a certain number of parking fines are actively doled out, the power of traffic wardens passively to influence our parking behaviour will also fade. A second point is that, since power is a capacity, and a capacity persists through periods when it is not being realized, power exists even while it is not being realized in action. Consider our traffic warden again. If a driver, in a crazy state of urban denial, pays no heed one afternoon to what traffic wardens can do, parking wantonly on red lines and double yellow lines entirely without constraint, then we have a situation in which the traffic warden's power is (*pro tem*) quite inoperative—it is idling. But it still exists. This should be an unproblematic metaphysical point, but it is admittedly not without dissenters, for Foucault famously claims that 'Power exists only when it is put into action'.[2] We should, however, reject the claim, because it is incompatible with power's being a capacity, and because even in the context of Foucault's interests, the idea that power is not a capacity but rather pops in and out of existence as and when it is actually operative lacks motivation. The nearby Foucauldian commitment to a metaphysically light conception of power, and the idea that power operates in a socially disseminated, 'net-like' manner do not depend on it, as we shall see.

So far, we have been considering power as a capacity on the part of social agents (individuals, groups, or institutions) exercised in respect of other social agents. This sort of power is often called 'dyadic', because it relates one party who is exercising power to another party whose actions are duly influenced. But since it might equally be pictured as influencing many parties (the traffic warden's power as constraining all drivers in the area), I shall focus on what is essential: namely, that this sort of power is exercised by an agent. So let us call it *agential* power. By contrast, power can also operate *purely structurally*, so that there is no particular agent exercising it. Consider, for instance, the case where a given social group is informally disenfranchised in the sense that, for whatever complex social reasons, they tend not to vote. No social agent or agency in particular is excluding them from the democratic process, yet they are excluded, and their exclusion marks an operation of social power. It seems in such a case that the power influencing their behaviour is so

---

[2] Michel Foucault, 'How Is Power Exercised?', trans. Leslie Sawyer from Afterword in H. L. Dreyfus and P. Rabinow, *Michel Foucault: Beyond Structuralism and Hermeneutics* (Hemel Hempstead: Harvester Press, 1982), 219.

thoroughly dispersed through the social system that we should think of it as lacking a subject. Foucault's work presents historical examples of power operating in purely structural mode. When he describes the kind of power at work in historical shifts of institutionalized discursive and imaginative habits—as when a practice of categorizing certain criminals as 'delinquents' emerges as part of a professionalized medical-legal discourse[3]—he illustrates some of the ways in which power can operate purely structurally. These sorts of changes come about as the result of a system of power relations operating holistically, and are not helpfully explained in terms of particular agents' (persons' or institutions') possession or non-possession of power. Further, in purely structural operations of power, it is entirely appropriate to conceive of people as functioning more as the 'vehicles'[4] of power than as its paired subjects and objects, for in such cases the capacity that is social power operates without a subject—the capacity is disseminated throughout the social system. Let us say, then, that there are agential operations of social power exercised (actively or passively) by one or more social agents on one or more other social agents; and there are operations of power that are purely structural and, so to speak, subjectless.

Even in agential operations of power, however, power is already a structural phenomenon, for power is always dependent on practical co-ordination with other social agents. As Thomas Wartenberg has argued, (what he calls) dyadic power relationships are dependent upon co-ordination with 'social others', and are in that sense 'socially situated'.[5] The point that power is socially situated might be made in a quite general way as a matter of the importance of social context taken as a whole: any operation of power is dependent upon the context of a functioning social world—shared institutions, shared meanings, shared

---

[3] 'Now the "delinquent" makes it possible to join [two figures constructed by the penal system: the moral or political "monster" and the rehabilitated juridical subject] and to constitute under the authority of medicine, psychology or criminology, an individual in whom the offender of the law and the object of scientific technique are superimposed' (Foucault, *Discipline and Punish: The Birth of the Prison*, trans. Alan Sheridan (London: Penguin Books, 1977), 256; originally published in French as *Naissance de la prison* by Editions Gallimard, 1975).

[4] '[Individuals] are always in the position of simultaneously undergoing and exercising this power. ... In other words, individuals are the vehicles of power, not its points of application' (*Michel Foucault, Power/Knowledge: Selected Interviews and Other Writings 1972–1977*, ed. C. Gordon, trans. C. Gordon, L. Marshall, J. Mepham, and K. Soper (Hemel Hempstead: Harvester Wheatsheaf, 1980), 198).

[5] Thomas E. Wartenberg, 'Situated Social Power', in T. Wartenberg (ed.), *Rethinking Power* (Albany, NY: State University of New York Press, 1992), 79–101.

expectations, and so on. But Wartenberg's point is more specific than that, since he argues that any given power relationship will also have a more significant, direct dependence on co-ordination with the actions of some social others in particular. He presents the example of the power that a university teacher has over her students in grading their work. This power is of course broadly dependent upon the whole social context of university institutions and systems of grading, and so on. But it is also more directly dependent upon co-ordination with the actions of a narrow class of social others: for instance, the potential employers who take notice of grades. Without this co-ordination with the actions of a specific group of other social agents, the actions of the teacher would have no influence upon the behaviour of the students, for her gradings would have no bearing on their prospects. Co-ordination of that more specific kind constitutes the requisite social 'alignment' on which any given power relation directly depends. Or rather, the social alignment is partly constitutive of the power relation.

Wartenberg's point is clearly right. It also helps one see what is right about the Foucauldian idea that power is to be understood as a socially disseminated 'net-like organisation'—even while it may equally lead one to reject as a piece of exaggeration his claim that power is 'never in anybody's hands'.[6] The individual teacher indeed possesses the power to grade the student; but her power is directly dependent upon practical co-ordination with a range of social others. She possesses her power, if you like, in virtue of her place in the broader network of power relations. Now, the mere idea of such practical co-ordination is thoroughly generic, applying to the power required to get anything at all done in the social world—my power to cash a cheque is dependent on practical co-ordination with the cashier at the bank and a range of other social agents. But we are trying to establish a conception of something called 'social power', which is on anybody's reckoning more specific than the mere notion of 'social ability' (such as is involved in my cashing a cheque). What, then, is distinctive of social power? The classical response to this question is to say that power involves the thwarting of someone's objective interests.[7] But this seems an unduly narrow and

---

6 '[Power] is never localised here or there, never in anybody's hands, never appropriated as a commodity or piece of wealth. Power is employed and exercised through a net-like organisation. And not only do individuals circulate between its threads; they are always in the position of simultaneously undergoing and exercising this power' (Foucault, *Power/Knowledge*, 98).

7 See Steven Lukes, *Power: A Radical View* (London: Macmillan, 1974).

negative conception of power, for there are many operations of power that do not go against anyone's interests—in grading their work the university teacher need not thwart her students' interests. Wartenberg's response to the question is to say that what makes the teacher's ability to grade her students' work a matter of social power is that the student encounters it 'as having control over certain things that she might either need or desire'.[8]

This way of putting it is appropriate for many agential relations of power; but the present aim is to establish a working conception of social power that is sufficiently broad to cover not only agential but also purely structural operations of power, and Wartenberg's idea of social alignment is not designed to do this. However, I believe that there is such a conception available, and that the notion of control, in slightly more generic guise, remains essential. The fundamental feature of social power that Wartenberg's notion of social alignment reflects is that the point of any operation of social power is *to effect social control*, whether it is a matter of particular agents controlling what other agents do or of people's actions being controlled purely structurally. In agential relations of power, one party controls the actions of another party or parties. In purely structural operations of power, though the power has no subject, it always has an object whose actions are being controlled—the disenfranchised group in our example of informal disenfranchisement, the 'delinquents' of Foucault's *Discipline and Punish*. In such cases there is always a social group that is properly described as being controlled, even while that control has no particular agent behind it, for purely structural operations of power are always such as to create or preserve a given social order. With the birth of the 'delinquent', a certain subject position is created as the subject matter for a certain professionalized theoretical discourse; with the disenfranchisement of a given social group, the interests of that group become politically expendable.

Putting all this together, I propose the following working conception of social power:

a practically socially situated capacity to control others' actions, where this capacity may be exercised (actively or passively) by particular social agents, or alternatively, it may operate purely structurally.

Although we tend to use the notion of social power as a protest concept—on the whole, we cry power only when we want to object—the

---

[8] Wartenberg, 'Situated Social Power', 89.

proposed conception reflects the fact that the very idea of social power is in itself more neutral than this, though it is never so neutral as the mere idea of social ability. It is right, then, to allow that an exercise of power need not be bad for anyone. On the other hand, placing the notion of control at its centre lends the appropriate critical inflection: wherever power is at work, we should be ready to ask who or what is controlling whom, and why.

1.2 IDENTITY POWER

So far the kind of social co-ordination considered has been a matter of purely practical co-ordination, for it is simply a matter of co-ordination with others' actions. But there is at least one form of social power which requires not only practical social co-ordination but also an *imaginative* social co-ordination. There can be operations of power which are dependent upon agents having shared conceptions of social identity—conceptions alive in the collective social imagination that govern, for instance, what it is or means to be a woman or a man, or what it is or means to be gay or straight, young or old, and so on. Whenever there is an operation of power that depends in some significant degree upon such shared imaginative conceptions of social identity, then *identity power* is at work. Gender is one arena of identity power, and, like social power more generally, identity power can be exercised actively or passively. An exercise of gender identity power is active when, for instance, a man makes (possibly unintended) use of his identity as a man to influence a woman's actions—for example, to make her defer to his word. He might, for instance, patronize her and get away with it in virtue of the fact that he is a man and she is a woman: 'Marge, there's female intuition, and then there are facts'—as Greenleaf says to Marge in *The Talented Mr Ripley*.[9] He silences her suspicions of the murderous Ripley by exercising identity power, the identity power he inevitably has as a man over her as a woman. Even a flagrant active use of identity power such as this can be unwitting—the story is set in the Fifties, and Greenleaf is ingenuously trying to persuade Marge to take what he regards as a more objective view of the situation, a situation which he correctly sees as highly stressful and emotionally charged for her. He may not be aware that he is using gender to silence Marge, and

---

[9] Minghella, *The Talented Mr Ripley*, 130.

what he does is perhaps well-intentioned and benevolently paternal. But it is no less an exercise of identity power.

Greenleaf's exercise of identity power here is active, in that he performs an action which achieves the thing he has the power to do: silence Marge. He pulls it off by effectively invoking a collective conception of femininity as insufficiently rational because excessively intuitive.[10] But in another social setting a man might not need to *do* anything to silence her. She might already be silenced by the mere fact that he is a man and she a woman. Imagine a social context in which it is part of the construction of gender not merely that women are more intuitive than rational, but, further, that they should never pitch their word against that of a man. In that sort of social situation, a Herbert Greenleaf would have exercised the same power over a Marge—his power as a man to silence her as a woman—but passively. He would have done it, so to speak, just by being a man. Whether an operation of identity power is active or passive, it depends very directly on imaginative social co-ordination: both parties must share in the relevant collective conceptions of what it is to be a man and what it is to be a woman, where such conceptions amount to stereotypes (which may or may not be distorting ones) about men's and women's respective authority on this or that sort of subject matter. Note that the operation of identity power does not require that either party consciously accept the stereotype as truthful. If we were to interpret Marge as thoroughly aware of the distorting nature of the stereotype used to silence her, it would still be no surprise that she should be silenced by it. The conceptions of different social identities that are activated in operations of identity power need not be held at the level of belief in either subject or object, for the primary *modus operandi* of identity power is at the level of the collective social imagination. Consequently, it can control our actions even despite our beliefs.

Identity power typically operates in conjunction with other forms of social power. Consider a social order in which a rigid class system imposes an asymmetrical code of practical and discursive conduct on members of different classes, so that, for instance, once upon a time (not so long ago) an English 'gentleman' might have accused a 'member

_____

[10] For an argument to the effect that intuition is not in general a source of cognitive failing but rather an essential cognitive resource, see my 'Why *Female* Intuition?', *Women: A Cultural Review*, 6, no. 2 (Autumn 1995), 234–48; a shorter version of which appears as 'Intuition and Reason', *Philosophical Quarterly*, 45, no. 179 (Apr. 1995), 181–9, without the discussion of female intuition in particular.

of the working classes' of 'impudence', or 'insolence', or 'cheek', if he spoke to him in a familiar manner. In such a society the gentleman might exercise a plain material power over the man by, say, having him sacked (maybe he was a tradesman from a company that needed the gentleman's patronage); but this might be backed up and imaginatively justified by the operation of identity power (the social conception of him as a gentleman and the other as a common tradesman is part of what explains his capacity to avenge the other's 'impudence'). The gentleman's identity carries with it a set of assumptions about how gentlemen are to be treated by different social types, and in virtue of these normative trappings the mere identity category 'gentleman' can reinforce the exercise of more material forms of social power. The identity power itself, however, is something non-material—something wholly discursive or imaginative, for it operates at the level of shared conceptions of what it is to be a gentleman and what it is to be a commoner, the level of imagined social identity. Thus identity power is only one facet of social identity categories pertaining to, say, class or gender, since such categories will have material implications as well as imaginative aspects.

Could there be a purely structural operation of identity power? There could; indeed, identity power often takes purely structural form. To take up our disenfranchisement example again, we can imagine an informally disenfranchised group, whose tendency not to vote arises from the fact that their collectively imagined social identity is such that they are not the sort of people who go in for political thinking and discussion. 'People like us aren't political'; and so they do not vote. Conversely, we can imagine that among those groups that do vote, identity power plays its part here too. Part of what encourages many of us to vote is a social self-conception in the collective imagination such that 'People like us are politically engaged'. Identity power, like social power in general, may be agential or purely structural; it may work positively to produce action or negatively to constrain it; and it may work in the interests of the agent whose actions are so controlled, or again it may work against them.

The reason for our particular interest in identity power is that we shall be concerned with how it is involved in the sort of discursive exchange in which knowledge can be imparted from speaker to hearer—in the broadest sense, testimonial exchange. I shall argue that identity power is an integral part of the mechanism of testimonial exchange, because of the need for hearers to use social stereotypes as heuristics in their spontaneous assessments of their interlocutor's credibility. This use of stereotypes may be entirely proper, or it may be misleading, depending on the stereotype. Notably, if the stereotype embodies a prejudice that works against the speaker, then two things follow: there is an epistemic dysfunction in the exchange—the hearer makes an unduly deflated judgement of the speaker's credibility, perhaps missing out on knowledge as a result; and the hearer does something ethically bad—the speaker is wrongfully undermined in her capacity as a knower. I now turn to the exploration of this dual epistemic and ethical dysfunction. The task is to home in on what is perhaps the most ethically and socially significant moment of identity power's impact on our discursive and epistemic relations, and to paint a portrait of the distinctive injustice that it entails: *testimonial injustice*.

1.3 THE CENTRAL CASE OF TESTIMONIAL INJUSTICE

Broadly speaking, prejudicial dysfunction in testimonial practice can be of two kinds. Either the prejudice results in the speaker's receiving more credibility than she otherwise would have—a *credibility excess*—or it results in her receiving less credibility than she otherwise would have—a *credibility deficit*. Consider the immediate discursive impact of a speaker's accent, for instance. Not only does accent carry a social charge that affects how a hearer perceives a speaker (it may indicate a certain educational/class/regional background), but very often it also carries an epistemic charge. Accent can have a significant impact on how much credibility a hearer affords a speaker, especially in a one-off exchange. I do not mean that someone's accent is especially likely to lead a hearer, even an intensely prejudiced one, automatically to reject outright some manifestly believable assertion or, conversely, to firmly believe some otherwise incredible assertion. No doubt these things are possible, but given that for the most part it is generally in the interests of hearers to believe what is true and not believe what is false, it would be a strong prejudice in an unusual context that would be single-handedly powerful enough to have that sort of effect. The idea is rather that prejudice will tend surreptitiously to inflate or deflate the credibility afforded the speaker, and sometimes this will be sufficient to cross the threshold for belief or acceptance so that the hearer's prejudice causes him to miss out on a piece of knowledge.

In face-to-face testimonial exchanges the hearer must make some attribution of *credibility* regarding the speaker.[11] Such attributions are surely governed by no precise science, but clearly there can be error in the direction of excess or deficit.[12] On the whole, excess will tend to be advantageous, and deficit disadvantageous. As a qualification, however, we should note that in localized contexts excess could bring disadvantage in its wake, and deficit could conceivably bring advantage. With regard to the former, consider an overburdened GP whose patients ask him medical questions that call for a more specialist training. He is not in a position to answer them fully responsibly; yet he must do his best to answer them, since the patients need an answer, and he is the only source they have access to. His patients assume that he is in a position to provide the information they need, and thus they attribute to him an excess of credibility on the matters in question. Let us add that any attempts to disabuse them of their inflated view of his expertise would damage the doctor–patient relationship by unduly undermining their confidence in him. All this is an ethical burden for our GP, because he is aware that his best advice might yet mislead them about an important health issue. For this GP, the credibility excess he receives from his patients brings an unwanted ethical burden, and so we see that credibility excess can be disadvantageous.[13] Alternatively, consider the example of a professor who gives a more junior colleague some work for comments and who is relying on that colleague's critical feedback to get the thing straight before a conference presentation. If the junior colleague is an admirer and gives too much benefit of the doubt, then his comments will be less critical than they might otherwise be, and the professor is effectively let down. Again, the credibility excess she receives on this occasion is only

---

[11] *Pace* two well-known views in the epistemology of testimony. First is Reid's view according to which we naturally operate counterpart principles of veracity and credulity in our testimonial exchanges (see Thomas Reid, *Inquiry into the Human Mind*, ch. 6, sect. xxiv: 'Of the Analogy between Perception and the Credit We Give to Human Testimony' (first published 1764)). Second is Tyler Burge's view, according to which we have an a priori entitlement for believing what others tell us, other things equal (see his 'Content Preservation', *Philosophical Review*, 102, no. 4 (Oct. 1992), 457–88). I shall discuss these views in Ch. 3, as I situate the phenomenon of testimonial injustice in the epistemology of testimony more generally.

[12] I sympathize with Coady's scepticism about there being any precise science here, any precise 'credibility ratio' to determine what degree of belief the hearer is entitled to (see C. A. J. Coady, *Testimony: A Philosophical Study* (Oxford: Clarendon Press, 1992), 210).

[13] I thank Hugh Mellor for this example, which I have elaborated somewhat.

a disadvantage to her. In such circumstances as these, then, credibility excess can be disadvantageous, though on the whole it is surely more usually an advantage.

What of the possibility that credibility deficit can in unusual circumstances be an advantage? Consider the stuttering Claudius, destined one day to be emperor of Rome, but who repeatedly escapes political murder on the way up owing to the fact that he is generally taken to be a fool. Or alternatively, recall that inimitable character from Seventies TV crime detection, Lieutenant Columbo, whose bumbling and shambolic style lures those he is investigating into a false sense of security and enables him to quiz them off-guard. Credibility deficit, then, in such specific and localized contexts, can be advantageous. In general, however, we shall see that credibility is a good that one needs to get enough of for all manner of well-functioning, and accordingly we should think of its deficit as generally disadvantageous.

On the face of it, one might think that both credibility deficit and credibility excess are cases of testimonial injustice. Certainly there is a sense of 'injustice' that might naturally and quite properly be applied to cases of credibility excess, as when one might complain at the injustice of someone receiving unduly high credibility in what he said just because he spoke with a certain accent.[14] At a stretch, this could be cast as a case of injustice as distributive unfairness—someone has got more than his fair share of a good—but that would be straining the idiom, for credibility is not a good that belongs with the distributive model of justice. Unlike those goods that are fruitfully dealt with along distributive lines (such as wealth or health care), there is no puzzle about the fair distribution of credibility, for credibility is a concept that wears its proper distribution on its sleeve. Epistemological nuance aside, the hearer's obligation is obvious: she must match the level of credibility she attributes to her interlocutor to the evidence that he is offering the truth. Further, those goods best suited to the distributive model are so suited principally because they are finite and at least potentially in short supply. (Recall Hume on the genealogy of justice: a situation of plenty is not one in

---

[14] In 'Rational Authority and Social Power: Towards a Truly Social Epistemology', *Proceedings of the Aristotelian Society*, 98, no. 2 (1998), 159–77, I wrote as if both deficit and excess were cases of epistemic injustice (the only type of which I considered was what I am here more specifically calling testimonial injustice), but the considerations I present here have changed my mind. I am also using the notion of 'credibility' rather more generically than I did in that paper.

which the distributive concept will naturally arise.[15]) Such goods are those for which there is, or may soon be, a certain competition, and that is what gives rise to the ethical puzzle about the justice of this or that particular distribution. By contrast, credibility is not generally finite in this way, and so there is no analogous competitive demand to invite the distributive treatment.

Accordingly, in cases of credibility deficit, the injustice we are aiming to track down is not to be characterized as non-receipt of one's fair share of a good (credibility), as this would fail to capture the distinctive respect in which the speaker is wronged. The idea is to explore testimonial injustice as a distinctively epistemic injustice, as a kind of injustice in which someone is *wronged specifically in her capacity as a knower*. Clearly credibility deficit can constitute such a wrong, but while credibility excess may (unusually) be disadvantageous in various ways, it does not undermine, insult, or otherwise withhold a proper respect for the speaker *qua* subject of knowledge; so in itself it does her no epistemic injustice, and *a fortiori* no testimonial injustice. On the contrary, our imagined professor and GP are overly esteemed in their capacity as knowers.

Yet, could it be (we should press the question) that there are some circumstances in which being overly esteemed in one's capacity as a knower would do one harm of a sort that merits the label 'testimonial injustice'? Suppose we imagine someone growing up who, because of various social prejudices overwhelmingly in his favour, is constantly epistemically puffed up by the people around him. Let's say that he is a member of a ruling elite, and that his education and entire upbringing are subtly geared to installing this message firmly in his psychology. Perhaps the pupils who attend his school even wind up with a distinctive accent and certainly a confident air that helps mark them out as epistemically authoritative. No doubt the credibility excess he tends to receive from most interlocutors in his class-ridden society will be advantageous: it is very likely to bring him lucrative employment and a certain automatic high status in many of his discursive exchanges, and so on. But what if all this also causes him to develop such an epistemic arrogance that a range of epistemic virtues are put out of his reach, rendering him closed-minded, dogmatic, blithely impervious to criticism, and so on? Is it not the case that such a person has in some degree quite literally been made a fool of? And if so, is there not something to the idea that

---

[15] David Hume, *A Treatise of Human Nature*, III. ii. 2, ed. L. A. Selby-Bigge, 3rd edn. (Oxford: Clarendon Press, 1975).

the catalogue of credibility excesses that have malformed his epistemic character amounts to some sort of testimonial injustice? Is he not, after all, precisely wronged in his capacity as a knower? I think the answer is probably Yes, and we are perhaps confronted with an interesting special case of testimonial injustice. Note, however, that it is *cumulative*, whereas our focus has been on token cases of the injustice. I do not think it would be right to characterize any of the individual moments of credibility excess that such a person receives as in itself an instance of testimonial injustice, since none of them wrongs him sufficiently in itself. It is only if enough of them come together in the semi-fanciful manner described that each moment of credibility excess takes on the aspect of something that contributes to the subject's being epistemically wronged over the long term. Consequently, I would suggest that while the example does indicate that some people in a consistently privileged position of social power might be subject to a variant strain of testimonial injustice: namely, testimonial injustice in its strictly cumulative form; none the less it does not show that any token cases of credibility excess constitute a testimonial injustice. The primary characterization of testimonial injustice, then, remains such that it is a matter of credibility deficit and not credibility excess.

Let us begin to home in on the concept of testimonial injustice, now duly conceived as a form of credibility deficit. A first point to notice is that prejudice is not the only thing that can cause credibility deficit, and so not all sorts of credibility deficit are cases of testimonial injustice. A credibility deficit might simply result from *innocent error*: error that is both ethically and epistemically non-culpable. One reason why there will always be cases of innocent error is that human judgement is fallible, and so it is inevitable that even the most skilled and perceptive hearers will on occasion come up with a mistaken judgement of a speaker's credibility. More specifically, a hearer may simply have a false belief about the speaker's level of expertise and/or motives, so that she gives him less credibility than she might otherwise have done. So long as her false belief is itself ethically and epistemically non-culpable (it does not, for example, result from an immoral hatefulness or from epistemic carelessness), there will be nothing culpable in her misjudgement of his credibility. It is simply an unlucky epistemic mistake of one or another familiar kind.

Consider an example in which the hearer—let us say that she is a philosopher, an ethicist—knows that her interlocutor is an academic at a certain institution, and having looked him up on the web she believes him to be a medic, since his name was listed under medical sciences. When the conversation turns to a certain current debate in the literature pertaining to her own specialism, moral fictionalism, and to her surprise he expresses a forthright critical view on the fictionalist approach, she affords his word a lower credibility than she would if she took him for a fellow ethicist. In fact, however, unbeknownst to her, he *is* an ethicist, with a specialism in medical ethics, employed in a medical department, and so her false belief about his professional identity has put him in credibility deficit for the duration. Yet I would suggest that her misjudgement does him no real testimonial injustice. It is simply an innocent error. An unlucky mistake of this sort, then, can cause a credibility deficit that does not constitute a case of testimonial injustice. At least, I suggest that we circumscribe the concept in this manner. Of course it would not be linguistically outrageous for our imagined hearer, embarrassed on learning the true professional identity of her interlocutor, to say she felt bad for doing him such an 'injustice'. But this would be a very weak sense of injustice; so much so that it is a mere shadow of our ordinary ethical and political sense of the word and lacks the usual implication of moral badness. This is largely a terminological point, so if others disagree, then they can regard cases of innocent error as producing a weak form of testimonial injustice. For my part, however, I shall reserve the term for cases in which there is something ethically bad about the hearer's misjudgement.

What about credibility deficit caused by ethically innocent but epistemically culpable error? If we revisit our example and alter it so that we picture our philosopher making her mistake as the result of a hopelessly careless web search, I suggest that we find that the credibility deficit she assigns her interlocutor still does not amount to a testimonial injustice. Her unduly deflated credibility judgement of him does not insult or undermine him as a knower, for she has simply made a stupid mistake. While her error is epistemically culpable, its ethical non-culpability still seems to prevent the resultant credibility deficit from constituting a testimonial injustice: an ethically non-culpable mistake cannot undermine or otherwise wrong the speaker. It seems that the ethical poison of testimonial injustice must derive from some ethical poison in the judgement of the hearer, and there is none such wherever the hearer's error is ethically non-culpable. The proposal I am heading for is that the ethical poison in question is that of *prejudice*. From different points in history one might draw on many depressing examples of prejudices obviously relevant to the context of credibility judgement, such as the idea that women are irrational, blacks are intellectually inferior to whites, the working classes are the moral inferiors of the upper classes, Jews are wily, Orientals are sly ... and so on in a grim catalogue of clichés more or less likely to insinuate themselves into judgements of credibility at different moments in history. But in order to furnish the philosophical imagination less crudely, let us turn to an example from literature that provides us with a historically truthful fiction.

The example is from Harper Lee's *To Kill a Mockingbird*. The year is 1935, and the scene a courtroom in Maycomb County, Alabama. The defendant is a young black man named Tom Robinson. He is charged with raping a white girl, Mayella Ewell, whose family's run-down house he passes every day on his way to work, situated as it is on the outskirts of town in the borderlands that divide where whites and blacks live. It is obvious to the reader, and to any relatively unprejudiced person in the courtroom, that Tom Robinson is entirely innocent. For Atticus Finch, our politely spoken counsel for the defence, has proved beyond doubt that Robinson could not have beaten the Ewell girl so as to cause the sort of cuts and bruises she sustained that day, since whoever gave her the beating led with his left fist, whereas Tom Robinson's left arm is disabled, having been injured in a machinery accident when he was a boy. The trial proceedings enact what is in one sense a straightforward struggle between the power of evidence and the power of racial prejudice, with the all-white jury's judgement ultimately succumbing to the latter. But the psychology is subtle, and there is a great complexity of social meanings at work in determining the jury's perception of Tom Robinson as a speaker. In a showdown between the word of a black man and that of a poor white girl, the courtroom air is thick with the 'do's and 'don't's of racial politics. Telling the truth here is a minefield for Tom Robinson, since if he casts aspersions on the white girl, he will be perceived as a presumptuous, lying Negro; yet, if he does not publicize Mayella Ewell's attempt to kiss him (which is what really happened), then a guilty verdict is even more nearly assured. This discursive predicament mirrors his practical predicament at the Ewell's house on that fateful day when Mayella grabbed him. If he pushes her away, then he will be found to have assaulted her; yet if he is passive, he will equally be found to have assaulted her. So he does the most neutral thing he can, which is to run, though knowing all the while that this action too will be taken as a sign of guilt. Mr Gilmer's interrogation of Tom is suffused with the idea that his running away implies culpability:

' … why did you run so fast?'
  'I says I was scared, suh.'
  'If you had a clear conscience, why were you scared?'[16]

Running away, it seems, is something a black man in Maycomb County cannot do without incriminating himself. Similarly, there are many things he cannot say in court and stand a chance of being heard as truthful. At a pivotal moment during the prosecution's interrogation, for instance, Tom Robinson makes the mistake of being honest about his kindly motivations for stopping off at Mayella Ewell's house as regularly as he did to help her out with odd jobs. The scene, like the whole story, is reported from the point of view of Scout, Atticus Finch's young daughter, who is secretly surveying the proceedings with her brother, Jem, from the 'Negro gallery'. Mr Gilmer, the prosecutor, sets him up:

'Why were you so anxious to do that woman's chores?'
  Tom Robinson hesitated, searching for an answer. 'Looked like she didn't have nobody to help her, like I says—'
  … Mr Gilmer smiled grimly at the jury. 'You're a mighty good fellow, it seems—did all this for not one penny?'
  'Yes suh. I felt right sorry for her, she seemed to try more'n the rest of 'em—'
  '*You* felt sorry for *her*, you felt *sorry* for her?' Mr Gilmer seemed ready to rise to the ceiling.
  The witness realized his mistake and shifted uncomfortably in the chair. But the damage was done. Below us, nobody liked Tom Robinson's answer. Mr Gilmer paused a long time to let it sink in.[17]

Here the 'damage' in question is done to any epistemic trust that the white jury has so far been human enough to feel towards the black testifier. For *feeling sorry for* someone is a taboo sentiment if you are black and the object of your sympathy is a white person. In the context of a racist ideology structured around dogmas of white superiority, the fundamental ethical sentiment of plain human sympathy becomes disfigured in the eyes of whites so that it appears as little more than an indicator of self-perceived advantage on the part of the black subject. A black man is not allowed to have feelings that imply a position of any

---

[16] Harper Lee, *To Kill a Mockingbird* (London: William Heinemann, 1960), 202.
[17] Ibid. 201.

sort of advantage relative to any white person, no matter how difficult and lonely her life might be. The fact that Tom Robinson makes the sentiment public raises the stakes in a way that is disastrous for legal justice and for the epistemic justice on which it depends. The trial is a zero-sum contest between the word of a black man against that of a white girl (or perhaps that of her father who has brought the case to court), and there are those on the jury for whom the idea that the black man is to be epistemically trusted and the white girl distrusted is virtually a psychological impossibility—Robinson's expressed sympathy in feeling sorry for a white girl only reinforces that impossibility.

As it turns out, the members of the jury stick with their prejudiced perception of the defendant, formed principally by the racial stereotypes of the day. Atticus Finch challenges them to dispense with these preju-dicial stereotypes; to dispense, as he puts it, with the 'assumption—the evil assumption—that *all* Negroes lie, that *all* Negroes are basically immoral beings, that *all* Negro men are not to be trusted around our women'.[18] But when it comes to the verdict, the jurors go along with the automatic distrust delivered by the prejudices that structure their perception of the speaker. They find him guilty. And it is important that we are to interpret the novel so that the jurors really do find him guilty. That is to say, they do not privately find him innocent yet cynically convict him anyway. Even allowing that the psychology here may be to some degree indeterminate, it is crucial that they genuinely fail to do what Atticus Finch in his summing-up describes as their 'duty':

' … In the name of God, do your duty.'

Atticus's voice had dropped, and as he turned away from the jury he said something I did not catch. He said it more to himself than to the court. I punched Jem.

'What'd he say?'

' "In the name of God, believe him," I think that's what he said.'[19]

Finch is trying to impress upon the jury that they have a *duty to believe Tom Robinson*, and this supports my interpretation of the jurors' psychology. Finch evidently takes it that what the jury need to be urged to do is to make the right judgement, to do the right epistemic thing. He does not urge them to focus on their moral and legal duty to convict only if they judge the defendant guilty, for he is aware that their prejudice goes psychologically deeper than that, all the way to the jurors'

---

[18] Ibid. 208.   [19] Ibid. 210.

very powers of judgement. When they do deliver the guilty verdict, this attests to their failure in their duty to make the proper testimonial judgement, in the light of the evidence. They fail, as Atticus Finch feared, precisely in their duty to believe Tom Robinson. Given the evidence put before them, their immovably prejudiced social perception of Robinson as a speaker leads at once to a gross epistemic failure and an appalling ethical failure of grave practical consequence. As it turns out, Tom Robinson does not survive long enough to go ahead with any appeal, for he is shot in the back as he tries, we hear it said, to escape over the prison fence right in front of the guards.

It is perhaps worth remarking that even the most hateful prejudicial ideologies may be sustained not only by explicitly hateful thought and talk but also by more domestic stereotypical ideas that are almost cosy in comparison. There is a relatively light-hearted theme of epistemic untrustworthiness that runs through the book as a leitmotif, softly echoing the deadly serious racist exclusion from epistemic trust of the sort that leads ultimately to the killing of Tom Robinson. We see this, for instance, when Scout is talking to her family's friend and neighbour, Miss Maudie, about the reclusive and mysterious young Boo Radley (aka Mr Arthur), about whom spooky stories abound and who is an object of unfailing fascination for the children. Scout quizzes Miss Maudie about him:

'Do you think they're true, all those things they say about B—Mr Arthur?'
'What things?'
I told her.
'That is three-fourths coloured folks and one-fourth Stephanie Crawford,' said Miss Maudie grimly.[20]

Given a culture where it is so utterly natural for white people to associate 'coloured folks' in general with irresponsible gossip (even in a spirit of independent-mindedness, as is the case with Miss Maudie's response to Scout), it is not hard to imagine a relation of support between this comparatively cosy side of the ideology and the far harsher, more squarely unjust associations that work to undermine the epistemic trustworthiness of black people. While there may be nothing hateful in the more light-hearted side of these attitudes, still it may be a significant nutrient to the hateful ideology overall.

Tom Robinson's case represents an extreme example of the sort of testimonial injustice I am aiming to portray philosophically. An initial

---

[20] Harper Lee, *To Kill a Mockingbird* (London: William Heinemann, 1960), 51.

sketch might lead us to capture it as *prejudicial credibility deficit*. But while this may serve as a general definition of testimonial injustice, it misses a crucial feature of the sort of testimonial injustice that Tom suffers. There are all sorts of prejudices that can cause credibility deficit, yet where the resultant testimonial injustice is highly localized and therefore lacking any of the structural social significance that a case such as Tom Robinson's clearly has. Imagine, for instance (I adapt an example proposed to me by a scientist), a panel of referees on a science journal who have a dogmatic prejudice against a certain research method. It might reasonably be complained by a would-be contributor that authors who present hypotheses on the basis of the disfavoured method receive a prejudicially reduced level of credibility from the panel. Thus the prejudice is such as to generate a genuine testimonial injustice (writing being one medium of testimony). Although such a testimonial injustice may be grievous for the careers of the would-be contributors, and perhaps even for the progress of science, none the less its impact on the subject's life is, let us assume, highly localized. That is to say, the prejudice in question (against a certain scientific method) does not render the subject vulnerable to any other kinds of injustice (legal, economic, political). Let us say that the testimonial injustice produced here is *incidental*.

By contrast, testimonial injustices that are connected, via a common prejudice, with other types of injustice, might appropriately be termed *systematic*. Systematic testimonial injustices, then, are produced not by prejudice *simpliciter*, but specifically by those prejudices that track the subject through different dimensions of social activity—economic, educational, professional, sexual, legal, political, religious, and so on. Being subject to a tracker prejudice renders one susceptible not only to testimonial injustice but to a gamut of different injustices, and so when such a prejudice generates a testimonial injustice, that injustice is systematically connected with other kinds of actual or potential injustice. Clearly the testimonial injustice suffered by Tom Robinson is systematic, for racial prejudice renders him susceptible to a panoply of injustices besides the testimonial kind. Systematic testimonial injustice constitutes our central case—it is central from the point of view of a guiding interest in how epistemic injustice fits into the broader pattern of social justice.

The main type (the only type?) of prejudice that tracks people in this way is prejudice relating to social identity. Let us call this sort of prejudice *identity prejudice*. It can come in positive or negative form—prejudice for or against people owing to some feature of their social identity—but since our interest is in cases of credibility deficit rather than excess, we shall be concerned only with negative identity prejudice. (Indeed, I shall tend to use 'identity prejudice' as short for 'negative identity prejudice'.) The influence of identity prejudice in a hearer's credibility judgement is an operation of identity power. For in such a case the influence of identity prejudice is a matter of one party or parties effectively controlling what another party does—preventing them, for instance, from conveying knowledge—in a way that depends upon collective conceptions of the social identities in play. In our *Mockingbird* example, racial identity power is exercised in this way by members of the jury as they make their deflated credibility judgements of Tom Robinson, with the result that he is unable to convey to them the knowledge he has of what happened at the Ewells' place. This is the essential exercise of identity power in the courtroom that seals Tom's fate, though of course it is not the whole story, for this operation of identity power is crucially supported by Mr Gilmer's simple but highly effective prosecution strategy, which is to invoke the usual collective negative imaginings of the Negro. Gilmer deliberately controls the jurors, and sure enough the jurors go on to control what Tom Robinson does, preventing him from conveying his knowledge to them.

With the concepts of identity prejudice and systematicity in place, we are now in a position to propose a refined characterization of the central case of testimonial injustice—the systematic case. The speaker sustains such a testimonial injustice if and only if she receives a credibility deficit owing to identity prejudice in the hearer; so the central case of testimonial injustice is *identity-prejudicial credibility deficit*. We should note, however, that there could be exceptions; that is, one can imagine cases of identity-prejudicial credibility deficit that are not cases of systematic testimonial injustice, and so not examples of our central case. Consider the following case (an anecdote recounted to me by a philosopher of science). There is a large international conference dominated by research scientists and some historians of science, with only a smattering of philosophers of science. It becomes clear that the philosophers of science are regarded by the majority of the other delegates as out of touch with the realities of scientific practice, so much so that they are, frankly, held in some intellectual disdain. In this context, it would seem, simply falling into the identity category 'philosopher of science' renders one's word likely to be dismissed as the vain speculations of an out-of-touch academic. Thus there are genuine cases of identity-prejudicial credibility deficit going on here. These testimonial injustices, however, do not instantiate our central case, for they are not systematic. Despite the prejudice's being an identity prejudice, it does not concern the kind of broad identity category that makes for a tracker prejudice; on the contrary, its social significance is highly localized to the specific conference context described. It therefore produces only an incidental testimonial injustice.

To categorize a testimonial injustice as incidental is not to belittle it ethically. Localized prejudices and the injustices they produce may be utterly disastrous for the subject, especially if they are repeated frequently so that the injustice is *persistent.* If, for instance, the practical context in which the injustices occur is that of a project, professional or otherwise, which is crucial to the person's life being worth living, then the accumulation of incidental injustices may ruin their life. The importance of systematicity is simply that if a testimonial injustice is not systematic, then it is not central from the point of view of an interest in the broad pattern of social justice. 'Persistent' labels the diachronic dimension of testimonial injustice's severity and significance, whereas 'systematic' labels the synchronic dimension. The most severe forms of testimonial injustice are both persistent and systematic. Such is the case for Tom Robinson, who lives in a society in which the prejudice that devalues his word also blocks his everyday pursuits repeatedly and in every social direction. By contrast, cases of testimonial injustice that are neither persistent nor systematic are on the whole unlikely to be very disadvantageous. Generally speaking, systematic injustice tends towards persistence, because the imaginative conceptions of social identity that feature in the relevant tracker prejudices are likely to be enduring features of the social imagination.

Now that I have identified our central case as systematic testimonial injustice, let us now inquire further into how identity prejudice enters in to make its impact on the discursive exchange. We must explore the role of stereotypes in hearers' judgements of speakers' credibility.

2

Prejudice in the Credibility Economy

2.1 STEREOTYPES AND PREJUDICIAL STEREOTYPES

What is the basic mechanism in testimonial exchange whereby prejudice corrupts hearers' judgements of speaker credibility? Prejudice can insinuate itself in a number of ways, but I shall pursue the idea that its main point of entry is via stereotypes that we make use of as heuristics in our credibility judgements. I use 'stereotype' in a neutral sense, as before, so that stereotypes may or may not be reliable; and while I shall argue that reliable stereotypes are a proper part of the hearer's rational resources in the making of credibility judgements, the picture I shall build up of our predicament as hearers is such that we are perpetually susceptible to invoking stereotypes that are prejudiced.

Let us begin by clarifying what, more precisely, is meant by 'stereotype' here. The social psychology literature presents an array of varying conceptions.[1] Since I am using the word neutrally, so that there can be empirically reliable stereotypes as well as unreliable and distorting ones, a fairly broad conception is in order. I shall say a little more about the nature of stereotypes later when I consider them as images, but for now let me state that stereotypes are *widely held associations between a given social group and one or more attributes*. This conception is broad in three ways. First, it is neutral with respect to whether the generalization embodied by the stereotype is reliable or not. Second, it allows that stereotypes may be held not only as beliefs but also in other dimensions of cognitive commitment: notably those that may have an

---

[1] See, e.g., Charles Stangor (ed.) *Stereotypes and Prejudice: Essential Readings* (Philadelphia: Psychology Press, 2000); C. Neil Macrae, Charles Stangor, and Miles Hewstone (eds.) *Stereotypes and Stereotyping* ((New York and London: The Guilford Press, 1996); and Craig McGarty, Vincent Y. Yzerbyt, and Russell Spears (eds.), *Stereotypes as Explanations: The Formation of Meaningful Beliefs about Social Groups* (Cambridge: Cambridge University Press, 2002).

affective aspect such as commitments which derive from the collective imagination and which may permit less transparency than beliefs.[2] And third, it allows that stereotypes may have a positive or negative valence, or indeed neither, depending on whether the attribute is derogatory or complimentary or indifferent, good or bad or neutral.[3] Some stereotypes may resist any definitive categorization because they can carry either a positive or a negative valence, depending on the context. The stereotype of women as intuitive is a case in point. In contexts where it is assumed that 'intuitive' suggests irrationality, the stereotype is derogatory; but in contexts where intuition is regarded as a cognitive asset, the stereotype is complimentary. There may also be contexts in which both the positive and the negative valence are somehow in play—the stereotype might work like a barbed compliment, for instance.

If stereotypes are widely held associations between a group and an attribute, then stereotyping entails a cognitive commitment to some empirical generalization about a given social group ('women are intuitive'). A generalization can of course be more or less strong. Accordingly, in extreme cases someone who stereotypes might be committed to the generalization as a universal ('all women are intuitive'); or, at the other end of the spectrum, one might be committed to it in very dilute form ('many women are intuitive'); or, again, one might be committed to something in between ('most women are intuitive').

The idea that we use stereotypes in our credibility judgements is in line with currents in social psychology:

The past few decades have witnessed a shift away from a view of judgments as the products of rational, logical decision making marred by the occasional presence of irrational needs and motives toward a view of the person as heuristic user. Empirical work on non-social judgments indicates that the perceiver employs

---

[2] Compare, e.g., a definition given in doxastic terms by co-authors Jacques-Philippe Leyens, Vincent Y. Yzerbyt, and Georges Schadron: 'shared beliefs about person attributes, usually personality traits, but often also behaviours, of a group of people' (*Stereotypes and Social Cognition* (London: Sage Publications, 1994), 11). Such a purely doxastic conception of what it is to hold a stereotype seems too narrow, certainly for present purposes.

[3] Compare Lawrence Blum's conception of stereotypes as false and negative associations between a group and an attribute. This certainly picks out the most ethically problematic kind of stereotyping, and therefore sits naturally in an analysis of what is morally wrong with stereotyping people; but it would be too narrow for present purposes—what he calls stereotypes I distinguish as negative identity-prejudicial stereotypes. See Blum, 'Stereotypes and Stereotyping: A Moral Analysis', in Ward E. Jones and Thomas Martin (eds.), *Immoral Believing*, Special Issue of *Philosophical Papers*, 33, no. 3 (Nov. 2004), 251–89.

shortcuts or heuristics to free capacity and transmit information as quickly as possible, and recent research in social psychology suggests that these processes also apply to the formation and use of social judgments.[4]

We are picturing hearers as confronted with the immediate task of gauging how likely it is that what a speaker has said is true. Barring a wealth of personal knowledge of the speaker as an individual, such a judgement of credibility must reflect some kind of social generalization about the epistemic trustworthiness—the competence and sincerity—of people of the speaker's social type, so that it is inevitable (and desirable) that the hearer should spontaneously avail himself of the relevant generalizations in the shorthand form of (reliable) stereotypes. Without such a heuristic aid he will not be able to achieve the normal spontaneity of credibility judgement that is characteristic of everyday testimonial exchange. Consider the stereotype of the dependable family doctor. In so far as the association crystallized in this stereotype means that it embodies an empirically reliable generalization about family doctors, it is epistemically desirable that the stereotype should help shape the credibility judgements we make when such doctors give us general medical advice. Much of everyday testimony requires the hearer to engage in a social categorization of speakers, and that is how stereotypes oil the wheels of testimonial exchange.

But what if an identity prejudice is at work in the stereotype? Many of the stereotypes of historically powerless groups such as women, black people, or working-class people variously involve an association with some attribute inversely related to competence or sincerity or both: over-emotionality, illogicality, inferior intelligence, evolutionary inferiority, incontinence, lack of 'breeding', lack of moral fibre, being on the make, etc. A first thing to say about such prejudicial stereotypes is that in so far as the association is false, the stereotype embodies an *un*reliable empirical generalization about the social group in question. But this alone is not sufficient to render a stereotype prejudicial, for a stereotype embodying an unreliable empirical generalization might yet amount to an entirely non-culpable mistake—the result perhaps of a piece of collective epistemic bad luck such as the available evidence being misleading. The idea of a prejudice is most basically that of a

---

[4] Shelley E. Taylor, 'The Availability Bias in Social Perception and Interaction', in D. Kahneman, P. Slovic, and A. Tversky (eds.), *Judgement under Uncertainty: Heuristics and Biases* (Cambridge: Cambridge University Press, 1982), 190–200, at 198. See also Daniel Kahneman and Amos Tversky, 'On the Psychology of Predication', *Psychological Review*, 80 (1973), 237–51; and Tversky and Kahneman, 'Judgment under Uncertainty: Heuristic and Biases', *Science*, 185 (1974), 1124–31.

pre-judgement, where this is most naturally interpreted in an internalist vein as a judgement made or maintained without proper regard to the evidence, and for this reason we should conceive of prejudice generally as something epistemically culpable.[5] As a qualification, we should note, however, that there might be rare exceptions to this general rule of epistemic culpability. There might, for instance, be mitigating circumstances such as when the subject's patterns of judgement are influenced by the prejudices of his day in a context where it would take a very exceptional epistemic character to overcome those prejudices. These might be circumstances in which it is simply too much to expect the subject to achieve awareness that a certain prejudice is structuring his social consciousness, let alone to realign his habits of credibility judgement accordingly. In such a situation the person making the prejudicial mistake is subject to 'circumstantial' epistemic bad luck—the epistemic counterpart to what Nagel calls 'circumstantial' moral bad luck.[6] We shall consider an example of this sort of exculpating circumstance in Chapter 4 when we revisit Herbert Greenleaf and the testimonial injustice he does Marge Sherwood.

Nomy Arpaly constructs an interesting example intended to illustrate the distinction between a non-culpable mistake (an 'honest mistake') and a prejudice. Consider Solomon. He is 'a boy who lives in a small isolated farming community in a poor country' who 'believes that women are not half as competent as men when it comes to abstract thinking, or at least are not inclined towards such thinking'.[7] He has never met a woman

---

[5] For an account that defines prejudice independently from the idea that it involves any misjudgement on the part of the subject, see Rupert Brown, *Prejudice: Its Social Psychology* (Oxford: Blackwell, 1995). He defines prejudice as, simply, 'a negative attitude, emotion, or behaviour towards members of a group on account of their membership of that group' (p. 14; see also p. 8). Depending on how one interprets it, the obvious worry with such a broad definition is that it would label a person as prejudiced if she has a negative attitude towards, say, members of a neo-Nazi political party on account of their membership of that group—something most people would not call a prejudice. There may well be methodological considerations in the social psychological setting in favour of adopting such a very broad definition, but philosophically it seems quite wrong to sever the link between prejudice and misjudgement.

[6] See Thomas Nagel, 'Moral Luck', in *Mortal Questions* (Cambridge: Cambridge University Press, 1979). It was a reply to Bernard Williams's paper of the same name—in *Moral Luck: Philosophical Papers 1973–1980* (Cambridge: Cambridge University Press, 1981). Both papers were originally published in *Proceedings of the Aristotelian Society*, supp. vol. 50 (1976). For a discussion of the analogy between moral and epistemic luck, see Daniel Statman, 'Moral and Epistemic Luck', *Ratio*, 4 (Dec. 1991), 146–56.

[7] Nomy Arpaly, *Unprincipled Virtue: An Inquiry into Moral Agency* (Oxford: Oxford University Press, 2003), 103.

who went in for abstract thinking; his local library contains only such books by men, and he has met many men who were abstract thinkers and among these men there seemed to be a consensus that women are not really up to it. So far, Arpaly suggests, Solomon could not be accused of any marked irrationality. But now she asks us to imagine that he goes to university, where he studies alongside able women students. If this counter-evidence to his view shifts the belief, then the belief is revealed as an honest mistake. If it does not shift the belief, however, then the belief is revealed as irrational, and moreover a prejudice: the stubbornness of Solomon's belief in the face of manifest counter-evidence would at once reveal him as both epistemically and ethically flawed. The ethical flaw stems from the fact that Solomon's maintaining his belief in the face of counter-evidence would be not just a piece of irrationality but a piece of motivated irrationality, where the motivation (presumably some sort of contempt for women) is ethically noxious.

Thus far I agree with the intended message, for I take it that Arpaly's example illustrates that a prejudiced judgement is (typically) culpably resistant to the evidence and thus irrational. I agree too that Solomon's envisaged prejudice would reveal him as ethically flawed, and that this ethical flaw consists in the ethically bad motivation behind the irrationality. Arpaly, however, seems to go on to imply that such an ethical flaw on the part of the subject is a definitive feature of prejudice *per se*. I am unsure whether she intends to commit herself on this score, but the point is worth raising in its own right. While it is surely correct to cast Solomon's imagined prejudice as constituting an ethical failing on his part, this is not so of prejudice in general. Not all prejudices involve an ethical flaw on the part of the subject. There are different sorts of prejudice. Solomon's prejudice against women's intellectual abilities is, in my terms, an instance of negative identity prejudice, and that sort of prejudice would indeed tend to have an ethically bad motivation behind it. Negative identity prejudice is certainly the most morally problematic kind of prejudice, and it is the kind we are most interested in (recall the white jurors' identity prejudice against Tom Robinson, behind which there lies one or more ethically noxious motivation, such as racial hatred or contempt). But prejudice taken generally is a broader notion.

It is broader in two respects. First, while prejudice is most certainly an idea of a judgement formed or maintained in a manner resistant to the evidence, and where this resistance is caused by some kind of motivation on the part of the subject, this permits motivations that are not ethically bad. Recall our example about the imagined science journal and its panel of referees who are prejudiced against a certain scientific method. We do not have to stipulate that the referees are host to an ethically bad motivation in order to represent them as prejudiced. It is sufficient that we cast their judgement about a given submission to the journal as resistant to the evidence because of some countervailing motivational investment—perhaps the panel members are insufficiently sensitive to the benefits of the new scientific method owing to a deep-seated feeling of loyalty to methodological orthodoxy, or perhaps they feel threatened by intellectual innovation. These are not admirable motivations, but nor are they in themselves ethically bad. Second, prejudice is not always *against* someone or something, for there can be prejudice *in favour*. Imagine a different but equally prejudiced panel of referees whose members are not prejudiced against any particular scientific method but prejudiced in favour of one, so that when a submission of that sort comes in, they are spontaneously over-impressed. Prejudice can have a positive valence.

We can summarize the general conception of prejudice that has now emerged as follows:

Prejudices are judgements, which may have a positive or a negative valence, and which display some (typically, epistemically culpable) resistance to counter-evidence owing to some affective investment on the part of the subject.

This affective investment may or may not be ethically bad, but given our central concern with systematic testimonial injustice, we have a special interest in negative identity prejudices, and these are, I take it, always generated by some ethically bad affective investment. Negative identity prejudices are prejudices with a negative valence held against people *qua* social type. Now if we put our conception of negative identity prejudice together with our conception of a stereotype, we can say what a negative identity-prejudicial stereotype is:

A widely held disparaging association between a social group and one or more attributes, where this association embodies a generalization that displays some (typically, epistemically culpable) resistance to counter-evidence owing to an ethically bad affective investment.

This is the sort of prejudice that is at work in systematic testimonial injustice.

We may now probe a little further into the mechanism by which such a prejudicial stereotype actually shapes a hearer's credibility judgement. I have already suggested that the hearer in everyday testimonial exchange will often make use of stereotypes as heuristics to facilitate his judgement of a speaker's credibility. Hearer and speaker are engaged in a form of social interaction, and they inevitably trade in social perceptions of each other. Anticipating the argument for a perceptual model of credibility judgement that I shall give in the next chapter, let us provisionally countenance the idea that in those everyday testimonial exchanges in which the hearer does not deliberate about how far to trust the speaker, the hearer *perceives* the speaker as trustworthy to this or that degree in what he is telling her. She perceives him in the light of a set of background assumptions about how far people like him are trustworthy about things like this in relation to people like her, and I have suggested that reliable stereotypes have an essential role to play here. This model of the interaction between speaker and hearer helps us to see the mechanism whereby identity prejudice can distort a hearer's credibility judgement: *it distorts the hearer's perception of the speaker*. Applying the perceptual idiom to our chief example, we can say that the judgement of the jurors of Maycomb County is so distorted by prejudicial racial stereotype that they cannot, in that courtroom context, perceive Tom Robinson as anything but a lying Negro. Now in this example the jurors' perceptions are shaped *inter alia* by prejudiced beliefs; the prejudicial racial stereotype determining their credibility judgements is in part doxastically mediated. But our focus will be chiefly on the operation of prejudice at the non-doxastic level; for concentrating on beliefs would lead us to underestimate the incidence of testimonial injustice. I believe that the right vision of epistemic relations is such that testimonial injustice goes on much of the time, and while it may be hard enough to police one's beliefs for prejudice, it is significantly harder reliably to filter out the prejudicial stereotypes that inform one's social perceptions directly, without doxastic mediation. Many instances of testimonial injustice will be importantly unlike Tom Robinson's case, for many cases will be owing not to prejudiced beliefs at all but only to stealthier, residual prejudices, whose content may even be flatly inconsistent with the beliefs actually held by the subject. Certainly we may sometimes perpetrate testimonial injustice because of our beliefs; but the more philosophically intriguing prospect is that we may very frequently do it in spite of them.

In order to clarify the idea that prejudicial stereotypes can sometimes be especially hard to detect because they influence our credibility judgements directly, without doxastic mediation, it might help to remind ourselves of the origin of the idea of a social stereotype. The political journalist Walter Lippmann is widely cited as popularizing our metaphorical use of 'stereotype' to mean social type.[8] Its literal meaning signifies the mould used in printing, and accordingly Lippmann described social stereotypes as 'pictures in our heads'. This seems as good an off-the-cuff description as any. If we think of a social stereotype as an *image* which expresses an association between a social group and one or more attributes, and which thereby embodies one or more generalizations about that social group, then it becomes clearer how its impact on judgement can be harder to detect than that of a belief with the same content. Images are capable of a visceral impact on judgement, which allows them to condition our judgements without our awareness, whereas it would take an unconscious belief to do so with comparable stealth.

This is most starkly illustrated when the influence of prejudicial images from the social imagination persists in a hearer's patterns of judgement even where their content *conflicts* with the content of her beliefs. Imagine, for example, a woman who has freed herself of sexist beliefs—a card-carrying feminist, as they say—and yet her psychology remains such that in many contexts she is influenced by a stereotype of women as lacking the requisite authority for political office, so that she tends not to take the word of female political candidates as seriously as that of their male counterparts. Such a conflicted figure exemplifies the phenomenon of (what we might call) residual internalization, whereby a member of a subordinated group continues as host to a sort of half-life for the oppressive ideology, even when her beliefs have genuinely moved on. Sometimes this might simply be a matter of the person's affective states lagging behind their beliefs (a lapsed Catholic's guilty conscience, a gay rights activist's feelings of shame). But other times it can be that cognitive commitments held in our imaginations retain their impact on how we perceive the social world even after any correlative beliefs have faded away. These commitments can linger in our psychology in residual form, lagging behind the progress of belief, so that they retain an influence upon our social perception.

Where prejudicial images subsist alongside conflicting beliefs, their influence will tend to be very difficult to identify. Why, after all, should one suspect that, despite everything one believes, one's judgements might in fact be shaped by ideas to the contrary? Imagine that our

---

[8] Walter Lippmann, *Public Opinion* (New York: Free Press, 1965; first published 1922).

card-carrying feminist came to political consciousness in the 1970s, so that there was a radical shift away from all the gender-related beliefs that first formed her as a girl. Given her newly wrought and strongly held feminist beliefs, why should she suspect that her social perceptions might remain shaped by sexist stereotypes? It takes a special feat of self-consciousness to be alert to this kind of prejudice in one's thinking, let alone to correct it. Perhaps, however, she comes to notice a certain dissonance between her beliefs and her perceptual judgements, and asks herself why it is that she tends not to perceive women political candidates as possessing the requisite gravitas. In a spirit of optimism, let us imagine that she confides her feelings and suspicions to others and gradually arrives at an enhanced self-awareness that helps limit the impact of the prejudicial residue on her credibility judgements. But many prejudices will not be so short-lived. The social imagination is a mighty resource for social change, and this is significantly due to its capacity for informing thought directly, and thus independently of beliefs that may remain tainted with the prejudices of the day. But where it is the images themselves that are tainted by prejudice, the very same capacity to impinge on judgement directly and without the subject's awareness can render the social imagination an ethical and epistemic liability.[9] The collective social imagination inevitably contains all manner of stereotypes, and that is the social atmosphere in which hearers must confront their interlocutors. No wonder the prejudicial elements in the social

---

[9] It is a merit of the idea of the 'social imaginary' that it explains how we can unintentionally give cognitive sanctuary to conflicting ideas and/or images. Thus, for instance, Moira Gatens: 'there are some ... who unreflectively endorse and perpetuate a sexual imaginary in which women embody the paradox of being considered as *both* free and rational members of a democratic political body *and* beings under the "natural" authority of men' (*Imaginary Bodies: Ethics, Power and Corporeality* (London: Routledge, 1996), 141). I do not make use of the idea of the social imaginary, however, since I find that there are real difficulties in attempting to cut it free from its psychoanalytic roots, so that one needs more or less to re-create the concept in order to use it independently from a body of background psychoanalytical theory to which one may not want to be committed. There is interesting work in such re-creation, but for present purposes the less heavily theoretical notion of the social imagination is a more straightforward option. (The idea of the social imaginary originated in the work of Cornelius Castoriadis. See, e.g., *World in Fragments: Writings on Politics, Society, Psychoanalysis, and the Imagination*, ed. and trans. David Ames Curtis (Stanford, Calif.: Stanford University Press, 1997).) For an account of different developments of the notion by feminist writers, see Susan James, 'Freedom and the Imaginary', in Susan James and Stephanie Palmer (eds.), *Visible Women: Essays on Feminist Legal Theory and Political Philosophy* (Oxford and Portland, Ore.: Hart Publishing, 2002), 175–95.

imagination can impinge on our credibility judgements without our say-so.

We can distinguish two ways in which a prejudicial residue from the collective social imagination may subsist in a subject's social consciousness even while it conflicts with her beliefs. We can capture them respectively under a diachronic and a synchronic aspect. The diachronic case is exemplified by our card-carrying feminist. Her beliefs have moved on, but contents carried in her social imagination have not, so they constitute a residual prejudicial force that continues to shape her judgements and motivations—not unconsciously in any strict, psychoanalytical sense, but without any focused awareness and without her permission, as we might put it. And an example of the synchronic case might be a lifelong committed anti-racist whose patterns of social judgement none the less betray a residue from racist elements that are contained in the collective social imagination. In such a case, the individual subject is unable to filter out prejudice in the atmosphere of social judgement wholly efficiently, so that a residue of atmospheric prejudice impinges on his own patterns of judgement, again without his permission. Residual prejudice, whether diachronic or synchronic in form, is the sort of prejudice that will bring about the most surreptitious and psychologically subtle forms of testimonial injustice.

I take it that an awareness of how such prejudice can, despite ourselves, shape our credibility judgements by stealth lends support to the idea that various degrees of testimonial injustice happen all the time. As Judith Shklar points out, the history of philosophy leads us to think falsely of justice as the norm and injustice as the aberration:

[T]here is a normal way of thinking about justice, which Aristotle did not invent but certainly codified and forever imprinted upon all our minds. This normal model of justice does not ignore injustice but it does tend to reduce it to a prelude to or a rejection and breakdown of justice, as if injustice were a surprising abnormality.[10]

Shklar persuasively develops the point that injustice is in fact a normal social baseline, while active cries of resentment and demands for rectification are the precious exception. I think that testimonial injustice is a normal part of discursive life, even though cries of resentment are relatively few and far between. One might offer various explanations for

---

[10] Judith Shklar, *The Faces of Injustice* (New Haven and London: Yale University Press, 1990), 17.

this last, including the fact that making the complaint that your boss has not given you your due credibility because, say, you are disabled is unlikely to be readily verifiable and might carry significant social risk (you might get a name as a trouble-maker, they might not want to promote you). But I believe that another reason is that our everyday moral discourse lacks a well-established understanding of the wrong that is done to someone when they are treated in this way. The idea that (what I am calling) testimonial injustice constitutes an ethical wrong that can be non-trivial, indeed profoundly damaging, and even systematically connected with other forms of injustice in society, is not much appreciated. If it were, perhaps we would be more ready to voice our resentments and argue them through to some sort of rectification; and perhaps a social shift would occur towards developing a better vocabulary and forum for airing and responding to such complaints. Perhaps too we would be more ready and able to change our patterns of credibility judgement so as to become less likely to inflict testimonial injustice on others.

In this section I have been arguing that prejudice will tend to go most unchecked when it operates by way of stereotypical images held in the collective social imagination, since images can operate beneath the radar of our ordinary doxastic self-scrutiny, sometimes even despite beliefs to the contrary. Where prejudice does indeed impact directly on hearers' perceptions of speakers, the hope must be that the hearers' beliefs may at some point serve as a corrective force (as in our example of the card-carrying feminist who overcomes her prejudiced perception of female political candidates). I should point out, however, that the converse possibility—of prejudiced beliefs being corrected by unprejudiced social perceptions—is another source of hope, and indeed the general idea that the social imagination can be a powerful positive force for social change depends on it. An example discussed by Arpaly illuminates this possibility. According to Arpaly's reading of Mark Twain's *Huckleberry Finn*, Huckleberry firmly and consistently believes that morality requires him to turn the escaped slave, Jim, over to the authorities in order that he may be returned to his legal owner. But Huckleberry's actions betray the conflict between these beliefs and his perceptual faculty: he crucially fails to turn Jim in when the opportunity arises. Arpaly characterizes Huckleberry as having an unprejudiced moral perception of Jim as a full human being in spite of his conventional but highly racially prejudiced beliefs, and she convincingly argues that he is morally praiseworthy for it. We might say that in not turning Jim in, Huckleberry proves himself to be perceptually unprejudiced, and indeed morally good, in spite of his genuinely held prejudiced beliefs.

I think this possibility of a subject's unprejudiced perception of another human being winning out against his prejudiced beliefs is crucially important for our understanding of how social change is possible, including the social change involved in reforming our patterns of credibility judgement. Whether, in any given case, hopes for effective self-criticism in a hearer reside in the possibility of her beliefs reforming her perceptions, or her perceptions reforming her beliefs, the more general point is that the possibility of dissonance between the two forms of cognitive commitment is a crucial epistemic and ethical resource for those who aim to reduce prejudice in their judgements of credibility.

2.2 TESTIMONIAL INJUSTICE WITHOUT PREJUDICE?

We have been exploring the nature of prejudice and its influence on credibility judgement because we are committed to a definition of testimonial injustice as necessarily involving prejudice, with the central case involving identity prejudice. But it might be objected that under certain circumstances of epistemic bad luck, a hearer could seemingly perpetrate a testimonial injustice without harbouring any prejudice at all. The sort of epistemic bad luck in play in the following example stems from the fact that even the most reliable, non-prejudicial stereotypes will permit of exceptions. Imagine that a hearer responsibly judges a speaker to be untrustworthy (because insincere) owing to the fact that the speaker avoids looking her in the eye, frequently looks askance, and pauses self-consciously in mid-sentence as if to work out his story.[11] The speaker's behaviour justifies the hearer's judgement inasmuch as it fits an empirically reliable stereotype of insincerity. In fact, however, this individual is speaking entirely ingenuously, and his shifty manner is simply due to the rather idiosyncratic manifestations of his extraordinary personal shyness. This speaker, let us agree, constitutes an exception to an empirically reliable rule, and thus the testimonial injustice he suffers is caused not by prejudice but simply by bad luck. What should be said about such an example?

---

[11] I thank Penelope Mackie for this example.

If we were to consider this shyness example to be an instance of testimonial injustice, then it would be a case of non-culpable testimonial injustice: clearly the hearer has done nothing for which she is blameworthy, either epistemically or ethically. While it is possible that an exceptionally perceptive hearer might have been able to discern that her interlocutor's idiosyncratic manner was a manifestation of shyness rather than insincerity, we do not hold ordinary hearers to exceptionally high standards any more than in ethical judgements we hold ordinary agents to exceptionally high standards. If a hearer cannot be blamed for the grounds of her flawed credibility judgement (whether these grounds are embodied in a heuristic or a deliberated argument), then she cannot be blamed for the harm that may result. In the present example, the hearer's flawed credibility judgement arises from a piece of circumstantial epistemic bad luck: she invokes a reliable stereotype of insincerity in a circumstance where the stereotype is, unluckily, misleading.

But I am inclined, ultimately, to say that we should not consider this case to be an instance of testimonial injustice. For if the shy person is deemed to have been wronged, it begins to seem that epistemically wronging someone through no fault of one's own is rather too easy to do, and testimonial injustice comes to be a much less clearly specified ethical idea. If we think of our shy person as wronged, then what about an honest second-hand car salesman? Given that he too is an exception to a reliable stereotype, shouldn't we allow that he is likewise wronged by the hearer's suspicion of him? And then, further down the line, consider Matilda, who told such dreadful lies that her reputation justifies the hearer's disbelief when she is exclaiming truthfully from the window that the house is on fire. Is she wronged too, however non-culpably? Clearly not, for it's her own fault that no one believes a word she says; nor is the second-hand car salesman wronged, though his case is less stark because it relies more on bad luck on his part (the bad luck of winding up in that trade, so to speak). Our shy person has even worse luck than the honest second-hand car salesman, given that we generally have little control over how shy we are or the forms that it takes in our behaviour. Still, the continuity with the other two examples should lead us to conclude that in the case of our shy person too there is no testimonial injustice, for what is common to all three cases is that the hearer has not put a foot wrong—she has made a credibility judgement that is in line with the evidence, yet, as bad luck would have it, the case proves an exception to the rule. All three examples are cases of innocent error on the part of the hearer: no epistemic culpability, and no ethical culpability. There is no testimonial injustice here, and our definition stands.

2.3 THE WRONG OF TESTIMONIAL INJUSTICE

I have here and there urged a picture of human discursive relations such that testimonial injustice is a normal feature of our testimonial practices. Sometimes it may do very little harm—indeed its impact may be trivial—but other times it may be seriously harmful, most of all when it is persistent and systematic. Can we say more about the nature of the harm in question? There is of course a purely epistemic harm done when prejudicial stereotypes distort credibility judgements: knowledge that would be passed on to a hearer is not received. This is an epistemic disadvantage to the individual hearer, and a moment of dysfunction in the overall epistemic practice or system. That testimonial injustice damages the epistemic system is directly relevant to social epistemologies such as Goldman's 'veritism',[12] for prejudice presents an obstacle to truth, either directly by causing the hearer to miss out on a particular truth, or indirectly by creating blockages in the circulation of critical ideas. Further, the fact that prejudice can prevent speakers from successfully putting knowledge into the public domain reveals testimonial injustice as a serious form of unfreedom in our collective speech situation—and on a Kantian conception, the freedom of our speech situation is fundamental to the authority of the polity, even to the authority of reason itself.[13] This is rich territory, and I believe that the concept of testimonial injustice has something to contribute to our understanding of the political importance of just and well-functioning

[12] See Alvin Goldman, *Knowledge in a Social World* (Oxford: Clarendon Press, 1999).
[13] See Onora O'Neill, 'Vindicating Reason', in Paul Guyer (ed.), *The Cambridge Companion to Kant* (Cambridge: Cambridge University Press, 1992), and her *Constructions of Reason: Explorations of Kant's Practical Philosophy* (Cambridge: Cambridge University Press, 1989), chs. 1 and 2. In a recent paper, Axel Gelfert pieces together Kant's view of testimony and its relation to the rule of reason, both conceptually and in our public institutions. Interestingly, it seems that Kant emphasizes a moral dimension to undue incredulity (the primary form of which is embodied in someone who does not want to accept anything as true except on theoretically conclusive grounds), but he identifies this moral dimension not in terms of any harm done to the speaker but rather in terms of the hearer's own loss of dignity in failing to show the proper moral commitment to sustaining those public practices of trust—most obviously promising—that are essential to social life. See Axel Gelfert, 'Kant on Testimony', *British Journal for the History of Philosophy*, 14, no. 4 (2006), 627–52.

practices of epistemic trust. However, present purposes call for a focus specifically on the ethical. The harm that concerns us here is not the epistemic harm incurred by the hearer or the epistemic system, nor any implied damage done to the foundations of the polity and its institutions, but rather the immediate wrong that the hearer does to the speaker who is on the receiving end of a testimonial injustice.

We should distinguish a primary from a secondary aspect of the harm. The primary harm is a form of the essential harm that is definitive of epistemic injustice in the broad. In all such injustices the subject is wronged in her capacity as a knower. To be wronged in one's capacity as a knower is to be wronged in a capacity essential to human value. When one is undermined or otherwise wronged in a capacity essential to human value, one suffers an intrinsic injustice. The form that this intrinsic injustice takes specifically in cases of testimonial injustice is that the subject is wronged in her capacity as a giver of knowledge. The capacity to give knowledge to others is one side of that many-sided capacity so significant in human beings: namely, the capacity for reason. We are long familiar with the idea, played out by the history of philosophy in many variations, that our rationality is what lends humanity its distinctive value. No wonder, then, that being insulted, undermined, or otherwise wronged in one's capacity as a giver of knowledge is something that can cut deep. No wonder too that in contexts of oppression the powerful will be sure to undermine the powerless in just that capacity, for it provides a direct route to undermining them in their very humanity.

The fact that the primary injustice involves insult to someone in respect of a capacity essential to human value lends even its least harmful instances a symbolic power that adds a layer of harm of its own: the epistemic wrong bears a social *meaning* to the effect that the subject is less than fully human. When someone suffers a testimonial injustice, they are degraded *qua* knower, and they are symbolically degraded *qua* human. In all cases of testimonial injustice, what the person suffers from is not simply the epistemic wrong in itself, but also the meaning of being treated like that. Such a dehumanizing meaning, especially if it is expressed before others, may make for a profound humiliation, even in circumstances where the injustice is in other respects fairly minor. But in those cases of testimonial injustice where the driving prejudicial stereotype explicitly involves the idea that the social type in question is humanly lesser (think of the sort of racism heaped upon

Tom Robinson—'*all* Negroes lie'[14]), the dimension of degradation *qua* human being is not simply symbolic; rather, it is a literal part of the core epistemic insult.

Epistemic trustworthiness has two distinct components: competence and sincerity. Now in a case of testimonial injustice it may often be that both components are impugned by the prejudice in the hearer, in which case the experience of the injustice will have a certain composite character. Equally, however, there might be cases in which the prejudice attacks only one of the distinct components, and in such cases the experience of the injustice may have one or another rather different character, depending on whether it is one's competence or one's sincerity that is undermined. Elisabeth Young-Bruehl characterizes three styles of prejudice, two of which are relevant here: the obsessional and the hysterical. The obsessionally prejudiced often construct or imagine their target group 'as descendants of great civilizations of the past—so they are considered highly literate'; and they are constructed as 'both terrifically intellectual ... and terrifically materialistic—and there is no felt contradiction here, as they are so totalitarian in their striving for control'. The hysterically prejudiced, by contrast, construct their target group as 'serflike or slavelike by nature and [such that they] can make their livings only from their physical strength. They are artless and unintelligent, without spiritual accomplishments, or with gifts for only nonliterate arts like music.'[15] One can see how these two different prejudicial stereotypes relate specifically to each of the two different components of epistemic trustworthiness: sincerity in the first case, competence in the second.

But despite the possibility that a prejudice might separate the twin components of epistemic trustworthiness, I suggest that the experience of testimonial injustice remains unified enough to warrant a unified ethical characterization in terms of being wronged *qua* giver of knowledge. Since epistemic trustworthiness requires the conjunction of competence and sincerity, a wrongful attack on either component is sufficient for being wronged in that capacity. The harm will take different forms, but they are both cases of identity-prejudicial exclusion from the community of epistemic trust, and so

---

[14] Harper Lee, *To Kill A Mockingbird* (London: William Heinemann, 1960), 208.
[15] Elisabeth Young-Bruehl, *The Anatomy of Prejudices* (Cambridge, Mass.: Harvard University Press, 1996), 344 and 364.

they both belong to the same category of injustice. (Compare the idea that human rights violations fall under a single ethical category even though they can involve attacks on quite different aspects of human personhood.)

Hobbes was entirely clear that (what I call) credibility judgements involve an assessment of two distinct things: 'in Beleefe are two opinions; one of the saying of the man; the other of his vertue'. Yet we find in his remarks on testimony a mirror-image precedent for the proposed unified conception of the wrong done in a prejudicial deflation of trust. He writes about the *honour* we accord an interlocutor when we believe them:

> When wee believe any saying whatsoever it be, to be true, from arguments taken, not from the thing itselfe, or from the principles of naturall Reason, but from the Authority, and good opinion wee have, of him that hath sayd it; then is the speaker, or person we believe in, or trust in, and whose word we take, the object of our Faith; and the Honour done in Believing, is done to him onely.[16]

When one is wrongfully mistrusted, regardless of whether it is one's competence or one's sincerity that is being impugned, one is *dishonoured* — this would not be an inappropriate term to use in connection with the primary harm of testimonial injustice.

Turning now to the secondary aspect of the harm, we see that it is composed of a range of possible follow-on disadvantages, extrinsic to the primary injustice in that they are caused by it rather than being a proper part of it. They seem to fall into two broad categories distinguishing a *practical* and an *epistemic* dimension of harm. First, practical: if someone is subject to even a one-off testimonial injustice in a courtroom, so that he is found guilty instead of innocent, he may face a fine or worse; or, alternatively, a background experience of persistent testimonial injustice may mean that in someone's working life she comes across as lacking the sure judgement and authority required for a managerial role, and this may make her seem (indeed, in a context where appearances matter, it may truly render her) not management material. I have twice given talks about prejudice and credibility at gatherings of women professionals from a large and male-dominated multinational corporation, and some of the stories they related present examples of considerable professional disadvantage being caused to them by, as I would put it, the everyday

---

[16] Thomas Hobbes, *Leviathan*, ed. Richard Tuck (Cambridge: Cambridge University Press, 1991), ch. 7; quotations from pp. 48 and 49.

testimonial injustices they put up with in the workplace.[17] One Egyptian woman, working in Cairo, said that when she is at a meeting and wants to make a suggestion about policy, she actually writes down the suggestion on a little piece of paper, surreptitiously passes it to a sympathetic male colleague, has him make the suggestion, watches it be well received, and then joins in the discussion from there. She adopted this policy after mounting frustration at the incredulous reception that her ideas typically got from her male colleagues when she presented them as her own. I think I am right in saying that her attitude was feisty resignation that this was how she got things done, and also perhaps that somewhere in the process she probably got more credit than was allowed to show on the surface. She was clear none the less that she was considerably disadvantaged by the prejudicial attitudes towards her word as a woman.

Another woman, this time working for the company in the USA, told me that she tended not to worry too much about who got the credit for ideas she put forward, so long as the ideas got implemented. If she made a suggestion and it was not taken up until a male team member had verbalized it, never mind. Getting things done is what mattered to her and what gave her job satisfaction. She did note, however, that it had probably been an obstacle to the development of her career, for in her annual performance assessments her manager had on more than one occasion remarked how extraordinarily 'lucky' she had seemed to be in the teams she had been a member of—all so successful! Were it part of the corporate understanding and institutions of equal opportunities that an employee could complain that prejudice in the workplace was causing her to receive less than her due credibility and that this was holding back her career, these women would surely have a good case to make. Their experiences seem to be examples of the practical kind of secondary harm caused by testimonial injustice.

The second category of secondary harm caused by testimonial injustice is (more purely) epistemic harm: the recipient of a one-off testimonial injustice may lose confidence in his belief, or in his justification for it, so that he ceases to satisfy the conditions for knowledge; or, alternatively, someone with a background experience of persistent testimonial injustice may lose confidence in her general intellectual abilities to such an extent that she is genuinely hindered in her educational or other intellectual

---

[17] The events were put on by the Cambridge Programme for Industry and New Hall, University of Cambridge. I am grateful to Melissa Lane and her co-organizers for the opportunity to participate.

development. A speaker may incur a testimonial injustice in respect of a particular thing they've said, or with respect to their authority in a specific social role, or just generally; but in cases of systematic testimonial injustice, which are driven by an *identity* prejudice, these three forms of attack tend to come together, so that an identity-prejudicial reception of a particular claim made by a speaker represents an attack on the speaker's epistemic authority quite generally. Linda Martín Alcoff recounts a story of an untenured philosophy professor friend, a Chicana who fell prey to undermining complaints from a white male graduate teaching assistant. She believed, and according to the story had good grounds to believe, that his complaints were utterly unfounded; yet Alcoff tells how this young professor received precious little credibility from her colleagues in her account of the matter until a senior white professor suffered the same sort of complaints from the student: 'This senior professor then concluded that the student didn't really have a problem with my friend, but with authority in any form. And the rest of her colleagues then changed their view of her and made an effort to accept her back into the fold .... *She suffered two years of anguish and self-doubt because of this roadblock in her career.*'[18] In this example, as it is recounted, we see how someone might suffer a double testimonial injustice (first from the teaching assistant regarding what she told students about philosophy,[19] and then from her colleagues in respect of her account of the matter), so that she is doubly undermined as a giver of knowledge, and consequently suffers prolonged self-doubt and loss of intellectual confidence.

These examples of the sorts of practical and epistemic secondary disadvantages that may attend testimonial injustice illustrate how being subject to such injustice can have a wide-ranging negative impact on a person's life. But, as I say, the fact that such disadvantages are effects of the intrinsic injustice means that, strictly speaking, they should be understood as extrinsic. (This does not stop any such effects being unjust, as they will typically inherit the status of injustice from their causal origin. They may also constitute another sort of injustice in their own right, as in the Tom Robinson case, in which the practical outcome of the

---

[18] Linda Martín Alcoff, 'On Judging Epistemic Credibility: Is Social Identity Relevant?', in Naomi Zack (ed.), *Women of Color and Philosophy* (Oxford: Blackwell, 2000), ch. 10; quote on p. 248, italics added.

[19] I am assuming that his unfounded complaints were made ingenuously. Alternatively, if even from his own point of view they were entirely made up, then while he did a serious injustice to this professor, he did not do her a testimonial injustice. Testimonial injustice demands that the hearer genuinely judges the speaker's credibility too low.

testimonial injustice is itself a legal injustice.) Secondary consequences tend to ramify in a person's life, then, so that they are capable of alarming breadth; but they can also run much deeper than one might expect, as we shall see if we pursue the epistemic dimension of harm a little further.

Many definitions and conceptions of knowledge cast some sort of epistemic confidence as a condition of knowledge, whether it comes in as part of the belief condition or as part of a justification condition. If we are to name one seminal epistemological view in this connection, then it must surely be Descartes's idea that a state of absolute confidence in one's belief—a state of certainty—is requisite for knowledge, for the Cartesian internalist assumption has made itself felt in so many conceptions of knowledge subsequently. The significance for the present discussion is that, on any confidence-including conception of knowledge, the implications for someone who meets with persistent testimonial injustice are grim: not only is he repeatedly subject to the intrinsic epistemic insult that is the primary injustice, but where this persistent intellectual undermining causes him to lose confidence in his beliefs and/or his justification for them, he literally *loses knowledge*. Perhaps some piece of knowledge he possesses is washed away in a one-off wave of under-confidence. Or perhaps he suffers a prolonged erosion of epistemic confidence so that he is ongoingly disadvantaged, repeatedly failing to gain items of knowledge he would otherwise have been able to gain.[20]

A less direct way in which someone's general loss of epistemic confidence might result in an ongoing failure to gain knowledge is by preventing him from developing certain intellectual virtues. Most notably, for instance, loss of epistemic confidence is likely to inhibit the development of intellectual courage, the virtue of not backing down in one's convictions too quickly in response to challenge. This is an important feature of intellectual function. James Montmarquet categorizes the epistemic virtues as those of 'impartiality', 'intellectual sobriety', and 'intellectual courage', where this last category includes 'most prominently the willingness to conceive and examine alternatives to popularly held beliefs, perseverance in the face of opposition from others (until one is convinced one is mistaken), and the determination

---

[20] On a view such as Keith Lehrer's, for instance, which accounts for knowledge in coherentist terms that make it depend upon self-trust on the part of the subject, the connection between erosion of epistemic confidence and the capacity to possess knowledge is starkly direct. (I take it that loss of epistemic confidence is equivalent to, or at least entails, loss of epistemic self-trust.) See Lehrer, *Self-Trust: A Study of Reason, Knowledge, and Autonomy* (Oxford: Clarendon Press, 1997).

required to see such a project through to completion'.[21] These different virtues relating to intellectual courage require epistemic confidence, and are obviously susceptible to erosion by persistent testimonial injustice. So if a history of such injustices gnaws away at a person's intellectual confidence, or never lets it develop in the first place, this damages his epistemic function quite generally. The under-confident subject will tend to back down in the face of challenge, or even at the very prospect of it, and this tendency may well deprive him of knowledge he would otherwise have gained. In such a case there will be a series of specific deprivations of knowledge—beliefs or hypotheses that are given up too quickly—where some of these epistemic deprivations may constitute significant losses. More generally, and quite apart from the obvious fact that feelings of under-confidence are generally unpleasant in themselves, there is also an epistemic loss to the subject in terms of his intellectual character. The value of an intellectual virtue is not reducible to the value of those particular items of knowledge it might bring, but derives also from its place in the harmony of a person's overall intellectual character, a harmony which is spoiled by the loss of intellectual confidence that persistent testimonial injustice can cause.

In some cases it will be hard to say whether a given moment of epistemic under-confidence is one-off, or whether it should rather be seen as part of an ongoing process of erosion. A striking example is found in Simone de Beauvoir's *Memoirs of a Dutiful Daughter*. In it she recounts a philosophical skirmish with her friend and fellow student Jean-Paul, where one cannot help but read between the lines (despite de Beauvoir's uncritical authorial point of view) that he does her a testimonial injustice.[22] There is real pathos in the fact that even the mature de Beauvoir writes in apparent innocence of the wrongfulness of Sartre's undermining treatment of her, not to mention its tiresome bullishness, and she recounts the experience thus:

Day after day, and all day long I measured myself against Sartre, and in our discussions I was simply not in his class. One morning in the Luxembourg

---

[21] James A. Montmarquet, *Epistemic Virtue and Doxastic Responsibility* (Lanham, Md.: Rowman and Littlefield, 1993), 23.

[22] I use 'testimonial' here in an extended sense to include not only all cases of telling but also cases of the expression to an interlocutor of judgements, views, and opinions. I think that the real place of testimonial injustice in human discourse licenses this extended usage, though its ethical structure, and indeed its epistemology, is best anchored in cases of telling, since the fundamental communicative point of telling is to transmit knowledge.

Gardens, near the Medici fountain, I outlined for him the pluralist morality which I had fashioned to justify the people I liked but did not wish to resemble: he ripped it to shreds. I was attached to it, because it allowed me to take my heart as the arbiter of good and evil; I struggled with him for three hours. In the end I had to admit I was beaten; besides, I had realized, in the course of our discussion, that many of my opinions were based only on prejudice, bad faith or thoughtlessness, that my reasoning was shaky and my ideas confused. *'I'm no longer sure what I think, or even if I think at all,'* I noted, completely thrown.[23]

Here is an (exceptionally successful) student of philosophy apparently feeling utterly flattened by an experience of testimonial injustice—she is rendered unsure whether she even thinks at all. Happily she has the resilience and intellectual discipline to bounce back, though, as it is presented in the memoir at least, the experience marks the turning point in her intellectual development at which she decides that philosophy is not really for her, and that she is destined instead for the life of a writer. This may have been the right decision, all things considered; but if so, it will not have been because her ideas about good and evil 'were based only on prejudice, bad faith, or thoughtlessness', her reasoning 'shaky' and ideas 'confused'.[24] Testimonial injustice, and the attack it makes on intellectual confidence, can change an intellectual trajectory in one fell blow, whether as a single event or, more likely, as the final straw in an ongoing experience of persistent petty intellectual underminings. However we might judge matters, it is clear how the experience at the time may constitute a wrongful epistemic humiliation of considerable personal and professional consequence.

Such are the secondary practical and epistemic effects of testimonial injustice. I have been arguing that these disadvantages can go broad and deep in a person's life. But now I would like to return to the primary aspect of testimonial injustice to see if the experience of being epistemically undermined might have a more profound significance for the subject's psychology than we have so far countenanced. In Bernard Williams's model of the psychological mechanism by which our various mental contents come to be sorted into (roughly) beliefs on the one hand and desires on the other, we find the mind depicted as containing

---

[23] Simone de Beauvoir, *Memoirs of a Dutiful Daughter* trans. James Kirkup (London: Penguin, 1959), 344, italics added; originally published in French as *Mémoires d'une jeune fille rangée* by Librairie Gallimard, 1958).

[24] I try to say a little more about her reasons in 'Life-Story in Beauvoir's Memoirs', in Claudia Card (ed.), *The Cambridge Companion to Simone de Beauvoir* (Cambridge: Cambridge University Press, 2003).

a stratum of contents that are entertained with no determinate attitude attached: 'wishes'. Wishes are beliefs or desires in waiting, so that any given wish may be on its way to becoming either. And the process by which wishes come to be sorted into one or another category (not a deliberative activity on the part of the subject, needless to say, but rather a process in the subject's psychology) Williams calls 'steadying the mind':

> The basic mechanism depends on the fact that there are others who need to rely on our dispositions, and we want them to be able to rely on our dispositions because we, up to a point, want to rely on theirs. We learn to present ourselves to others, and consequently also to ourselves, as people who have moderately steady outlooks or beliefs.[25]

A mental state cannot count as a belief at all unless it has a reasonable life expectancy. It must be the sort of thing that one is disposed to assert not only now but in the future too. And Williams's proposal is that engagement in mutually reliant, and so mutually trustful, dialogue with others is the chief impetus for this process by which the mind becomes settled. This is because if my interlocutor asks me a question, and given that I come to the exchange in the frame of mind of someone with an interest in ongoing trust with such an interlocutor (in due course she may be able to tell me something I need to know), then her question calls on me to ask myself how the world is in order that I may answer truthfully. This creates a pressure for me to avoid fantasy in my thinking (most specifically to avoid desires slipping through as beliefs to produce wishful thinking), and to tell her something I believe to be true, thus contributing to the steadying of my mind. We might say, then, that trustful conversation with others is the basic mechanism by which the mind steadies itself. Such dialogue pressurizes the subject into having attitudes of belief towards only those propositions that merit it. It draws the subject away from assertoric caprice and towards doxastic stability:

> [The subject] is engaged in trustful conversation with another who relies on him, and the question is whether he can give that person to believe the proposition. In doing that, he may well, in such a case, give himself to believe it as well. It is the presence and needs of others that help us to construct even our factual beliefs.[26]

---

[25] Bernard Williams, *Truth and Truthfulness: An Essay in Genealogy* (Princeton: Princeton University Press, 2002), 192.

[26] Ibid. 194. Williams continues with the claim that 'similar factors can help us to construct our desires', but I am uncertain what these factors are. There is the general idea that the pressure to have a belief attitude towards only those propositions that merit

But now we must add to this conception of the role of trustful dialogue in our psychological formation something further. Williams suggests that this process of settling the mind is the most basic mechanism whereby we come to be who we are. It settles not only one's mind, but thereby (some basic aspects of) one's identity too. As not only our beliefs and desires but also our opinions and value commitments settle themselves through social dialogue into more or less stable states, so an important dimension of our identity thereby takes shape: 'Drawn to bind myself to the others' shared values, to make my own beliefs and feelings steadier ... I become what with increasing steadiness I can sincerely profess; I become what I have sincerely declared to them.'27 The conception of identity in question concerns the most important part of an individual's social identity: an individual's self-acknowledged affiliation to a group identity (racial, political, sexual, religious), where the affiliation tends, in our culture at least, to be experienced by the individual as essential to who she or he really is. We can come to see that we, or others, have made mistakes about what affiliations these are or should be, and this gives substance to the idea that we not only construct but also discover who we are. The process by which the mind is steadied, then, is also the process by which we may become who we deeply, perhaps essentially, are.

The depth of significance that this picture of our psychology and social identity gives to the phenomenon of testimonial injustice is perhaps now coming into view. Testimonial injustice excludes the subject from trustful conversation. Thus it marginalizes the subject in her participation in the very activity that steadies the mind and forges an essential aspect of

---

it entails that one should not believe things that merit only an attitude of desire. Thus the fundamental social pressure to avoid fantasy in thinking and to become mentally steady. But if Williams's remark is intended more specifically to concern the very genesis of desires, then perhaps the idea is that the presence and needs of trustful and trusted interlocutors help us construct and stabilize our desires because it gears them to sincerely asserted expressions of those desires.

27 Ibid. 204. The connection between mental steadiness and others' ability to rely on one for a degree of consistency in one's assertions and actions suggests that there may be an internal relation between becoming a subject of thought and language and becoming an *ethical* subject. Sabina Lovibond explores the idea that there is such an internal relation between meaning what one says and the development of a responsible self. In her account, one learns to be an 'author' of one's words—one learns to be 'serious'—by gaining 'mastery of the social practice of reason giving' (p. 85), where this mastery is conceived as involving the achievement of accountability, so that 'we say only what we are prepared to be called to account for' (p. 84). See her *Ethical Formation* (Cambridge, Mass.: Harvard University Press, 2002), ch. 4.

identity—two processes of fundamental psychological importance for the individual. Further, testimonial injustice is not merely a moment of exclusion from this doubly psychologically valuable activity, it is a prejudicial exclusion. Earlier I made the point that some prejudices are relatively local, giving rise to incidental testimonial injustices, whereas others (identity prejudices) are more socially structural, so that the injustices they give rise to are systematic. But Williams's conception of identity allows us to see how the prejudice working against a speaker in a given discursive exchange may concern a category of social identity (racial, political, sexual, religious) that is *essential* to his identity, essential to who he is. Thus we now understand better how, when this is the case, the injustice cuts him to the quick. Not only does it undermine him in a capacity (the capacity for knowledge) that is essential to his value as a human being, it does so on grounds that discriminate against him in respect of some essential feature of him as a social being. Keeping one's dignity in the face of such a double assault on one's personhood can take great courage, especially if the assault is persistent and systematic. A character such as Tom Robinson may only be able to do it owing to the happily fragmentary nature of social identity taken as a whole. His membership of his own racial community means that an essential dimension of his identity will in part be forged through trustful conversation and other activities of reciprocated trust and respect within that community, in which he may find solidarity and shared resources for psychological resistance.

It would be melodramatic to suggest that whenever someone suffers testimonial injustice they are thereby inhibited, at least a tiny bit (whatever that would mean), in the formation of their identity. But I do not think it an exaggeration to suggest that persistent cases of this sort of wrongful epistemic exclusion could, especially if they are also systematic, genuinely inhibit the development of an essential aspect of a person's identity. Somebody subject to this sort of injustice may not *have* the sort of community in which to find resources for resistance, since the formation of such a community is itself a social achievement and not a social given. The mere fact that one might live around other individuals in the same predicament is insufficient for affiliation to a community in the relevant sense. Imagine a nineteenth-century middle-class woman who entertains a keen but frustrated interest in political affairs in a climate in which women lack the vote and are generally considered out of place in public life on the grounds that they are intellectually and temperamentally unsuited to political judgement. If when this woman expresses her beliefs and opinions around the dinner table she receives a blank wall of incredulity from her hoped-for conversational partners, is she not likely over time to be inhibited precisely in the development of an essential aspect of who she is? Excluded from the trustful conversation of the only people apparently allowed to talk politics, is she not blocked from becoming, in some significant aspect, the person that she is? And unless she takes the risky social leap of becoming a suffragist of one or another stripe, is she not precisely lacking the sort of community that might provide resources for solidarity and resistance? The answer to these questions is surely Yes, and thus the role of trustful conversation in steadying the mind and forging identity helps us to understand just how profoundly the experience of persistent testimonial injustice might penetrate a person's psychology, and just how debilitating it might be in circumstances where psychological resistance would be a social achievement that is more or less out of the subject's reach. Persistent testimonial injustice can indeed inhibit the very formation of self.

A final twist is that, in some contexts, the prejudice operating against the speaker may have a self-fulfilling power, so that the subject of the injustice is socially *constituted* just as the stereotype depicts her (that's what she counts as socially), and/or she may be actually *caused* to resemble the prejudicial stereotype working against her (that's what she comes in some measure to be). When either constitutive or causal construction occurs, we have a case of identity power operating 'productively', as the Foucauldian idiom would term it.[28] The terminology is suggestive, but we will do better not to adopt it for the present case with any real commitment, since it is crucial in the present context that identity power at once constructs and *distorts* who the subject really is, and that is an idea which finds no home in the Foucauldian conception. Take our pre-suffrage, politically minded woman again. Her experience

---

[28] For Foucault, power is productive in at least two senses. In connection, for instance, with the establishment of psychiatric discourse around the 'delinquent', it is not hard to see how power might be productive rather than merely repressive. Power can be at work, first, in producing the conceptual and discursive innovation itself, so that the idea of a certain social identity is created ('delinquent'); and, secondly, it is at work in categorizing people so that they are constitutively and perhaps even causally constructed as delinquents. Concepts such as 'delinquent' or 'pervert', newly invoked as means of categorization and institutional organization, render a given social scientific discourse—psychology, criminology—its own distinctive subject matter, thus helping that discourse to establish itself as scientific; see Foucault, *Discipline and Punish: The Birth of the Prison*, trans. Alan Sheridan (London: Penguin Books, 1997), 256. Power, then, can produce changes in conceptual practices; and it can thereby produce new categories of social subject that are fit for a newly created function.

of persistent testimonial injustice in respect of matters political might well, in the absence of community, not only help rigidify what sort of social being she is allowed to count as, but may actually cause her to become something closer to the prejudicial stereotype that is directed against her: a social type intellectually and temperamentally unsuited to political judgement. Thus the construction of gender; thus identity power's ability to shape the people it cramps.[29]

Constitutive construction does not lend itself easily to empirical verification. But there is an empirical literature on the self-fulfilling power of stereotypes that illustrates the causal constructive mechanism. Stereotypes make themselves felt in the form of expectations, and expectations can have a powerful effect on people's performances. Many contexts in which the performance in question is intellectual and discursive are like this. There is evidence from educational studies, for instance, that pupils respond to teachers' expectations of them. In Robert Rosenthal and Lenore Jacobson's much discussed[30] study, they summarize the results of an experiment as follows:

20 percent of the children in a certain elementary school were reported to their teachers as showing unusual potential for intellectual growth. The names of these 20 percent of the children were drawn by means of a table of random numbers, which is to say that the names were drawn out of a hat. Eight months later these unusual or 'magic' children showed significantly greater gains in IQ than did the remaining children who had not been singled out for the teachers' attention. The change in the teachers' expectations regarding the intellectual performance of these allegedly 'special' children had led to an actual change in the intellectual performance of these randomly selected children.[31]

---

[29] For related discussions of social construction, see Rae Langton, 'Subordination, Silence, and Pornography's Authority', in Robert Post (ed.), *Censorship and Silencing: Practices of Cultural Regulation* (Los Angeles: Getty Research Institute for the History of Art and the Humanities, 1998), 261–84; and Sally Haslanger, 'Ontology and Social Construction', in S. Haslanger (ed.), *Philosophical Topics: Feminist Perspectives on Language, Knowledge, and Reality*, 23, no. 2 (1995), 95–125.

[30] It seems that certain aspects of the method used in this study were initially controversial, though later vindicated. For a brief discussion to this effect see Lee Jussim and Christopher Fleming, 'Self-fulfilling Prophecies and the Maintenance of Social Stereotypes: The Role of Dyadic Interactions and Social Forces', in C. Neil Macrae, Charles Stangor, and Miles Hewstone (eds.), *Stereotypes and Stereotyping* (New York and London: The Guilford Press, 1996), 161–92.

[31] Robert Rosenthal and Lenore Jacobson, *Pygmalion in the Classroom: Teacher Expectation and Pupils' Intellectual Development* (New York: Holt, Rinehart and Winston Inc., 1968), pp. vii–viii. See esp. chs. 6–7. Richard Nisbett and Lee Ross also cite later studies which provide 'particularly persuasive evidence of people's tendency to elicit behavior from others according to their initial hypotheses' (*Human Inference: Strategies*

This study was not a study of the influence of prejudicial stereotypes on teacher expectation, for the teachers in question were simply fed pseudo-information about the pupils' relative signs of ability. But it is not hard to imagine how in general prejudicial stereotypes might help determine teacher expectation in a negative and unjust manner (to think otherwise would be to set teachers implausibly apart from the rest of us). If we envisage classroom contexts in which students are asked by teachers for factual answers to questions, for interpretations, for views and opinions, we can well imagine that a negative prejudicial stereotype will tend to do two things. First, it will tend to deflate the credibility judgement that the teacher makes of the pupil's expressed views. So far, so recognizable: prejudicial stereotypes issue in testimonial injustice. But second, the stereotype may actually exert a causal force towards its own fulfilment, as in the experiment recounted above. Just as the quality of our driving, say, might be responsive to a censorious passenger's negative expectations of our performance, so that we are actually caused to drive badly in the company of such a person, it seems entirely plausible that our intellectual performances might take a similar route in educational contexts, not to say quite generally. In other, more recent empirical trials, for example, which were designed to establish whether negative stereotypes of African-Americans in relation to intelligence have a causal impact on their academic performance, it was indeed found that if the test was advertised as a test of academic ability, black students performed worse than white students, whereas this was not the case if it was billed as not designed to test intelligence. This result is taken as demonstrating the 'stereotype threat', according to which a member of a group that is subject to a negative stereotype (what I call a negative identity-prejudicial stereotype) will tend to behave in ways that fulfil that stereotype. 'Stereotype threat' effectively labels a certain social predicament: the predicament of susceptibility to a disadvantageous causal construction.[32]

and Shortcomings of Social Judgement (Englewood Cliffs, NJ: Prentice-Hall, 1980). A particularly relevant study described is M. Snyder, E. D. Tanke, and E. Berscheid, 'Social Perception and Interpersonal Behavior: On the Self-fulfilling Nature of Social Stereotypes', *Journal of Personality and Social Psychology*, 35 (1977), 656–6. For a more recent survey of similar trials demonstrating the power of stereotypes for self-fulfilment, see Jussim and Fleming, 'Self-fulfilling Prophecies and the Maintenance of Social Stereotypes' in Macrae, Stangor, and Hewstone (eds.).

[32] See Claude M. Steele and Joshua Aronson, 'Stereotype Threat and the Intellectual Test Performance of African Americans', in Stangor (ed.), *Stereotypes and Prejudice*, 369–89.

The implication for persistent testimonial injustice is that the subject's intellectual performance may be inhibited long-term, their confidence undermined, and development thwarted. How far this is so, and for whom, are of course empirical questions, but the social psychological research is very suggestive. I offer these thoughts about the self-fulfilling power of prejudicial stereotypes concerning trustworthiness as pregnant speculation as to the ramifications in a person's life, and in a group's social trajectory, of persistent testimonial injustice. Testimonial injustice may, depending on the context, exercise real social constructive power, and where such construction ensues, the primary harm of the injustice is grimly augmented—the epistemic insult is also a moment in a process of social construction that constrains who the person can be. Putting the primary harm together with the extensive secondary harms it can cause, we now have a portrait of an injustice that shows it to be capable of running both deep and wide in a person's psychology and practical life. Where it is not only persistent but also systematic, testimonial injustice presents a face of oppression.

Oppression can be explicitly repressive (as it was for Tom Robinson) or it can be a silent by-product of residual prejudice in a liberal society. Iris Marion Young characterizes the latter as 'the disadvantage and injustice some people suffer not because a tyrannical power intends to keep them down, but because of the everyday practices of a well-intentioned liberal society'.[33] In this chapter it is the everyday practices of well-intentioned hearers, operating in a social-imaginative atmosphere of residual prejudice, that we have been exploring. For this is the social context in which we find the most surreptitious and philosophically complex forms of testimonial injustice. Discussing the nature of oppression, Sandra Lee Bartky quotes Frantz Fanon's idea of 'psychic alienation', where the alienation in question consists in 'the estrangement of separating off a person from some of the essential attributes of personhood'.[34] I think it is obviously an essential attribute of personhood to be able to participate in the spread of knowledge by testimony and to enjoy the respect enshrined in the proper relations of trust that are its prerequisite. A culture in which some groups are separated off from that aspect of personhood by the experience of

[33] Iris Marion Young, 'Five Faces of Oppression', in Thomas E. Wartenberg (ed.), *Rethinking Power* (Albany, NY: State University of New York Press, 1992), 175–6.
[34] Sandra Lee Bartky, 'On Psychological Oppression', in her *Femininity and Domination: Studies in the Phenomenology of Oppression* (New York and London: Routledge, 1990), 30.

repeated exclusions from the spread of knowledge is seriously defective both epistemically and ethically. Knowledge and other rational input they have to offer are missed by others and sometimes literally lost by the subjects themselves; and they suffer a sustained assault in respect of a defining human capacity, an essential attribute of personhood. Such a culture would indeed be one in which a species of epistemic injustice had taken on the proportions of oppression.

3

Towards a Virtue Epistemological
Account of Testimony

3.1 SKETCHING THE DIALECTICAL POSITION

The phenomenon I call testimonial injustice is not in fact confined to testimonial exchange, even allowing that we intend testimony in its broadest sense to include all cases of telling. Prejudicial credibility deficit can, after all, occur when a speaker simply expresses a personal opinion to a hearer, or airs a value judgement, or tries out a new idea or hypothesis on a given audience. But telling is the parent case of testimonial injustice, since the basic wrong of testimonial injustice is the undermining of the speaker *qua* knower, and, while other sorts of utterance may sometimes communicate knowledge, it is distinctive of telling that conveying knowledge is its most basic and immediate point—its illocutionary point, as we might put it.[1] (I hope this claim is intuitive enough in its

---

[1] It should not go without mention that C. A. J. Coady, in his ground-breaking book *Testimony. A Philosophical Study* (Oxford: Clarendon Press, 1992), casts the illocutionary point of testimony not in terms of the communication of knowledge but specifically as the provision of evidence. He effectively casts the conveying of knowledge as an especially felicitous case of providing evidence; but it seems to me that this requires too much of a stretch. To characterize as *evidence* what I offer to my interlocutor when he asks me my date of birth and I tell him my date of birth puts too much strain on the idea—which it is Coady's main aim to vindicate—that testimonial knowledge can be direct or non-inferential.

Coady is sensitive to this line of objection, and responds by emphasizing that the conception of evidence he intends is epistemologically minimal; and he also says that, like asserting, objecting, and arguing, the more general illocutionary point of testimony is to inform, so that the giving of evidence is just the distinctive way that testimony does it (p. 43). But I think that it is very hard to hear 'evidence' as minimally as Coady wants us to, and certainly the claim that the speaker 'offers' her word as evidence seems psychologically quite wrong for the normal case.

Coady takes formal courtroom testimony as his starting model for everyday informal testimony, and one might think that he is right to suppose that this supports the idea that the point of informal testimony is to provide evidence. I do not think this is so. Certainly,

own right, but we shall in any case see it substantiated in Chapter 5 by way of a certain genealogy of the concept of knowledge.) For this reason the epistemology of testimony is the relevant framework within which to place all cases of prejudicial credibility deficit.

Accounts of the epistemology of testimony can be seen as falling into two broad varieties: inferentialist and non-inferentialist. There is room for a diversity of views, to be sure, but a key motivation for any will be the author's inclinations *vis-à-vis* inferentialist and non-inferentialist pictures of the obligations upon a hearer if she is to gain knowledge from her interlocutor. One might be inclined to put a familiar picture of justification to the fore and argue that in order to gain knowledge that *p* from somebody telling her that *p*, the hearer must in some way (perhaps very swiftly, perhaps even unconsciously) rehearse an argument whose conclusion is *p*.[2] Alternatively, one might be inclined to put phenomenological considerations to the fore and argue that our everyday spontaneous reception of the word of others can bring

what courtroom witnesses are doing by testifying is giving evidence; but most of the testimony given in a court of law is solicited because of its evidential bearing on some *other* matter which it is the court's business to settle (is the defendant guilty as charged?). It remains quite open whether a witness's testimony that *p* should be conceived as also *evidence for p*. This seemed odd as an account of informal testimony, and now it seems odd even as an account of formal testimony. Certainly the procedural or institutional point of formal testimony is to give evidence, but the illocutionary point may yet be, simply, to pass on knowledge.

2 The key historical source for the inferentialist outlook is surely Hume; see David Hume, *An Enquiry Concerning Human Understanding*, sect. 10 (first published 1739). But let me register some caution here, as I think it is a bad interpretive strategy to assume that the inferentialist view that Hume sets out in respect of astonishing reports—the only thing he wrote on testimony is 'Of Miracles'—can be taken as a position on testimony generally. One can readily imagine an alternative, equally Humean, view that he might have taken of the epistemology of everyday non-astonishing reports, to the effect that the human mind is conditioned by experience to spontaneously move from a speaker's word that *p* to the truth of *p*. Michael Welbourne has argued a case for reading Hume as advancing such an associationist default of acceptance (see his *Knowledge* (Chesham, Bucks: Acumen, 2001), ch. 5); Paul Faulkner warns against interpreting Hume as a sceptical reductionist (see his 'David Hume's Reductionist Epistemology of Testimony', *Pacific Philosophical Quarterly*, 79 (1998), 302–13); and Robert Fogelin suggests that Hume's position is neutral on the matter (see *A Defense of Hume On Miracles* (Princeton: Princeton University Press, 2003), 90, n. 3).

For some recent inferentialist approaches, see Elizabeth Fricker, 'Against Gullibility', in B. K. Matilal and A. Chakrabarti (eds.), *Knowing from Words: Western and Indian Philosophical Analysis of Understanding and Testimony* (Dordrecht: Kluwer, 1994), and 'Second-hand Knowledge', forthcoming in *Philosophy and Phenomenological Research*; Jack Lyons, 'Testimony, Induction and Folk Psychology', *Australasian Journal of Philosophy*, 75, no. 2 (1997), 163–77; and Peter Lipton, 'The Epistemology of Testimony', *Studies in History and Philosophy of Science*, 29 (1998), 1–31.

knowledge even without the making of any such argument. Those inclined towards this latter, non-inferentialist picture tend to argue for some sort of *default* of credulity or acceptance of what others tell us. Perhaps this default is argued for on the grounds that we have a natural proclivity towards both veracity (as speakers) and credulity (as hearers), so that, generally speaking, the former provides an empirical justification for the latter.[3] Or perhaps the default is advanced as a priori justified, so that we are a priori entitled to the default of uncritically accepting what others tell us.[4] One way or the other, we see non-inferentialism taking shape as a default of uncritical receptivity on the part of the hearer, as this seems to render the epistemology consonant with the phenomenology. Roughly speaking, then, in the epistemology of testimony it can seem as though we must plump for one of two epistemological stories. One story presents the hearer as gaining knowledge only if he rehearses an appropriate inference. The other story seems to present the hearer as gaining knowledge by way of one or another default of uncritical receptivity such that he is entitled to accept what he is told without exercising any critical capacity.

The shortcoming of each is the allure of the other. Inferentialism, as Coady presents it, says 'that all knowledge by testimony is indirect or inferential. We know that *p* when reliably told that *p* because we make some inference about the reliability and sincerity of the witness'.[5] In an alternative formulation, John McDowell presents the inferentialist model as resting on the following assumption:

If an epistemically satisfactory standing in the space of reasons, with respect to a proposition, is mediated rather than immediate, that means the standing

---

[3] The key historical figure for the view that a default of accepting what we are told is innate is Thomas Reid; see his *An Inquiry into the Human Mind on the Principle of Common Sense* (first published 1764), ch. 6, sect. xxiv, 'Of the Analogy between Perception and the Credit We Give to Human Testimony'. The twin principles of 'credulity' and 'veracity', instilled in our nature by God, together ensure that we are entitled to accept what we are told, except in so far as the experience of the mature subject may give rise to doubt in any particular case. For some recent non-inferentialist approaches, see Coady, *Testimony*; John McDowell, 'Knowledge by Hearsay', in *Meaning, Knowledge, and Reality* (Cambridge, Mass.: Harvard University Press, 1998), essay 19; and for a specifically communitarian form of non-inferentialism, see Martin Kusch, *Knowledge by Agreement: The Programme of Communitarian Epistemology* (Oxford: Oxford University Press, 2002), Part I.

[4] The view that a default of acceptance is justified a priori is advanced by Tyler Burge, 'Content Preservation', *Philosophical Review*, 102, no. 4 (Oct. 1992), 457–88; see also his 'Interlocution, Perception, and Memory', *Philosophical Studies*, 86 (1997), 21–47.

[5] Coady, *Testimony*, 122–3.

is constituted by the cogency of an *argument* that is at its occupant's disposal, with the proposition in question as conclusion.[6]

On whichever formulation, the inferentialist model is obviously well designed to calm anxieties about the justification of accepting what others tell us, as it requires that the hearer go in for a piece of reasoning that provides just such a justification. Inevitably this will usually be some sort of inductive argument: for instance, an argument about the individual speaker's past reliability on these matters, or about the general reliability of people like that about things like this. But the trouble now is that the requirement that the hearer avail herself of such an argument seems too strong because too laborious intellectually. It simply does not match our everyday phenomenology of informal testimonial exchange, which presents learning something by being told as distinctly *un*-laborious and spontaneous. Surely an epistemic practice as basic to human life as being-told-things-by-someone-who-knows cannot demand that level of intellectual effort, not to mention accomplishment? If the hearer were genuinely supposed competently to attend (in however rule-of-thumbish a way) to the likelihood that she has been told a truth, then that would take a few moments' hard-nosed assessment of a sort which simply does not tally with the easy spontaneity that is characteristic of so much of our everyday testimonial exchange. The advocate of the inferential model will naturally respond by emphasizing that the mature hearer will normally rehearse her argument very readily and easily. But the more he is at pains to emphasize that such justificatory argumentation can be so swift as barely to be noticed, and might even be altogether unconscious, the more the model strikes one as a piece of intellectualism in a tight corner.

This problem with the inferentialist model leads one to look to non-inferentialism for an alternative. Here we find a picture according to which the hearer enjoys some sort of default of uncritical receptivity to what she is told. This certainly seems to tally better with the

---

[6] McDowell, 'Knowledge by Hearsay', 415. He takes it that inferentialism demands that such an argument equip the hearer with *knowledge* of what he is told; but this would be a particularly strong form of inferentialism, since it requires that one be in possession of an argument that guarantees the truth of what one is told. A more modest inferentialism would require only that the argument equip the hearer with a *justification* for believing what he is told. It seems to me, therefore, that one of the chief arguments that McDowell uses against inferentialism—that there would never be an argument available to the hearer that was strong enough to supply the requisite guarantee—is ineffective against the more modest form of inferentialism.

phenomenology of our everyday exchanges. In the absence of cues for doubt, we surely accept most of what we are told without going in for any active critical assessment, and so our experience as hearers can seem to be that we are trustful unless and until some prompt for doubt is picked up on. This is something that a view depicting us as constitutionally open to the word of others, such as is advanced by Thomas Reid, is well placed to explain. An everyday example might be that, as I make my way hurriedly to the train station, I ask a stranger what the time is, he tells me it's 2 p.m. and I simply, unreflectively, accept what he says. This unreflectiveness is underlined by the fact that if I do pick up on some cue for doubt—such as his saying it is 2 p.m. when I know it must be later than that because it's already getting dark—then I experience a sort of intellectual shift of gear, out of that unreflective mode and into a reflective, more effortful mode of active critical assessment. It is only with this shift of gear that I might start to bring some active reflection to bear on the matter of my interlocutor's trustworthiness.

But now we may feel that the intuitive relevance of the evidence of past experience in how we are conditioned to receive the word of others has gone missing from the ordinary unreflective case. It is not only one's awareness of (for instance) whether it is light or dark that conditions one's responses as a hearer, but also one's background assumptions about the probability of a speaker like this telling one the truth about a subject matter like that. Surely these sorts of assumptions must be doing some justificational work? If such broadly inductive considerations are wholly absent from our unreflective exchanges, imposing no constraint upon what the hearer may properly accept, then this surely leaves our ordinary unreflective exchanges in an unacceptable rational vacuum. Certainly this worry applies to views in which the default is supposed to be justified on empirical grounds, since the idea that a natural human propensity to tell the truth could justify a general policy of uncritically receiving what one is told seems over-optimistic, to put it mildly. A natural propensity is one thing, but discursive life brings in too many countervailing factors for such an underlying propensity to be relied on. Of course there are confined contexts in which such a practice would turn out all right, but a general practice of credulity would not be a success. First, people get things wrong—we make mistakes, we have bad luck, and sometimes perhaps we fancy ourselves as knowing when really we don't; and secondly, people sometimes deliberately mislead or withhold information from others because it is in their interests to do so.

A general default of accepting the word of others critically unmediated would be justificationally lax. Our testimonial exchanges will always be subject to luck, but that sort of default would leave us implausibly defenceless against routine testimonial hazards.

Where the default is argued to be justified a priori, however, as on Tyler Burge's account, the problem of over-optimism need not arise. It can be avoided by emphasizing, as Burge does, that the justification is precisely not dependent upon the empirical likelihood of speaker veracity.[7] The justification is sourced elsewhere, in the conceptual connections between intelligibility, rationality, and veracity (though this last is thoroughly problematic, for, as Burge is aware, the conceptual connection between rationality and truth may just as well issue in an instance of rational lying as one of truth telling[8]). An a priori default entitlement to accept what we are told can hold even if, in a given context, it is most usually the case that speakers cannot be trusted. In a context where distrust was more usually called for than trust, the a priori entitlement to the default would still hold; it is just that, as a matter of fact, the default would usually be lapsed. The problem of over-optimism, then, applies only to the empirical version of the idea that we enjoy a default of credulity. But there is a closely related problem that afflicts both sorts of default account: they both effectively represent the hearer's critical faculties as in snooze mode at the very moment when she takes in knowledge from an interlocutor. This should strike one as ultimately unsatisfactory, for while this aspect of the default accounts may seem on the face of it to be in tune with the hearer's phenomenology in respect of the spontaneous unreflectiveness with which we usually take

---

[7] See Burge, 'Content Preservation', 468.

[8] Burge tries to patch things up with a functional argument:

One of reason's primary functions is that of presenting truth, independently of special personal interests. Lying is sometimes rational in the sense that it is in the liar's best interests. But lying occasions a disunity among functions of reason. It conflicts with one's reason's transpersonal function of presenting the truth, independently of special personal interests (Ibid. 475).

Such an argument, however, is too weak for the job and could only furnish something like the idea that truth telling is functionally prior to lying, which it surely is. From this priority it follows that there could not be a society whose practice of testimony was universally unreliable, but it does not follow that we are entitled to presume veracity, other things equal, even allowing that the entitlement itself need only hold at a high level of idealization. For the awkward fact remains that in any given case the conceptual connection being realized might not be that between rationality and veracity but rather that between rationality and mendacity. Determining which is in fact being realized in any given case can only be an empirical matter.

in the word of others, none the less it is signally out of tune with the phenomenology in two other important respects.

First, the idea of an uncritical default position on the part of the hearer misrepresents the mental 'shift of gear' that is experienced on detecting a reason for doubt. Any default model—whether it takes the form of Reid's innate twin principles of credulity and veracity, or Burge's a priori justified Principle of Acceptance—represents the hearer as having his critical faculties in snooze mode unless and until he is alerted to some cue for doubt that flicks a switch to reawaken his critical consciousness. On any such account, then, the shift of gear is represented as a shift from uncritical to critical reception of what one is told. But I believe that the more faithful characterization (and it is certainly *as* faithful as the alternative) is one that presents it as a shift from unreflective to reflective modes on the part of the hearer, where *either* mode is one in which the hearer may give a critical reception to her interlocutor's word.

Second, and accordingly, I suggest that our experience of unreflectively taking in what we are told is not, after all, best characterized by an account that represents our critical faculties as entirely inoperative, but by an account that represents our critical faculties as ongoingly operative in a lower-level, more automatic manner. Without actively assessing or reflecting on how trustworthy our interlocutor is, the responsible hearer none the less remains unreflectively alert to the plethora of signs, prompts, and cues that bear on how far she should trust. This, I suggest, is the more faithful description of the phenomenology, and I shall develop a view below which makes epistemological sense of it. We shall take up the idea, mooted in the previous chapter, that a credibility judgement can be a perception. More specifically, such judgements are 'theory'-laden perceptions, the 'theory' in question being a body of generalizations about human cognitive abilities and motivational states relating to the two aspects of trustworthiness, competence and sincerity. This idea of a credibility judgement as a perception of the speaker will help characterize the responsible hearer's stance as one of *critical openness* to the word of others, where this stance allows her to take in knowledge as effortlessly as the phenomenology suggests. Both empirical and a priori default accounts seem to assume that if no inference is made by the hearer, then her reception of her interlocutor's word must be uncritical; hence the need to source justification somewhere off-stage, in a natural propensity, or else in something a priori. Indeed, this is an assumption they share with their inferentialist opponents, whose mirror response is to demand that a piece of argument be written into the hearer's script. But the assumption is false, or so I shall attempt to show.

3.2 THE RESPONSIBLE HEARER?

McDowell argues for the view that a hearer gains knowledge by testimony in virtue of exercising 'doxastic responsibility'; and what it is to exercise doxastic responsibility is explained in characteristic Sellarsian terms of a sensitivity to one's place in the 'space of reasons'. The idea of a 'mediated standing in the space of reasons' is the idea of a state—a state of knowledge, for example—which has been arrived at by way of an appropriate sensitivity to the reasons for and against the proposition. And this sensitivity need not manifest itself in the making of inferences or arguments. Indeed, precisely not. As McDowell says:

> What I am proposing is a different conception of what it is for a standing in the space of reasons to be mediated. A standing in the space of reasons can be mediated by the rational force of surrounding considerations, in that the concept of that standing cannot be applied to a subject who is not responsive to that rational force.[9]

So, if the standing in the space of reasons is 'knowing that p', then McDowell's proposal is that this knowing that p has as a precondition that the knower has somehow exercised a sensitivity to surrounding reasons for and against taking it that p.

If one accepts this eminently acceptable proposal, then it is natural to move to the next question and ask, If not by our usual faculties of argumentation and inference, then by what rational capacity *is* the hearer able to be responsive to the rational force of surrounding reasons? The idea that the fulfilment of doxastic responsibility need not require argumentation is surely crucial to explaining how testimonial knowledge can be mediated yet direct (or, as I am framing the issue, critical yet non-inferential); but something further needs to be said to explain how the hearer does it. If she is not exercising her capacity for inference and argumentation, what rational capacity is she exercising?

McDowell seems minded to say that there is nothing to be explained here:

> If we are not to explain the fact that having heard from someone that things are thus and so is an epistemic standing by appealing to the strength of an argument

9 McDowell, 'Knowledge by Hearsay', 430.

that things are that way ... do we need some other account of it? I would be tempted to maintain that we do not. The idea of knowledge by testimony is that if a knower gives intelligible expression to his knowledge, he puts it into the public domain, where it can be picked up by those who can understand the expression, as long as the opportunity is not closed to them because it would be doxastically irresponsible to believe the speaker.[10]

Supposing we can agree that quietism is in order on the question of what constitutes the transaction whereby a speaker uses language to put a piece of knowledge into the public domain so that another speaker might pick up on it. It might be said that having expressed the puzzle in the right way, free of certain peculiarly philosophical hang-ups that lead us to plumb fantasized depths, there is no longer any cause for puzzlement here. Agreed. None the less, something more is surely needed as regards the question of *how* we exercise doxastic responsibility. That does remain puzzling, and it is surely a puzzle that non-inferentialists need to address. If the hearer's exercising doxastic responsibility is not a matter of her making an inference, then what *is* it a matter of? It is surely right to say that a hearer can exercise responsibility without making any inferences; but this should leave one wondering *how*—by what capacity of reason—she is supposed to do it.

The same question arises, in slightly different terms, on Burge's default account. He argues for an Acceptance Principle, according to which the hearer 'is a priori entitled to accept a proposition that is presented as true and that is intelligible to him, unless there are stronger reasons not to do so'.[11] Thus we are entitled to accept what another tells us so long as the default of acceptance holds; or, as Burge glosses it, we are entitled to accept 'other things equal'. But the more we focus on this question of the default, the less Burge's account seems to have achieved in terms of realizing the non-inferentialist ambition. The traditional puzzle about how the hearer may be justified in accepting without inference what he is told is more displaced than solved, for we remain entirely in the dark about how hearers may live out the Acceptance Principle in practice. We are still groping for illumination when it comes to the remaining obligations on the hearer in terms of his on-stage display of sensitivity to whether or not the default holds in any particular case.

---

[10] McDowell, 'Knowledge by Hearsay', 437–8.
[11] Burge, 'Content Preservation', 469.

The question of how the hearer is to be non-inferentially sensitive to the status of the default is just a new version of the original problem that a non-inferentialist account has to solve: namely, the problem of how the hearer can exercise sensitivity to the balance of reasons for and against acceptance without making an inference. The Acceptance Principle bids us to 'accept ... unless there are stronger reasons not to', so in exercising a sensitivity to the status of the default of acceptance, the hearer can only be exercising a sensitivity to the very thing that the Acceptance Principle was supposed to save her wrestling with: namely, the balance of reasons for and against accepting what she is told. Of course, on Burge's account, the hearer's exercise of this sensitivity is not the source of the justification—the whole point of the account is to source that independently from anything in the hearer's performance. But now one is left wondering quite how much is gained by sourcing justification off-stage, since we see that the hearer *still* needs to exercise an unexplained non-inferential rational sensitivity to the balance of reasons for and against acceptance. The only difference is that she must exercise it in respect of the status of the default (does it hold?) rather than in respect of the status of the testimony itself (is it to be accepted?). It seems that non-inferentialism might be well served by a renewed direct look at the responsible hearer's on-stage performance. Indeed, I propose that if we can get clear about the role played by the responsible hearer's on-stage rational sensitivity, then we shall have arrived at a non-inferentialist account of the hearer's responsibilities that renders an a priori justification (indeed, any off-stage justification) surplus to requirement.

Let us pursue the idea of the hearer's critical openness to what she is told, an idea that might make sense of the phenomenology (as I characterized it) of unreflective alertness to the plethora of prompts and cues that bear on how far one should trust. We are looking for a rational sensitivity such that the hearer may critically filter what she is told without active reflection or inference of any kind. A brief comment of Coady's supplies a suggestive starting point. He describes a 'learning mechanism' which operates in the hearer critically, though non-inferentially, to determine the balance of trust. In his words:

What happens characteristically in the reception of testimony is that the audience operates a sort of learning mechanism which has certain critical capacities built into it. The mechanism may be thought of as partly innate, though modified by experience, especially in the matter of critical capacities.

It is useful to invoke the model of a mechanism here since the reception of testimony is normally unreflective but is not thereby uncritical.[12]

I think this is exactly right, although in itself it does not get us very far. We still need to find some fuller explanation of the formation and operation of our learning mechanism in order to understand how it can be spontaneously operative so that there is no need for any active reflection on our parts, and further how it can be responsive to new discursive experiences so that it develops and modifies itself accordingly. Let us look again at the phenomenology, and an example from Robert Audi. He imagines being on a plane and conversing with the person in the neighbouring seat. At the start of the conversation, one does not take her word all that seriously, but by the end one has come to find her entirely credible. Reflecting on the different possible explanations for such an attitude shift, he says:

One possibility is an unconscious inference, say from the general credibility of her account to the conclusion that this proposition, as an essential part of it, is true. But perhaps the cognitive *influence* of my standing beliefs, such as a newly formed belief that she is credible, need not proceed through an *inference* from them. Another possible explanation is more moderate: even apart from my forming beliefs about her credibility, her eventually becoming, in my eyes, a quite credible person, can in some fairly direct way produce in me a general disposition to believe her.[13]

But what account should be given of this 'fairly direct way' in which speakers are or become more or less credible in their interlocutors' eyes? As Hobbes says, in testimony it is first and foremost the *person* one sizes up:

When a mans Discourse beginneth not at Definitions, it beginneth either at some other contemplation of his own. … Or it beginneth at some saying of another, of whose ability to know the truth, and of whose honesty in not deceiving, he doubteth not; and then the Discourse is not so much concerning the Thing, as the Person; and the Resolution is called Beleefe, and Faith: *Faith* in the man.[14]

In the last chapter we began to explore the idea that we should think of the hearer's credibility judgement in terms of the hearer *perceiving*

    [12] Coady, *Testimony*, 47.
    [13] Robert Audi, *Epistemology: A Contemporary Introduction to the Theory of Knowledge* (London: Routledge, 1998), 133.
    [14] Thomas Hobbes, *Leviathan*, ed. Richard Tuck (Cambridge: Cambridge University Press, 1991), ch. 7; p. 48.

the speaker as more or less trustworthy on the matter in question. A perceptual model certainly fits the phenomenon that Audi describes of a hearer's changing 'in a fairly direct way' his view of a speaker's credibility during a conversation. So let us further develop the idea that a hearer's sensitivity to the many prompts and cues that bear on trust *is* his capacity for a certain sort of social perception. What sort of perceptual capacity would this be? In order for the hearer to, so to speak, see his interlocutors in epistemic colour, the perceptual capacity would have to be informed by a background 'theory' (body of generalizations) not simply of human competences and motivations *per se*, but, more specifically, a socially situated 'theory' of the competences and motivations of this or that social type in this or that context. He needs to receive the word of his interlocutor in the light of the probability that someone like that would (be able and willing to) tell someone like him the truth about something like this in circumstances like these. So the hearer's credibility judgement must trade in the likely competences and motivations of different social types, including how the speaker's likely social perception of the hearer may affect his motivation pertaining to sincerity. That the hearer must trade in social types in this way was why, in the previous chapter, we found stereotypes to be a proper part—indeed, an essential part—of credibility judgements. It is only when the stereotypes are prejudiced that something alien—a counter-rational current of identity power—has entered in.

So much is familiar from the previous chapter, but in order that we may now substantiate more fully the idea that the responsible hearer perceives his interlocutor in a way that is epistemically loaded—he perceives her as more, or less, credible in what she is telling him—let us look to ethics for an instructive analogy. There is a form of moral cognitivism in the virtue ethical tradition which advances the idea of moral perception. In this neo-Aristotelian tradition, the sensibility of the virtuous subject is conceived as 'trained' or socially educated, so that the subject comes to see the world in moral colour. By building an analogy with the idea of a virtuous agent's ethical sensibility, I hope to arrive at an account of how the responsible hearer exercises rational sensitivity, without inference, so as to be critically open to the word of others. Thus the account offered will supply the framework for a virtue epistemological account of testimony. The main idea is that where a hearer gives a suitably critical reception to an interlocutor's word without making any inference, she does so in virtue of the perceptual deliverances of a well-trained *testimonial sensibility*.

3.3 VIRTUOUS PERCEPTION: MORAL AND EPISTEMIC

The analogy I aim to build up between the virtuous agent's moral perceptual capacity and the virtuous hearer's testimonial perceptual capacity depends upon five closely related points of parallel. To anticipate, these are: (1) that in the testimonial as in the moral sphere, the model for judgement is perceptual, and so non-inferential; (2) in both spheres, good judgement is uncodifiable; (3) in both spheres, the judgement is intrinsically motivating and (4) intrinsically reason-giving; (5) and in both spheres the judgement typically contains an emotional aspect that is a proper part of the cognition. Let me elaborate.

According to the kind of cognitivism that grows out of the virtue tradition in ethics, the virtuous agent is marked out by his possession of a capacity for moral perceptual judgement. He is someone who, thanks to a proper moral 'upbringing' or (as I would prefer) a proper moral socialization, has come to see the world in moral colour. When he is confronted by an action or a situation with a certain moral character, he does not have to work out that the action is cruel or kind or charitable or selfish; he just sees it that way. Now this kind of perceptual judgement is spontaneous and unreflective; it involves no argumentation or inference on the agent's part. The virtuous agent's perceptual capacity is accounted for in terms of a sensitivity to morally salient features of the situation confronting him. In the testimonial case, the parallel suggestion is that the virtuous hearer's perceptual capacity be understood in terms of a sensitivity to epistemically salient features of the situation and the speaker's performance. These epistemically salient features are the various social cues that relate to trustworthiness—cues relating to the sincerity and competence of the speaker on the matter at hand. This sensitivity is underwritten by a set of background assumptions about the trustworthiness of different social types in different sorts of contexts—a socially situated 'theory' of trustworthiness, as I put it. Just as the morally virtuous subject's perception is morally enriched, so the virtuous hearer's perception is epistemically enriched. The analogy points us to a way of philosophically substantiating the idea that credibility judgements can be perceptual, and I suggest that we have here what the epistemology of testimony cries out for: a model for non-inferential judgement.

We should be especially cautious at this juncture with the idiom of 'theory' and 'theory-ladenness', however, since using it now carries a serious risk of misleading. For it is an important feature of the moral cognitivism we are focused on, and the second key feature of the analogy we are developing, that neither the morally virtuous agent nor the epistemically virtuous hearer comes to her perceptual judgement (a moral judgement and a credibility judgement, respectively) by applying generalizations to the case confronting her. She does not apply a *theory*, nor does she *apply* a theory—it isn't a theory, and she doesn't apply it. On the contrary, although some relevant generalizations or principles are surely formulable (and invaluable in contexts where the shift to a more reflective mode of judgement is called for) the virtuous subject does not arrive at her perceptual judgement by way of obedience to any codification of the endlessly complex norms implicit in her judgement. Free from any such dependence on advance rules, she is able to adapt and rework her thinking to the indefinitely diverse contexts liable to confront her. Reliance on rules would be rather the mark of someone who had not yet achieved full virtue, being still in the imitative phase. Martha Nussbaum makes a telling comparison with artistic improvisation:

Good deliberation is like theatrical or musical improvisation, where what counts is flexibility, responsiveness, and openness to the external; to rely on an algorithm here is not only insufficient, it is a sign of immaturity and weakness. It is possible to play a jazz solo from a score, making minor alterations for the particular nature of one's instrument. The question is, who would do this, and why?[15]

Of course it may well be possible to characterize many of the deliverances of a virtuous perceptual capacity in generalized terms, but this does not entail that any codification as such is available—no set of rules could capture in advance the educated improvisations of a virtuous moral perceptual sensitivity. Any such rules are after the fact of virtuous judgement. They may be useful as guidance to those who have not yet reached full virtue, just as the behaviour and judgements of the fully virtuous are useful as guidance to those *en route* to full virtue, but they could never be a substitute for virtue. The kind of judgement that we are suggesting is common to the moral and the

[15] Martha Nussbaum, 'The Discernment of Perception: An Aristotelian Conception of Private and Public Rationality', in *Love's Knowledge: Essays on Philosophy and Literature* (Oxford: Oxford University Press, 1990), 74.

testimonial case is irreducibly just that: a matter of *judgement*. McDowell again:

> To an unprejudiced eye it should seem quite implausible that any reasonably adult moral outlook admits of any such codification. As Aristotle consistently says, the best generalizations about how one should behave hold only for the most part. If one attempted to reduce one's conception of what virtue requires to a set of rules, then, however subtle and thoughtful one was in drawing up the code, cases would inevitably turn up in which a mechanical application of the rules would strike one as wrong—and not necessarily because one had changed one's mind; rather, one's mind on the matter was not susceptible of capture in any universal formula.[16]

The idea that moral knowledge is uncodifiable becomes clearer, I think, if one bears in mind that a virtuous moral perceptual capacity is a sensitivity to patterns of moral salience, a sensitivity to how different sorts of value configure in a new situation, action, or indeed person. It is a sensitivity that allows the virtuous person to see the world in a certain light, where this has an intrinsic practical import, but where it would be misleading to boil the sensitivity down to nothing more than an alternative to deliberation. There is more to ethical consciousness than deciding what to do.[17] A virtuous perception gives us a moral understanding of experiences, people, situations, and events—a view of the world in moral colour, as I put it—and it is part and parcel of this way of seeing that even the morally wisest person remains open to surprises. Or, rather, the fact that she is open-hearted enough to resist the dishonest safety of fixed moral understandings *is* the crowning mark of her moral wisdom. This is what Iris Murdoch means when she says: 'Moral tasks are characteristically endless not only because "within", as it were, a given concept our efforts are imperfect, but also because as we move and as we look our concepts themselves are changing.'[18] With virtuous perception understood this way, we can more clearly see how the very idea of codifiability is anathema to virtuous moral perception.

[16] John McDowell, 'Virtue and Reason', in *Mind, Value, and Reality* (Cambridge, Mass.: Harvard University Press, 1998), essay 3, pp. 57–8; originally published in *The Monist*, 62 (1979).

[17] See Cora Diamond, 'Wittgenstein, Mathematics and Ethics: Resisting the Attractions of Realism', in Hans Sluga and David Stern (eds.), *The Cambridge Companion to Wittgenstein* (Cambridge: Cambridge University Press, 1996), 226–60; and Sabina Lovibond's sympathetic rejoinder in *Ethical Formation* (Cambridge, Mass., and London: Harvard University Press, 2002), ch. 2.

[18] Iris Murdoch, 'The Idea of Perfection', in *The Sovereignty of Good* (London: Routledge, 1970), 28.

The aspiration to codification—not to be confused with the (entirely honourable) ambition to make explicit any general principles that may usefully be extrapolated from virtuous sensibility—is revealed as an impulse to take refuge in a bogus objectivity; an impulse, that is, to evade the indefinite creative demands made on one by ethical life.

The ultimate uncodifiability of ethical knowledge locates our second point of parallel with the testimony case. For the beginnings of the parallel thought, here is a remark of Coady's:

The mathematical tradition is full of talk about witnesses who tell the truth twice as often as they say what is false or who have a credibility ratio of .8 or whatever, but, as C. S. Peirce pointed out long ago, this kind of talk is very close to fantasy. It is not only that, in the case of real people, we have no way of computing such ratios. More importantly, the idea of such ratios fosters the illusion that people are like coins in having a quite general tendency to come down on one side or the other, a tendency which a long enough trial of their utterances would reveal. But people are not like that. They do not have quite general tendencies to lie, whatever the context or subject-matter, nor to make mistakes in abstraction from particular circumstances.[19]

This seems right, though we should allow that the quest for precise credibility ratios might well incorporate some sensitivity to context, and we should note too that probabilistic models need not require that real speakers have credibility ratios or that hearers make any such computations—their concern may be rather to chart the rationality of what sorts of changes in evidence increase or decrease the credibility of what is said, and by how much.[20] I think that the nub of the sceptical point here has to be that the sheer range of contexts to which the ordinary human hearer needs to be sensitive in her credibility judgements is so vast, the contexts so finely differentiated by the innumerable prompts and cues relating to trustworthiness in different social contexts, that it is simply not realistic to think that any sufficiently complex codification will be available, or if there were such, that it could be any use. This is the heart of the non-codification point in moral cognitivism, and the testimony side of our parallel contains an exact counterpart. The virtuous hearer does not arrive at her credibility judgement by

---

[19] Coady, *Testimony*, 210–11.

[20] See e.g. Luc Bovens and Stephan Hartmann, *Bayesian Epistemology* (Oxford: Clarendon Press, 2003), ch. 5, in which they construct a model for 'too-odd-not-to-be-true' reasoning, where we award more credibility to a surprising story told by multiple independent witnesses than to an unsurprising story told by multiple independent witnesses.

applying pre-set principles of any kind, for there are none precise or comprehensive enough to do the job. She 'just sees' her interlocutor in a certain light, and responds to his word accordingly. We can, of course, in the testimony case as in the moral case, benefit by making explicit certain general principles that should govern our judgements. The point is that such general principles are after the fact of virtuous judgement; they cannot substitute for virtue.[21] Having explained the moral case in terms of a sensitivity to the moral saliences of situations, actions, and people, we can see that, in the testimony case, the hearer must exercise a parallel sensitivity to the epistemic saliences—the many aspects of the speaker's performance in the context that relate to trustworthiness.

The uncodifiability of a virtuous agent's moral perception and a virtuous hearer's epistemic perception of a speaker, then, constitute our second point of parallel. But perhaps, as an addendum, it is worth noting an even closer relation here. Some of the things our virtuous hearer needs to be sensitive to simply concern the speaker's competence to know what he is talking about; but others concern his sincerity. Sincerity being a moral notion, these latter epistemic saliences also constitute moral saliences. They are cues relating to the speaker's moral attitude towards the hearer: how easily he may be motivated to deceive her, for instance, or to what extent he sees her as deserving a helpfully full account of things, or perhaps how far he regards her as his equal in terms of ability to stomach unpalatable truths. Epistemic trust incorporates ethical trust, because epistemic trustworthiness incorporates one kind of moral trustworthiness: namely, sincerity. Accordingly, the virtuous hearer's sensitivity to epistemic saliences will involve a sensitivity to some moral saliences—seeing a speaker in epistemic colour entails seeing them in some moral colour.

Moving now to our third and fourth points of parallel, it is a feature of the morally virtuous agent that her sensitivity to saliences carries a motivational charge—moral perception is intrinsically motivating. Even if I give a moral response to something I am told about that is in the past, so that there is no question of any practical intervention on my

---

[21] For an illuminating discussion that presents certain norms pertaining to astonishing reports, notably in contexts where prejudice might be at work, see Karen Jones, 'The Politics of Credibility', in Louise M. Antony and Charlotte E. Witt (eds.), *A Mind of One's Own: Feminist Essays on Reason and Objectivity*, 2nd edn. (Boulder, Colo.: Westview Press, 2002). Jones too is clear that while such principles feed into 'final assessments of credibility', they do not determine them. All-things-considered judgements of credibility remain a matter of judgement.

part, still my perception of what was good or bad, unjust, kind, brave or mean-spirited, is a perception of a sort which is such as to motivate action. Seeing a situation through the moral lens is to see it as calling for one or another practical response from relevant parties. More than this, however, moral perceptions are thereby justificationally charged too, since the motivation provided is rational: the facts virtuously perceived constitute a reason for acting in a certain way. Accordingly, one can explain and justify an action morally by citing the relevant circumstances as perceived by the virtuous agent. Thus McDowell: 'if [actions] manifest a virtuous person's distinctive way of seeing things, they must be explicable … in terms of exercises of that perceptual capacity, which need no supplementing with desires to yield full specifications of reasons'.[22]

In respect of both these points—motivation and justification—we can see a direct parallel in the testimony case. The virtuous hearer's epistemically enriched perception of her interlocutor—a perception of him as, for instance, trustworthy in what he is telling her—provides a motivation to accept what he is saying. This is obvious: if you perceive someone as offering you a piece of knowledge, you are thereby motivated to accept what he is telling you. Further, the virtuous hearer's perception of her interlocutor as trustworthy provides a justification for accepting what he says—the motivation to accept is rational. This is crucial for the general picture of testimony that we are building up here. The virtuous hearer's perception of her interlocutor as trustworthy in what he is telling her not only motivates her to accept what he says, but justifies her in so doing. If challenged after the fact, the hearer may or may not be able to reconstruct her reason, but so long as her credibility judgement was issued by a well-trained sensitivity to the epistemically salient features of the testimonial performance in the context—that is, if the judgement was the product of a virtuous testimonial sensibility—then it was justified. Consequently, if it is knowledge she is offered, then it is knowledge she receives. The virtuous hearer can get what she's given, without argument.

In the moral context the question of how something cognitive—a perception—may be intrinsically motivating is of course vexed. It is vexed because the moral cognitivist is committed to the view that the

[22] John McDowell, 'Are Moral Requirements Hypothetical Imperatives?', in *Mind, Value, and Reality*, essay 4, p. 85; originally published in the *Proceedings of the Aristotelian Society*, supp. vol. 52 (1978), 13–29.

virtuous agent needs no independent desire-like state to bring him to action; the perception is enough. By contrast, the parallel point we are making in the testimony case does not strictly depend on showing that such a perception is sufficient to motivate, since we have no special investment in showing that the virtuous hearer does not need to possess an independently identifiable desire for truth, or knowledge, in order to be motivated to accept when he trusts. Perhaps, however, it is worth exploring this point, since I do believe that the parallel with moral cognitivism holds up in this particular, so long as we have before us the proper understanding of emotion's constitutive role in certain sorts of cognition. If one comes to the issue with the empiricist *idée fixe* that there is cognition on the one hand and emotion on the other, where the former has intentional content and the latter does not, then it will be terminally puzzling to suggest that a cognitive state, such as a perception, could motivate an action.[23] If, however, one comes to the issue with a conception of emotion as capable of cognitive content, and/or a conception of cognition as permitting emotional content, then the question of motivation does not present itself as a problem.[24] Nussbaum's interpretation of Aristotle is helpful on this score:

[Aristotle] holds that the truly good person will not only act well but also feel the appropriate emotions about what he or she chooses. ...

Lying behind this is a picture of the passions as responsive and selective elements of the personality. Not Platonic urges or pushes, they possess a high degree of educability and discrimination. Even appetitive desires for Aristotle are intentional and capable of making distinctions; they can inform the agent of the presence of a needed object, working in responsive interaction with perception and imagination. Their intentional object is 'the apparent good.' Emotions are composites of belief and feeling, shaped by developing thought and highly discriminating in their reasons. ... In short, Aristotle does not make a sharp split between the cognitive and the emotive.[25]

---

[23] The principal source for this empiricist commitment is Hume, *A Treatise of Human Nature*, ed. L. A. Selby-Bigge, 3rd edn. (Oxford: Clarendon Press, 1975), II. iii. sect. 3.

[24] For early feminist work on this issue, and especially the power of emotions to tell us things about the moral and political world, see Alison Jaggar, 'Love and Knowledge: Emotion in Feminist Epistemology', and Elizabeth Spelman, 'Anger and Insubordination', both in A. Garry and M. Pearsall (eds.), *Women, Knowledge, and Reality: Explorations in Feminist Philosophy* (Boston: Unwin Hyman, 1989), 129–55, 263–74; and Miranda Fricker, 'Reason and Emotion', *Radical Philosophy*, 57 (1991), 14–19.

[25] Nussbaum, 'Discernment of Perception', 78. For an extended cognitivist treatment of emotion, see her *Upheavals of Thought: The Intelligence of the Emotions* (Cambridge: Cambridge University Press, 2003). For a different account, in which the intentionality

With emotion conceived as intentional and as a proper part of moral perception, we have a philosophical picture on which no puzzle about how states of moral perception could motivate action is going to arise. The answer is built in as a proper part of moral cognition. If one were to extract the emotion from the perception, it would cease to be a virtuous perception.

How does this point about the presence of emotion as a proper part of moral perception tally with our conception of the virtuous hearer? The many prompts and cues that our virtuous hearer must be sensitive to in his interlocutor's performance pertain to her trustworthiness in what she is telling him. If the hearer perceives that the speaker is trustworthy, then other things being equal he will indeed trust her and accept what she tells him. Now such an attitude of trust towards another person is not a purely intellectual attitude; such an attitude of trust contains a *feeling* of trust. I think this would be so even if it were only the speaker's competence that were at stake, but the fact that the hearer must also be sensitive to the speaker's sincerity towards him makes the point irresistible. A speaker's sincerity is not the sort of attitude one could pick up on without some kind of personal emotional response to them. When the virtuous hearer perceives his interlocutor as trustworthy in this or that degree, then, this cognitive achievement is inevitably partly composed of an emotion: a feeling of trust. Thus the hearer, like the moral subject, makes judgements that (at least typically) have an emotional aspect.

But this point of parallel is further substantiated by the fact that there is also a more general emotional engagement involved in the hearer's perception of her interlocutor's sincerity or insincerity: she must empathize sufficiently with him to be in a position to judge, and empathy typically carries some emotional charge.[26] A hearer with minimal powers of empathy is at a notable disadvantage when it comes to making credibility judgements, for she may often fail to see the speaker's performance in the proper light. If, for instance, her lack of empathetic skill renders her unable to pick up on the fact that her interlocutor is afraid of her (perhaps he is a school pupil and she the head teacher), then she may well misperceive his manner, taking him, for instance,

---

of the emotions is rendered in terms of 'feeling towards', see Peter Goldie, *The Emotions: A Philosophical Exploration* (Oxford, Clarendon Press, 2000).

[26] Karen Jones argues that trust involves empathy; see 'Trust as an Affective Attitude', *Ethics*, 107, no. 1 (Oct. 1996), 4–25.

to be insincere when he is not. Empathy, I take it, is an emotional cognitive capacity, and so in this regard too, the well-trained testimonial sensibility entails some well-trained emotions, and the hearer's perception of the speaker includes whatever emotional responses are associated with a particular empathetic engagement (a feeling of sympathy, or suspicion; of common purpose, or competition; of respect, or contempt, and so on). Were we to be committed to the empiricist dualist conception of cognition and emotion, this fact about the hearer's perception of his interlocutor might seem an embarrassment to be explained away as a merely accompanying emotion. But the more Aristotelian conception of emotion allows us to represent the hearer's feeling of trust or distrust, or any other feelings associated with a particular empathetic engagement, as making a positive cognitive contribution to her epistemically loaded perception. Sometimes it might even be, quite properly, the dominating aspect of the perception. When it comes to epistemic trust, as with purely moral trust, it can be good advice to listen to one's emotions, for a virtuous hearer's emotional responses to different speakers in different contexts are trained and honed by experience. The feeling of trust in the virtuous hearer is a sophisticated emotional radar for detecting trust-worthiness in speakers. Thus the fifth point of parallel: virtuous moral perceptions and virtuous testimonial perceptions both feature emotion as a positive cognitive input.

What, finally, should be said about our phenomenology as hearers? The five points of parallel explored above—that moral/testimonial judgement is non-inferential, uncodifiable, intrinsically motivating, intrinsically reason-giving, and typically has an emotional aspect—are all consistent with the spontaneous, unreflective phenomenology of testimony that has provided so much impetus for non-inferentialism. Indeed, they explain how our phenomenology as hearers can be of an entirely unreflective and spontaneous piece of cognitive activity even while it is critical activity. More specifically, these points of parallel fit the description of the phenomenology that I gave above to the effect that the hearer typically has an experience of unreflective alertness to the many prompts and cues relating to her interlocutor's trustworthiness. Granted that our everyday on-the-spot credibility judgements are as I have depicted them—trained, socially situated perceptual judgements typically made spontaneously—then it is not surprising that the phenomenology should be unreflective and yet, as I suggested, abused if characterized as plain uncritical. The interpretation of the hearer's phenomenology as an unreflective yet critical alertness is made sense of and vindicated if we accept the analogy with the moral perceptual model.

3.4 TRAINING SENSIBILITY

In advancing the idea of a testimonial perceptual capacity analogous to the virtuous person's moral perceptual capacity, I have been invoking the Aristotelian notion of moral training. But I need to say a little more about how this notion applies to the testimonial side of the parallel. In the Aristotelian picture, the training of the virtuous person consists in habituation by way of practice and example. Contrasting the virtues with the senses, Aristotle says:

> But the virtues we do acquire by first exercising them, just as happens in the arts. Anything that we have to learn to do we learn by the actual doing of it: people become builders by building and instrumentalists by playing instruments. Similarly we become just by performing just acts, temperate by performing temperate ones, brave by performing brave ones.[27]

We also find in his picture the risk that one's training may not be up to the mark, for habituation can work both ways, in the direction of virtue or of vice:

> Again, the causes or means that bring about any form of excellence are the same as those that destroy it, and similarly with art; for it is as a result of playing the harp that people become good and bad harpists. The same principle applies to builders and all other craftsmen. Men will become good builders as a result of building well, and bad ones as a result of building badly. ... Now this holds good also of the virtues.[28]

This is relevant for what I want to say about the hearer's testimonial sensibility. So far we have focused on the idea of the well-trained sensibility, but it is well to remember the source of bad training that is of central interest to our project: prejudice, and most particularly prejudicial stereotypes. The hearer's perception of her interlocutor may be virtuous, or it may fail to be virtuous in one or another way. There have always been prejudices (think of Aristotle on slaves and women), but the prejudices that may be in the air at any given time change

---

[27] Aristotle, *The Ethics of Aristotle: The Nicomachean Ethics*, trans. J. A. K. Thomson (London: Penguin, 1976), 91–2; II. 1; 1103^a 14–25.

[28] Ibid. 92; 1103^b 1–25.

with history. We need a conception of human beings as formed by the attitudes of their time yet capable too of taking a critical stance towards those attitudes, and so we need a more historicist and more reflexive conception of ethical training than we find in Aristotle.

Ethical sensibility is given its first form by our being inculcated into the attitudes of the day. But we are soon in a position to criticize these attitudes, and so we may, social pressures permitting, come to distance ourselves from any given commitment. Historicism brings responsibility for our own ethical way of life—an immersed, or immanent responsibility for who we are.[29] Accordingly, I suggest that we think of the training of an ethical sensibility as involving at least two distinct streams of input: social and individual—in that order. One develops an ethical sensibility by becoming inculcated into a historically and culturally specific way of life—or, as Alasdair MacIntyre puts it, an ethical 'tradition'[30]—where this is to be construed as a matter of ongoing ethical socialization. There again, it is from an irreducibly individual life experience that one gains a particular sentimental education, and in that respect the ongoing formation of one's sensibility is something distinctly individual. Together these two streams of input—collective and individual—continually generate a person's moral sensibility. The deliverances of an individual's sensibility, then, are shaped by a set of background interpretive and motivational attitudes, which are in the first instance passively inherited from the ethical community, but thereafter actively reflected upon and lived out in one or another way by the reflective individual. Ethical responsibility demands that the individual generate an appropriate critical link between the traditional moment in which she gains her primary ethical socialization and the experiences that life offers her—experiences which may sometimes be in tension with her ethical socialization so as to prompt critical reflection on the sensibility which she has otherwise simply inherited.[31]

I suggest that the epistemic socialization through which virtuous hearers gain their testimonial sensibility has a similar structure. As in the moral case, we should think of the virtuous hearer's sensibility as

---

[29] This theme of our responsibility for who we are runs through Sabina Lovibond's *Realism and Imagination in Ethics* (Oxford: Blackwell, 1983); and her *Ethical Formation* (see e.g. ch. 9, sect. 5).

[30] See Alasdair MacIntyre, *After Virtue: A Study in Moral Theory* (London: Duckworth, 1981), ch. 15.

[31] I have tried to develop this theme in my 'Confidence and Irony', in Edward Harcourt (ed.), *Morality, Reflection, and Ideology* (Oxford: Oxford University Press, 2000).

formed by way of participation in, and observation of, practices of testimonial exchange. There is, in the first instance, a passive social inheritance, and then a sometimes-passive-sometimes-active individual input from the hearer's own experience. Together the individual and collective streams of input are what explain how our normal unreflective reception of what people tell us is conditioned by a great range of collateral experience—our informal background 'theory' of socially situated trustworthiness. Just as the experiences pertinent to the training of ethical virtues are internalized in the sensibility of the virtuous person, so is the body of collective and individual testimonial experience internalized by the virtuous hearer, rendering it immanent in her testimonial sensibility. It is through the broadly inductive influence of this body of experience that we may learn, reliably enough, to assume trust when and only when it is in order. Thus our perception of speakers and their assertions comes to be informed by a wealth of individual and collective experience relating to different sorts of speakers' trustworthiness regarding different sorts of subject matter in different sorts of context. As hearers, our perceptions of our interlocutors are judgements conditioned by a vast wealth of diverse testimony-related experiences, individual and collective.

What of our ability as hearers to form a critical link with this great passive inheritance that conditions the credibility judgements we make? Here again the task is to identify an analogy with the ethical case. I have said that an individual's testimonial sensibility is in the first instance passively inherited. But once light has dawned for a hearer, she will come to find that sometimes her experiences of testimonial exchange are in tension with the deliverances of the sensibility she has passively taken on, in which case responsibility requires that her sensibility adjust itself to accommodate the new experience. Her experience of politicians might, for instance, be that there are proportionally just as many female politicians she respects as male politicians she respects. And she might notice a certain cognitive dissonance between her beliefs on the one hand—her belief, for instance, that women are the equal of men in political life—and the spontaneous deliverances of her testimonial sensibility on the other—a sensibility which time and again leaves her not quite taking women's political word as seriously as men's. As she reflects on her judgement processes, she might detect the influence of a traditional stereotypical image of women as not cut out for political life, even while her own experience has led her to believe that stereotype to be mere prejudice. On sensing any such dissonance, the responsible hearer might find her testimonial sensibility directly aligning itself with her beliefs, and this new alignment may occur without the need for any mediating critical reflection. More likely, however, she will need actively to bring critical thought to bear on her internalized habits of hearer response in order to shake them up sufficiently to effect any adjustment.

If the adjustment is direct, then she will undergo a kind of *gestalt* switch in how she perceives women political speakers, so that the adjustment to her testimonial sensibility is more or less instantaneous. If it is indirect, then active critical reflection on her patterns of credibility judgement may first produce some sort of corrective policy external to her sensibility (perhaps she actively focuses her mind on women's intellectual equality to men when she listens to women talking politics, or perhaps she tries to correct for the influence of prejudice in her judgement after the fact). Given time, such a corrective policy may become internalized as an integral part of her testimonial sensibility, so that it comes to be implicit in her newly conditioned powers of testimonial perception of women in politics. Whether direct or indirect, then, we can see how the responsible hearer's sensibility can mature and adapt in the light of ongoing testimonial experience. Such a process of self-critical maturation and adaptation is how one may increasingly approximate virtue as a hearer. The claim that testimonial sensibility is a capacity of reason crucially depends on its capacity to adapt in this way, for otherwise it would be little more than a dead-weight social conditioning that looked more like a threat to the justification of a hearer's responses than a source of that justification.

In this adaptiveness we can also see how our conception of testimonial sensibility bears out Coady's description of the critical 'learning mechanism'. We saw that he envisages hearers operating a mechanism which is 'modified by experience, especially in the matter of critical capacities', and I suggest that we have arrived at something that fits the bill: our idea of testimonial sensibility is an idea of a spontaneous critical sensitivity that is permanently in training and continuously adapting according to individual and collective experience. This proposal for how inductive rationality can be embodied in the spontaneous perceptual deliverances of testimonial sensibility shows that the making of an explicit inferential step is not the only way that a hearer may be justified in accepting what he is told. An appropriately trained testimonial sensibility enables the hearer to respond to the word of another with the sort of critical openness that is required for a thoroughly effortless sharing of knowledge. This idea of a testimonial sensibility gives us a picture of how judgements can be rational yet unreflective, critical yet non-inferential. It presents us with a rational capacity which comprises virtues, which is inculcated in the subject through a process of socialization, and which permits ongoing correction and adjustment in the light of experience and critical reflection. Thus we are confronted with a rational capacity unlike anything commonly entertained in epistemology *per se*, but which has ancient precedent in moral epistemology. We might think of testimonial sensibility as a part—indeed, an essential part—of our epistemic 'second nature'.[32]

---

[32] I echo John McDowell's use of this term, which he finds 'all but explicit in Aristotle's account of how ethical character is formed', and which he extends to apply not simply to our ethical upbringing (Aristotle's 'practical wisdom') but, more generally, to our epistemic upbringing. See McDowell, *Mind and World* (Cambridge, Mass.: Harvard University Press, 1994), 84.

4

The Virtue of Testimonial Justice

4.1 CORRECTING FOR PREJUDICE

We have so far developed a picture on which the hearer perceives the speaker in an epistemically loaded way—she sees him as more, or less, credible in what he is telling her. This perceptual faculty is trained in real historical human society, and this means that the presence of identity prejudice in the collective social imagination is an endemic hazard in the ongoing training of testimonial sensibility. Wherever there are identity prejudices in the discursive environment, there is a risk of testimonial injustice of our central sort (identity-prejudicial credibility deficit). This raises the question whether we can identify a particular virtue that the hearer needs to have in order to counteract the risk of letting such prejudice distort his perceptions of speakers. We need to ask about the specifically *anti-prejudicial* current that the virtuous hearer's sensibility needs to contain in order that the hearer may not be led into perpetrating testimonial injustices, possibly missing out on valuable knowledge into the bargain. In order to home in on the nature of this particular virtue, let us look more closely than before at Minghella's screenplay for *The Talented Mr Ripley*, in which Herbert Greenleaf unjustly silences Marge Sherwood.[1] I shall concentrate initially on the testimonial injustice he does her, in order to move on to the question of what epistemic virtue Greenleaf was lacking, and what exactly Greenleaf's moral status is, given the historical context.

It is the Fifties, and we are in Venice. Herbert Greenleaf, a rich American industrialist, is visiting, accompanied by a private detective whom he has hired to help solve the mystery of the whereabouts of

---

[1] Anthony Minghella, *The Talented Mr Ripley—Based on Patricia Highsmith's Novel* (London: Methuen, 2000). Minghella's screenplay is closely based on Patricia Highsmith's novel, though crucially for present purposes, the character of Marge Sherwood and her relationship with Dickie Greenleaf are developed differently.

his renegade son, Dickie. Dickie Greenleaf recently got engaged to his girlfriend, Marge Sherwood, but subsequently spent a great deal of time travelling with their 'friend' Tom Ripley—until Dickie mysteriously disappeared. Marge is increasingly distrustful of Ripley because he seems to be obsessed with Dickie and suspiciously bound up with his strange disappearance. She also knows very well that it is unlike Dickie—unreliable philanderer though he undoubtedly was—simply to do a bunk, let alone to commit suicide, which is the hypothesis that Ripley is at pains to encourage. Ripley, however, has all along done a successful job of sucking up to Greenleaf senior, so Marge is entirely alone in her suspicion—her correct suspicion—that Dickie has been murdered, and that Ripley is his killer.

Herbert Greenleaf has just asked Ripley to be as helpful as he can in 'filling in the blanks' of Dickie's life to MacCarron, the private detective, and Ripley responds:

Ripley: I'll try my best, sir. Obviously I'll do anything to help Dickie.
Marge looks at him in contempt.
Herbert Greenleaf: This theory, the letter he left for you, the police think that's a clear indication he was planning on doing something … to himself.
Marge: I just don't believe that!
Herbert Greenleaf: You don't want to, dear. I'd like to talk to Tom alone—perhaps this afternoon? Would you mind? Marge, what a man may say to his sweetheart and what he'll admit to another fellow—
Marge: Such as?[2]

Here Marge is being gently, kindly, sidelined by Greenleaf senior, who pathologizes her conviction that Dickie would not kill himself as a sweetheart's wishful thinking. He also assumes, wrongly at least to some extent, that Marge is innocent of the more tawdry facts of Dickie's life, so that his primary attitude towards her on the one hand and the-truth-about-Dickie on the other is that *she* needs protection from *it*. (Ripley exploits and reinforces this. Later that day, when Greenleaf and Ripley are alone, Greenleaf gloomily reflects: 'No, Marge doesn't know the half of it.' And Ripley responds: 'I think it might hurt her to know'.[3]) Greenleaf's everyday theory about what a man may say to his sweetheart etc.—though quite possibly true enough—has the effect of undermining Marge as a possessor of knowledge about the lover she had been living with for some time. Greenleaf is only too aware of how little he himself knows of his son—pathetically enthusiastic as he is at the prospect that the private detective might help make good this ignorance—and yet he fails to see Marge as the source of knowledge about Dickie that she manifestly is.

This attitude leads Greenleaf to ignore one of Marge's key reasons for her correct hypothesis that Dickie has died at the hands of Ripley: she finds Dickie's rings at Ripley's place, one of which had been a gift from her and which he had sworn never to remove. Greenleaf ignores it, partly because he underestimates Dickie's commitment to Marge, so that in his eyes any promise to Marge on Dickie's part is virtually worthless; but mostly because Ripley successfully constructs Marge as 'hysterical'. Indeed, not only Greenleaf but also Marge's friend, Peter Smith-Kingsley, comes to perceive her that way, so that the net result is a collusion of men against Marge's word being taken seriously. The theme of knowledge ever to the fore in the dialogue, we at one point hear her off-screen, shortly after she finds the rings, her powers of expression seemingly reduced to a self-contradictory mantra, repeating emphatically to the incredulous Greenleaf, 'I don't know, I don't know, I just know it'; and it is at this point that Greenleaf replies with the familiar put-down, 'Marge, there's female intuition, and then there are facts—.' A number of these sorts of exchange build up to the scene in which Marge, being taken back to America, is being ushered on to a boat but breaks away to lunge at Ripley, exclaiming, 'I know it was you—I know it was you, Tom. I know it was you. I know you killed Dickie. I know it was you.' MacCarron, the private detective, comes out of the waiting boat physically to restrain her, and the stage direction reads: 'Ripley looks at him as if to say: What can you do, she's hysterical. MacCarron nods, pulls her onto the boat.'[4]

Here we see poor Marge in some measure actually becoming what she has been constructed as: a hysterical female, apparently expressing herself in semi-contradictions, sticking to intuitions in the face of others' reasons, unable to keep a grip on her emotions. Thus the sinister mechanism of causal construction. Perversely, we catch a whiff here of how such causal construction might seem to supply an eleventh-hour justification for the original prejudiced credibility judgement—such is the power that some prejudices have for self-fulfilment. Greenleaf's wrongful credibility judgement of Marge cannot itself be retrospectively

---

[4] Minghella, *The Talented Mr Ripley*, 135.

justified, however, for when the judgement was made, the evidence did not support it; still, it must be acknowledged that the frustrated and semi-articulate expressive form that Marge's suspicions come to take, creates a terrible justificatory loop so that, given Greenleaf's point of view, there is no irrationality on his part if he views her behaviour as confirming his perception of her as non-trustworthy. As the viewer is aware, however, the construction was and remains radically unfair. Marge was right. She knew Dickie well, infidelity and all, and her clear-eyed accommodation to him is in large part what led her to the permanently lonely knowledge she now possesses, that Ripley has killed him. (She knew she could not rely on his sexual fidelity, but she also knew that he would not have given away that ring.) Marge's suspicions should have been listened to; *she* of all people should have been given some credibility. But Ripley cynically exploits the gender attitudes of the day so that the kindly and well-meaning men around her effectively collude with him to make her appear epistemically untrustworthy.

This example, like our earlier example of the fatal testimonial injustice suffered by Tom Robinson, presents us with a case of a hearer's testimonial sensibility delivering a prejudiced perception of the speaker. Thus we are presented with a fault in judgement occurring at the spontaneous, unreflective level. The spontaneous operation of Greenleaf's testimonial sensibility is flawed, for it is trained in part by the gender prejudices of the day. Sometimes there can be a fault at the reflective level too, however, depending on how far the context places the onus on the hearer to shift intellectual gear and engage in active, self-critical reflection concerning the deliverances of his testimonial sensibility. Certainly, in the formal context of a courtroom, for instance, jurors are under an obligation to reflect actively on the spontaneous deliverances of their testimonial sensibility, and they are seriously at fault if they fail to do so. One way or another, both our examples illustrate a hearer or hearers *failing to correct for* identity prejudice in their testimonial sensibility. In both cases, hearers fail to exercise any critical awareness regarding the prejudice that is distorting their perception of the speaker, so that the distorted spontaneous deliverance of their testimonial sensibility is left unchecked. I shall suggest below that Greenleaf's prejudiced perception of Marge is ultimately non-culpable because of the historical context. By contrast, this cannot be said for the jurors at Tom Robinson's trial, who have ample opportunity to grasp and make good the conflict between the distrust which their corrupted sensibility spontaneously delivers and the trust which a proper attention to the evidence would inspire—a proper attention which others present, white as well as black, are clearly able to give. Even if members of the jury were to be partially forgiven for the way in which their sensibility has been hitherto saturated with the powerful racial prejudices of the day, they remain starkly culpable in failing to respond appropriately to the heightened testimonial experience afforded by the trial, given the overwhelming evidence in favour of the judgement that Tom is telling the truth.

What sort of critical awareness is needed for a hearer to be able to correct for identity prejudice in a given credibility judgement? In the case of Herbert Greenleaf, he fails to correct for the way in which his habits of hearer response are saturated with the sexist constructions of gender—notably, ideas of women's innocence of the truths of men, and their need to be protected from such truths; ideas of feminine intuitiveness being an obstacle to rational judgement; and even ideas of a female susceptibility to hysterics. Similarly, the jurors of Maycomb County fail to correct for the way in which their habits of hearer response are saturated with racist constructions of the 'Negro'—'that *all* Negroes lie, that *all* Negroes are basically immoral beings, that *all* Negro men are not to be trusted around our women'.[5] In both examples, the influence of a prejudicial stereotype in the hearer's testimonial sensibility marks a corrupt operation of identity power between speaker and hearer. Social-imaginative ideas of 'Negro' or 'woman' distort the hearer's credibility judgement, and this operation of identity power controls who can convey knowledge to whom and, by the same token, who can gain knowledge from whom. Depending on which aspects of the scenario one wants to highlight, one will focus either on the agential identity power being actively exercised by Greenleaf over Marge, and by the jurors over Tom Robinson; or, alternatively, one will focus on the purely structural operation of identity power that is effectively controlling Greenleaf and Marge, jurors and Tom Robinson alike. This latter, purely structural description is appropriate if one wishes to highlight the fact that all parties are to some extent under the control of a gender or racial ideology. But since my aim is to highlight the injustice that is occurring, and the sense in which the hearers are preventing the speakers from conveying knowledge, it is the agential description that

<hr />

[5] The quotation is from Atticus Finch's closing speech (Harper Lee, *To Kill a Mockingbird* (London: William Heinemann, 1960), 208).

is most relevant here. On either construal, the hearer is represented as failing to correct for the counter-rational operation of identity power that is distorting their judgement of credibility.

For a hearer to identify the impact of identity power in their credibility judgement they must be alert to the impact not only of the speaker's social identity but also the impact of their *own* social identity on their credibility judgement. The jurors fail to take account of the difference it makes to their perception of Tom Robinson as a speaker not only that he is black but equally *that they are white*. What Greenleaf fails to take account of in his sceptical responses to Marge is the difference her being a woman makes to his testimonial perception *given that he is a man*. Our two examples, then, demonstrate that testimonial responsibility requires a distinctly *reflexive* critical social awareness. The hearer must factor into his net credibility judgement the likely impact on his spontaneous perception—and if possible the impact on the speaker's actual performance too—of the relation of identity power that mediates between himself and the speaker. Had Marge somehow been able to make her accusations instead to *Mrs* Greenleaf, she might have been heard differently. That things would have gone differently at Tom Robinson's trial if the members of the jury had been black goes without saying. In testimonial exchanges, for hearers and speakers alike, no party is neutral; everybody has a race, everybody has a gender. What is needed on the part of the hearer in order to avert a testimonial injustice—and in order to serve his own epistemic interest in the truth—is a corrective anti-prejudicial virtue that is distinctively *reflexive* in structure.

Such reflexive critical awareness of the likely presence of prejudice, then, is a prerequisite in the business of correcting for prejudice in one's credibility judgement. But what exactly is meant by 'correcting for' here? When the hearer suspects prejudice in her credibility judgement—whether through sensing cognitive dissonance between her perception, beliefs, and emotional responses, or whether through self-conscious reflection—she should shift intellectual gear out of spontaneous, unreflective mode and into active critical reflection in order to identify how far the suspected prejudice has influenced her judgement. If she finds that the low credibility judgement she has made of a speaker is due in part to prejudice, then she can correct this by revising the credibility upwards to compensate. There can be no algorithm for her to use in determining how much it should be revised upwards, but there is a clear guiding ideal. The guiding ideal is to neutralize any negative impact of prejudice in one's credibility judgements by compensating upwards to reach the degree of credibility that would have been given were it not for the prejudice. And this is at least an ideal that can regulate our practice of credibility judgement. The upshot of approximating this ideal in any given case may indeed be a reflation of the credibility level in the judgement; or, alternatively, it may be that all we are able to do is to render our judgement more vague and more tentative. In cases where the whole business of judging credibility becomes too indeterminate, we may need to suspend judgement altogether; or, alternatively, if we have a responsibility to arrive at some definite verdict, we may have resources to seek out further evidence. At any rate, since it is not always possible to 'correct for' the impact of prejudice by making a neat compensatory reflation of credibility, let us say that, one way or another, the virtuous hearer *neutralizes the impact of prejudice in her credibility judgements.*

This, then, is the anti-prejudicial virtue we are looking for. Its possession requires the hearer to reliably neutralize prejudice in her judgements of credibility. Let us call it (what else?) the virtue of *testimonial justice*. In order to avoid confusion, however, we should note that this label also invites a much more general idea: namely, that of a totally just testimonial encounter where not only our specifically anti-prejudicial virtue is in play, but all the virtues relevant to receiving the word of another—something a complete virtue epistemological account of testimony would supply. Aristotle makes such a distinction in connection with the concept of justice. He distinguishes 'universal justice' as the whole of virtue and 'particular justice' as a specific (distributive) virtue.[6] Keeping to our own terminology, then, let us allow that there is a general notion of testimonial justice such that it is the whole complex of intellectual virtues pertinent to a hearer's reception of another's word, and a specific sense of testimonial justice that speaks (most centrally) to the particular risk of letting negative identity prejudice shape one's credibility judgement. This last is the virtue we are interested in.

What more can we say, then, about how a hearer may display our specific virtue of testimonial justice? We have said that the hearer must exercise a certain reflexive critical awareness; but what form should it take? Need it always be a matter of conscious, deliberative reflection, or can the virtue sometimes be displayed more spontaneously? The virtue is, most basically, a matter of one's credibility judgements being

---

[6] Aristotle, *The Ethics of Aristotle. The Nicomachean Ethics*, trans. J. A. K. Thomson (London: Penguin, 1976), 174–5; V. 2; 1129^b30–1130^b8.

*un*prejudiced. That they should be unprejudiced might result from their being prejudice-free from the start, or it might result from the influence of prejudice being somehow neutralized. So let us first of all acknowledge that the virtue might be displayed altogether *naïvely*—that is, the subject's credibility judgements are free from prejudice from the start, without her having done any self-monitoring (conscious or otherwise), let alone any correcting; or alternatively, the virtue may be displayed in *corrective* form, so that the subject does engage in some sort of self-monitoring and corrects her judgements, or not, as appropriate.

How might someone possess the virtue naïvely? One can imagine it being displayed naïvely, for instance, in a society which was entirely free from prejudice (if one can imagine such a society). More realistically, a hearer brought up in a society or subculture with its own set of atmospheric prejudices will obviously be free of at least some of the prejudices that are peculiar to another society or subculture with a different set. Thus, perhaps, it is possible that some people brought up in the south of England, for instance, are simply oblivious to the sorts of identity prejudices that hold between Protestants and Catholics in Northern Ireland, for these prejudices are simply foreign to their own social consciousness. The social world that shaped their epistemic character contained these categories, of course, but did not give them any significant social organizational role that might affect credibility judgements. To qualify as possessing the virtue, they would need to have a suitably entrenched general motivation to make unprejudiced credibility judgements, but the particular religious prejudices we have in mind would, as it happens, never pose a threat. In relation to these particular prejudices, then, they would possess the virtue of testimonial justice naïvely.

A different circumstance in which the virtue would take naïve form would be where someone was brought up in a relevantly prejudiced society but whose native capacity for unprejudiced social perception remained sufficiently untouched. Recall the discussion of prejudice and prejudicial stereotypes in Chapter 2. Belief and credibility judgements can come apart because credibility judgements are perceptions shaped not only by belief but also by emotional responses and by contents in the social imagination. Someone whose capacity for perceiving speakers in a relatively unprejudiced manner, despite having prejudiced beliefs against them of a sort undermining to credibility, is someone whose native perceptual capacity has somehow escaped the prejudicial corruptions of the day. Given that their beliefs had not escaped the prejudice, there would be a dissonance between such a person's beliefs on the one hand and their perceptual judgements on the other—a dissonance which does them credit relative to the majority of their peers, whose cognitive faculties are more consistently prejudiced. Such a person would present an epistemic counterpart to Arpaly's Huckleberry Finn, whose moral perception of Jim has somehow escaped the racist prejudices that hold sway in his beliefs.

Perhaps a child—someone in the fast-moving initial phases of ethical and epistemic socialization—growing up in a relevantly prejudiced society might present an example of a person who (partially at least) displays the virtue of testimonial justice more or less naïvely. During the trial in *To Kill a Mockingbird*, we find young Scout, Atticus Finch's daughter, at an interesting staging post *en route* to acquiring the virtue of testimonial justice. Appropriately to her age, she is still at a stage of imitation, active reflection, and experimentation with respect to the virtue. At the trial, Atticus asks Tom Robinson:

'Did you ever ... at any time, go on the Ewell property—did you ever set foot on the Ewell property without an express invitation from one of them?'
'No suh, Mr Finch, I never did. I wouldn't do that, suh.'
Atticus sometimes said that one way to tell whether a witness was lying or telling the truth was to listen rather than watch: I applied his test—Tom denied it three times in one breath, but quietly, with no hint of whining in his voice, and I found myself believing him, in spite of his protesting too much. He seemed to be a respectable Negro, and a respectable Negro would never go up into somebody's yard of his own volition.[7]

Scout lets the evidence of her social experience direct her judgement without prejudice—her experience of how different social types are actually likely to behave—and the generalizations she draws upon concerning what a 'respectable Negro' would be motivated to do are, as presented, sound. This excerpt shows her as well on her way to possessing the anti-prejudicial virtue of testimonial justice, yet she is growing up in a highly prejudiced social world. Of course her father is, explicitly here, a key influence upon the formation of her testimonial sensibility, and her familiarity with certain other anti-prejudicial figures such as Calpurnia, who works for the family, has its influence too. But she is inevitably also influenced by other figures and the attitudes of the generality of Maycomb County. Scout's virtuousness here is broadly naïve, for she is

---

7 Lee, *To Kill a Mockingbird*, 196.

too young to be reflectively aware of the force of the prejudice all around her, and so too young for corrective deliberation as such. Happily, her testimonial sensibility is for the time being such that she directly perceives Tom as a speaker in an unprejudiced manner (she tells us that she listened to his voice, and 'found [herself] believing him'). But there is also a corrective aspect to her judgement—she runs a test in which one becomes blind to the colour of the speaker's skin—for she cannot, and could not possibly, be entirely free from prejudice. Her thoughts are naturally couched in the rotten terminology of the day, so that she sometimes gives voice to the standard racist attitudes. This is partly because children try out almost any forms of thought made available to them precisely in order to become critical beings, but also partly because their consciousness inevitably finds its first form by way of these attitudes. We are reminded of this when young Dill, who had accompanied Scout and Jem to the Negro gallery, starts to cry at Mr Gilmer's hateful way of talking to Tom Robinson, with the result that Scout has to take him outside. While she is trying to comfort him beneath an old oak tree, she good-naturedly tries to explain away Gilmer's performance by voicing a thought that encapsulates much of the atmospheric racism in which they must both grow up: 'Well, Dill, after all he's just a Negro.'[8]

In so far as Scout displays the virtue of testimonial justice, then, she does so in a manner that has a corrective aspect but is none the less broadly naïve. More usually, however, the virtue will simply be displayed in corrective form. Indeed, one might expect that as she gets older, the possibility of possessing the virtue naïvely will diminish, reinforcing the need to possess it in its corrective form. We should remember the pessimism of Mr Dolphus Raymond—a white man, originally from a 'fine old family', and now a self-made social outcast who 'preferred the company of Negroes'.[9] He predicts for young Dill a gradual habituation to the everyday spectacle of racial hatred that will soon leave his eyes dry. Having overheard Dill's tearful protestations against Gilmer's hatefulness towards Tom Robinson in the courtroom, Dolphus emerges from behind a tree to talk to the two children. He says of Dill: 'Things haven't caught up with that one's instinct yet. Let him get a little older and he won't get sick and cry. Maybe things'll strike him as being—not quite right, say, but he won't cry not when he gets a few years on him.'[10] If this is an inevitable part of first maturation in the society, the only hope for testimonial justice is that the virtue be

[8] Lee, To Kill a Mockingbird, 203.   [9] Ibid. 196.   [10] Ibid. 205.

acquired as a corrective virtue. But generally speaking too, the virtue will take corrective form, because human societies have prejudices in the air, and these prejudices will tend to shape hearers' credibility judgements regardless of whether they have succeeded in eliminating prejudice from their beliefs or not. Our predicament as hearers is a matter of needing to neutralize the impact of all sorts of prejudices endemic in the climate of testimonial exchange.

If a hearer is to display the virtue of testimonial justice correctively, what forms can this take? Obviously the corrective move of revising one's credibility judgement upwards can be made by way of active reflection, but can it also be done more spontaneously? Yes, and we can see two ways in which this can be so. First, plain personal familiarity can melt away the prejudice that presented an initial obstacle to an unprejudiced credibility judgement being made: an initially socially loaded accent gets normalized with habituation; a socially alien conversational style becomes familiar; the colour of someone's skin becomes irrelevant; their sex no longer impinges; their age is forgotten. Suppose a hearer's first impression of a speaker is such that she is not inclined to give him much credibility in what he is telling her, and this is due to some prejudice or other. Yet with the degrees of familiarity—gained over the duration of a conversation, or perhaps a more sustained acquaintance—the preju-diced first impression melts away, and the hearer's credibility judgement corrects itself spontaneously. Her perception of the speaker shifts owing to the power that familiarity can have (on a sufficiently receptive sen-sibility) to disable certain sorts of prejudice. One might think that, in the context of a society where all sorts of prejudices are in the social atmosphere, a good measure of a hearer's virtuousness in respect of testimonial justice is precisely how quickly her prejudices disappear spontaneously with the familiarity of actual testimonial contact and the evidence of trustworthiness it may furnish. This must be right, but with the proviso that in order for the hearer to count as displaying the *virtue* as such, the disappearance of the prejudice would have to be not only swift enough but also reliable enough, through time and across a suitable span of different prejudices.

The second way in which a hearer may make virtuously anti-prejudicial credibility judgements in a spontaneous manner is provided by an ideal of full possession of the virtue of testimonial justice. If full possession of the virtue is the ideal, then ideally hearers will possess the virtue entirely spontaneously and immediately—without any prejudiced first impression having to melt away, and without any active reflection, imitation, or rehearsal. According to such an ideal, then, our virtuous hearer's testimonial sensibility would spontaneously furnish *ready-corrected* credibility judgements. I said before that the hearer's testimonial sensibility is conditioned by innumerable testimony-related experiences, individual and collective, so that she may directly perceive speakers in an epistemically loaded way. Now, one sort of experience that contributes to the perpetual reconditioning of testimonial sensibility will be the experience of reflectively correcting one's spontaneous credibility judgements in order to compensate for the counter-rational impact of prejudice. Perhaps, for instance, one realizes after the fact that one's credibility judgement was too low and identifies a prejudice as part of the cause. Or perhaps one is reflectively aware at the time that prejudice is shaping one's perception of an interlocutor, and so one reserves judgement. Other sorts of experience will be relevant too. For instance, a hearer's experiences as a speaker too will feed into this process. Perhaps she has experienced being on the receiving end of testimonial injustice in respect of one sort of prejudice, and consequently gains a better understanding of how other sorts of prejudice may surreptitiously have an influence in her own testimonial sensibility. The fully virtuous hearer, then, as regards the virtue of testimonial justice, is someone whose testimonial sensibility has been suitably reconditioned by sufficient corrective experiences so that it now reliably issues in ready-corrected judgements of credibility. She is someone whose pattern of *spontaneous* credibility judgement has changed in light of past anti-prejudicial corrections and retains an ongoing responsiveness to that sort of experience. Full possession of the virtue, then, in a climate that has a range of prejudices in the social atmosphere, requires the hearer to have internalized the reflexive requirements of judging credibility in that climate, so that the requisite social reflexivity of her stance as hearer has become second nature.

It may be that the ever changing and self-renewing nature of prejudice in society means that the best we can really hope for is to achieve the required social reflexivity of judgement through repeated efforts of critical reflection, in which case in so far as we may achieve the virtue, our possession of it will be not full but partial. Certainly it seems improbable that any given hearer would be able to possess the virtue with respect to every prejudice that may suggest itself to her testimonial sensibility in practice (unless her social experience remained reliably narrow), for that would require her to have gained sufficient experience relating to testimonial exchange with all social types against whom there are atmospheric prejudices. Obviously the question of how broad someone's testimonial experience is depends on the contingencies of their life and place in the social scheme. But if, generally speaking, our testimonial experience is anything less than maximally broad, then the extent to which we could display the virtue fully (spontaneously rather than reflectively) will remain patchy across the span of identity prejudices. This puts partial possession in a more ideal-seeming light after all, for it reveals a general reason to expect most virtuous hearers to need to engage in active critical reflection some of the time. Perhaps some combination of spontaneity and reflectiveness may be the ideal: perhaps we should think of the ideal hearer as someone for whom correcting for familiar prejudices has become second nature, while the requisite alertness to the influence of less familiar prejudices remains a matter of ongoing active critical reflection. This seems about right. What matters is that somehow or other one succeeds, reliably enough (through time and across a suitable span of prejudices), in correcting for prejudice in one's credibility judgements. If one succeeds in that, then one has got the virtue of testimonial justice.

4.2 HISTORY, BLAME, AND MORAL DISAPPOINTMENT

The picture of the virtue of testimonial justice that we now have before us is of a virtue that is bound to be hard to achieve, owing to the psychologically stealthy and historically dynamic nature of prejudice. Prejudice is a powerful visceral force, especially when it is expressed less at the level of belief than at the level of those social-imaginative and emotional commitments that more surreptitiously shape hearers' perceptions of speakers. And even if one were faced only with correcting for prejudice at the level of belief, this too can be very hard while those beliefs are propped up by imaginative and emotional contents. (As Christopher Hookway has argued, there is the usual room for *akrasia* in the practical business of managing one's epistemic habits.[11]) It remains for the most part, however, something that we can and should aim for in

---

[11] Christopher Hookway, 'Epistemic *Akrasia* and Epistemic Virtue', in A. Fairweather and L. Zagzebski (eds.), *Virtue Epistemology: Essays on Epistemic Virtue and Responsibility* (Oxford: Oxford University Press, 2001); see e.g. p. 182.

practice. If we are able to achieve it only rather patchily across different sorts of prejudice, that is already a valuable achievement.

There are circumstances, however, under which the virtue *cannot* be achieved, for it is an ethically significant feature of this virtue that it displays a special sort of cultural-historical contingency. In order to explain this, let me follow Linda Zagzebski's reading of Aristotle such that virtues are defined as having both a motivational component and a component of reliable success in bringing about the end of that motivation.[12] In the case of intellectual virtues there will always be a motivation to achieve truth in one or another guise, but usually there will also be a more proximal aim to achieve something that is conducive to truth—notably here, the aim of neutralizing the impact of prejudice in one's credibility judgements. As a matter of definition, then, our virtuous hearer will be reliably successful in fulfilling that proximal aim of neutralizing prejudice. She will succeed in this in so far as her judgements are inflected with a certain reflexive critical awareness of the prejudicial distortions mediating between herself as hearer and her particular interlocutor, and in so far as she is able to correct for that distortion. As is always the case, some people will be better motivated and better able to achieve these things than others. But in the case of testimonial justice, it is not only personal differences that explain the fact that some will and some won't possess the virtue. It is also a matter of the cultural-historical setting. A setting in which there is little critical awareness of the construction of gender, say, is a setting in which people are not generally in a position to possess the virtue of testimonial justice *vis-à-vis* identity prejudice against women.

There is a sense in which just about any virtue may be thought of as historically contingent: one can always imagine a society in which nobody exhibited a given ethical or intellectual virtue—charity or open-mindedness, say—and consider that it would be well nigh impossible for anyone to cultivate the virtue in soil so barren of good example. But the special respect in which the achievement of testimonial justice depends on the historical setting is over and above this general dependence, for it concerns the specific critical reflective tools that are required to achieve the virtue. Even in a society in which the virtue of testimonial justice was possessed in respect of some prejudices, there might be other prejudices in respect of which the virtue was out of reach

---

[12] Linda Zagzebski, *Virtues of the Mind: An Inquiry into the Nature of Virtue and the Ethical Foundations of Knowledge* (Cambridge: Cambridge University Press, 1996).

(except to those, that is, who possess it naïvely; but I have already said that the naïve form of the virtue must be very much the exception). This would seem to mark out the virtue as unusual, though the ethical virtue of justice presumably exhibits the same historical dependence for the same reasons: there might be judgements of justice that cannot be made because they require a line of reflection for which the concepts are not socio-historically available. If there are other virtues of justice (other virtues with justice as their ultimate end), then perhaps their achievement would exhibit the same historical contingency. At any rate, on the face of it, this particular form of historical contingency seems to be special to matters of justice.

In the case of Herbert Greenleaf, we see this historical contingency played out in respect of the absence of a critical awareness of gender prejudice in the society in which his ethical and epistemic second nature were formed. While the Herbert Greenleafs of this world were always at fault in failing to exhibit the virtue, I suggest they were not *culpably* at fault until the requisite critical consciousness of gender became available to them. As we might put it, they were not culpably at fault until they were in a position to know better. There is no precise answer to the question at what point a Herbert Greenleaf comes to be in a position where he should know better than to neglect the possibility that Marge is right. And this question is surely best construed as a matter of degree, not least because the requisite collective gender consciousness is something that is likely to dawn only gradually. But no doubt a figure such as Herbert Greenleaf would be in that position long before he actually lived up to it by taking on board the gender-critical insights made newly available to him. Thus there will tend to be some period of historical transition in which a Herbert Greenleaf, well-intentioned as he may remain, moves from non-culpable fault to culpable fault. He lacks the virtue of testimonial justice with regard to gender prejudice throughout, but the relevant advance in collective consciousness is needed to render the shortcoming in his epistemic conduct blameworthy. Under the historical circumstances, then, my suggestion is that Greenleaf is not blameworthy for the testimonial injustice he inflicts on Marge.

Given that blame is out of order, the epistemic wrong that Green-leaf does Marge presents a genuine case of non-culpable testimonial injustice.[13] The suggestion rests on the idea that one cannot be blamed

---

[13] Previously, in Ch. 2, we discussed the case of the extraordinarily shy speaker whose manner fitted a reliable stereotype of insincerity so that the hearer was justified in

for failing to do something if one was not in a position to access the reason to do it. This presents a special case of 'ought' implies 'can', since in our example the 'can' part is a matter of whether Greenleaf could reasonably be expected to achieve the critical perspective on gender that would have enabled him to question his lack of trust in Marge in the requisite way. We do not blame people for things they objectively cannot do or cannot help doing—though that is not to say that their life will not be ethically tarnished (in an extreme case someone might be torn apart by what they have done, even if they wholly accepted they were not blameworthy for it[14]). Greenleaf could not neutralize the impact of gender prejudice in his judgement of Marge because the critical concepts he needed were not historically available to him.

This points to an interesting kind of epistemic and moral bad luck. On an external interpretation[15] of what it is to have a reason, the situation is fairly straightforward. Greenleaf has a reason to doubt his spontaneous distrust of Marge's word, but his historical situation is such that he cannot access that reason. He is thereby subject to a piece of epistemic and moral bad luck. On an internal interpretation of reasons,

judging insincerity. If we had found this to be a genuine case of testimonial injustice, it would have been of the non-culpable sort; but I argued that it was not in fact a case of testimonial injustice.

[14] As Bernard Williams says of Oedipus, 'The terrible thing that happened to him, through no fault of his own, was that he did those things' (*Shame and Necessity* (Berkeley and Los Angeles: University of California Press, 1993), 70). Oedipus was torn apart by feelings of shame, but in another historical context with a different repertoire of moral emotions, it seems to me that someone who through no fault of their own had done something terrible might be racked by any of the other forms of moral regret: not only shame, but remorse and guilt. The different forms of moral regret present some regretted deed on the part of the subject to her consciousness in slightly different ways. Shame, however internalized, is most basically a feeling of wanting to *hide* from disapproving eyes; remorse is focused on the person one has harmed, and primarily involves an empathetic feeling of *shared pain*; the feeling of guilt, being a matter of bad conscience, is characterized by a desire for *catharsis*, a desire to rid oneself of something bad and off-load a 'heavy' conscience, perhaps through some sort of confession. (But compare Gaita, who broadly identifies all 'guilt feeling' with remorse: Raimond Gaita, *Good and Evil: An Absolute Conception*, 2nd edn. (Abingdon, Oxon.: Routledge, 2004), 51.) I believe that none of these differently focused forms of moral regret is incompatible with a context in which even the agent herself is perfectly aware that she is not blameworthy for what she has done.

[15] See Bernard Williams, 'Internal Reasons and the Obscurity of Blame', in *Making Sense of Humanity and Other Philosophical Papers* (Cambridge: Cambridge University Press, 1995), ch. 3, p. 35). The relevant earlier paper is 'Internal and External Reasons', in *Moral Luck: Philosophical Papers 1973–1980* (Cambridge: Cambridge University Press, 1981).

the situation is slightly less straightforward. While Greenleaf has a subjective motivation to know the truth about his son's disappearance, and not to be taken in by his ingratiating killer, the 'sound deliberative route' he would need to take from there in order to arrive at the motivation to doubt his distrust of Marge is blocked by his historical circumstances. On the internal reasons conception, then, Greenleaf is unable to *possess* a reason to doubt his distrust of Marge. Even while, objectively speaking, there is a deliberative route running between the reason and actual motivations in Greenleaf's subjective motivational set, the fact that Greenleaf's historical situation prevents him from treading that deliberative route means that it cannot be a reason *for him*. This adds another dimension to Greenleaf's epistemic and moral bad luck, as it renders it bad luck not merely about what reasons he can access—which affects what he does—but moreover about what reasons he can have—which affects who he is.[16]

Whatever one thinks about the disagreements between internal and external reasons theorists, if one is inclined towards the internal idiom to describe cases of testimonial injustice such as that which Greenleaf perpetrates, it is worth noting that it could not be controversial in anything like the way that purely ethical cases inevitably are. This is because it could not be controversial to assume that epistemic subjects considered as such possess in their actual set of motivations some general motivation to truth, and *a fortiori* some motivation to more proximal ends which are in the service of truth (such as neutralizing prejudice in one's habits of trust, for instance). That is why it makes little difference whether one prefers to construe our present example according to the internal reasons model or the external reasons model, for all may agree that, in general, any epistemic subject will have a reason to get at the truth. This is not to underestimate the complex and often troubled nature of our relationship with truth. Human beings are obviously subject to all sorts of powerful motivations, and

---

[16] As these alternative descriptions of Greenleaf's case testify, while there is really very little difference in practice between the internal and external interpretations, there is none the less a significant difference in their respective conceptions of how individuals relate to reasons. Driving the internal conception is a spirit of political individualism, for what the internal reasons theorist most fundamentally maintains and the external reasons theorist most fundamentally denies is that, at the limit, a rejection of moral reasons that are not one's own remains a rational option. There is a Humean inheritance here, of course, but I think the Nietzschean streak in Williams's ethical philosophy is also part and parcel of this fundamental commitment to the sovereignty of the individual as the subject of reasons.

indeed reasons, for shielding themselves from painful truths through mechanisms of denial or repression. On the whole, however, one must see such mechanisms against a background of a more general motivation to truth. Given this, it is clear that not just Herbert Greenleaf, but even the most virulent, dyed-in-the-wool sexist version of Herbert Greenleaf, possesses a motivation (to truth) from which there is a sound deliberative route to questioning his spontaneous lack of trust in Marge.

On this as yet rather charitable interpretation of Greenleaf's moral status, then, he is unlucky, both epistemically and morally. More precisely, he is subject to two kinds of moral and epistemic bad luck: circumstantial—bad luck in the socio-historical context that puts the requisite reflexive critical awareness out of his reach—and constitutive—bad luck in the kind of person he is. More precisely, his case exemplifies a compound of circumstantial and constitutive bad luck, for it is specifically historical circumstance that has constituted him as someone who is unable to have a reason to doubt his lack of trust in Marge. Let us say, then, that Greenleaf is subject to a *historical-constitutive* form of bad epistemic and moral luck. The significance of this sort of luck is that its constitutive power is not at the level of the agent's personality (the kind of person one happens to be as an individual), but rather at the level of historical type, so that it is one's place in history that constrains what thoughts are available to one, and thus what reasons one can have. The upshot for Greenleaf is that he misses out on a truth that he is especially interested in acquiring (Marge is right; Ripley is Dickie's murderer), and he is guilty of doing something very bad to someone he cares about. Marge is treated as a hysterical female who cannot handle the truth, someone who deserves protection and sympathy, but not epistemic trust. If one's rationality is an essential part of one's humanity, then Greenleaf gently undermines Marge in her very humanity.

But now we need to qualify our exculpation of Greenleaf, for surely he is not altogether off the hook. If history puts blame out of court, is there some other form of moral resentment that remains in play? The line between what we should and should not blame people for, what we may and may not properly expect of them (and of ourselves), is surely fuzzy, and especially so across historical distance. Given what Greenleaf does to Marge, and given the moral conceptual resources that he *did* have available (which surely included ideas about the wrongs of condescension, respect for the sort of hard evidence that she in fact produces, some general ideas about prejudice being unfair, and so on), we might well feel some sort of qualified moral resentment towards him. It is disappointing, after all, that he colludes with the gender ideology of the day quite so readily, and ignores with such ease Marge's attempts to bring her evidence to his attention. At the very least, he might have held out longer, listened to her more, been more circumspect with regard to Ripley's dismissive comments about her being hysterical.[17] In short, we want to complain that he could have done better, where this registers not just an epistemic disappointment but also an ethical one. We may well feel, then, a certain *resentment of disappointment*—an attitude which is closely related to the resentment of blame, but falls short of it. The resentment of disappointment is still focused on the individual, but the individual conceived in a historically situated manner.

Can we say more to vindicate the resentment of disappointment across historical distance? We need to resist thinking of a culture's moral discourse (moral 'system' as it is sometimes called) as a finite monolith. The resources for moral judgement and moral thought offered up by any moral discourse are not like a set of building bricks with which one can build a finite number of different structures. Conceptual resources are resources for generating indefinitely many *new* meanings, whether as new applications of old concepts or coinings of new concepts. Such resources for meaning are generative and dynamic, never exhausted by the set of meanings actually realized in practical use at any given historical moment. With this generative conception of moral meaning in place, we are able to introduce a distinction between *routine* discursive moves in a moral discourse and *exceptional*, more imaginative moves in which existing resources are used in an innovative way that stands as a progressive move in moral consciousness. An example of such an imaginative move might be the extension of a notion of respect to all humanity as made by someone ethically formed in a society that routinely reserved respect for the ruling classes; or the new application of the concept 'cruel' to violent punishments of children routinely meted out in the name of ordinary discipline. Most of us most of the time make routine moves and exhibit routine moral thinking, and we are lucky if we live in a culture where this means that our ethical thinking is on the whole decent; but sometimes people can rise to a challenge and succeed in something more imaginative. Here, once again, we can draw a helpful parallel in the epistemic dimension. The relevant epistemic contrast

---

[17] A helpful email exchange with Karen Jones stimulated this point.

is between routine credibility judgements and exceptional credibility judgements, where the relevant sort of exceptional judgement might be a judgement that succeeds in correcting for a sort of prejudice not hitherto understood as such.

If we judge Greenleaf in the light of the full ethical resources of his day, then while we may find that the epistemic injustice he does Marge is not culpable (he judged routinely), we may still see it as less than it might have been (less than exceptional). For even Greenleaf might have risen to the occasion and done something morally and epistemically more imaginative than get drawn in to Ripley's conspiratorial story about Marge's female hysteria. There is admittedly nothing very much about Greenleaf to inspire high hopes in this regard, but still he is a decent man who has known Marge for longer than he has known Ripley, and who has a strong personal interest in knowing the truth; so one might well feel some pang of moral resentment over the ease with which he is drawn in to the epistemically insulting construal of her suspicions. Any such disappointment is grounded in the conviction that it *was* historically possible, in our newly extended sense, for him to have made a better credibility judgement: even Greenleaf *could* have judged exceptionally. By judging merely routinely in these heightened circumstances, he does something disappointing that it seems appropriate to hold him responsible for in some way; but the sense in which his moral and epistemic character is besmirched by his failure to rise above the routine is not enough to warrant anything as strong as blame. One cannot be blamed for making a routine moral judgement. But one can none the less be held responsible for making a merely routine judgement in a context in which a more exceptional alternative is, as a matter of historical possibility, just around the corner, and I have suggested that it is appropriate to register this responsibility by way of the resentment of disappointment. The distinction between exceptional and routine moral judgement, then, points to the possibility of a more nuanced range of moral attitudes to historically and culturally distant others—regardless of whether one holds to the internal or the external interpretation of reasons—for it allows us to avoid the hubris of deeming them blameworthy for actions not routinely regarded as wrong in their culture, while still holding them morally responsible to this or that extent, depending on how nearly available the exceptional moral move is judged to have been.

If this is right, then the distinction between exceptional and routine moral discursive moves can help us better understand the issues at stake in the topic of moral relativism. When we judge the behaviour of people in historically or socially distant moral cultures, we need not and should not confine ourselves to the routine moral discourse of that culture (except in so far as we are only interested in issues of blame), since more appropriately nuanced judgements of the moral performance of people in distant cultures will become available only when we also consider what non-routine, more exceptionally imaginative moral judgements might have been made had they better exploited their own moral resources. In the meta-ethical literature we find a fundamental tension rehearsed and re-rehearsed in different ways, and from different sides of the debate, between the universalist pull of moral psychology and language and the apparent fact of cultural and historical contingency. Time and again we come up against the seeming dead end that we can imagine another culture in which there are morally accepted practices that we find unacceptable, and yet, while we are reticent, even unable, to adopt a policy of withholding judgement, we simultaneously sense an eerie lack of justification for blaming these distant others for their actions. But the distinction between the routine and the exceptional helps us see that there need be no dead end for moral thinking here, for it opens up a space for the resentment of disappointment—an attitude still directed to the individual agent, but one which acknowledges his or her historical predicament.

The 'vulgar' relativist idea that it is wrong to pass moral judgements on people in other moral cultures is incoherent,[18] but the related idea that judgements of blame may be out of order across even quite small historical distances ought to be defended: judgements of blame are out of order when people's behaviour is the product of ethical thinking that was routine in their ethical culture. When, for example, we consider the past practice of forcing unmarried mothers to put their babies up for adoption, we should not confine ourselves to the concepts, attitudes, and feelings we surmise were routinely invoked in the daily moral discourse of that society at that time. Rather, we are entitled to appeal to thoughts which *they* could have had, given their full ethical resources, but failed to. And we may contrast their deliberative performance with that of their peers who succeeded in making the exceptionally imaginative moves that gradually gained critical mass so as to propel the community towards a more liberal practice, factoring in of course

---

[18] See Bernard Williams, 'Interlude: Relativism', in *Morality: An Introduction to Ethics* (Cambridge: Cambridge University Press, 1972).

the moral cognitive advantage had by those most directly involved with the practice itself—those who witnessed or felt for themselves the pain of the mother's separation, the effects on the child, and so on. The distinction between routine and exceptional moral judgement helps to explain how a piece of moral progress—the move away from a practice of forced adoption, for instance—is possible. For how else, but through the morally exceptional discursive moves of the few, is a community able to come to see things differently as a matter of routine?

To judge historical others in this way is not hubris, for we can acknowledge that 'could do better' will be our own ethical epitaph too—it is a matter of luck how far living up to what is morally routine is an achievement that leaves one immune from the resentment of disappointment on the part of distant others. It depends significantly on the contingencies that have formed one, and on those that will form future generations. I am often conscious, for instance, of the fact that while I eat meat in semi-good conscience, a vegetarian future society would judge people like me with moral abhorrence. I believe that members of such a society would probably be entitled to real moral disappointment in, say, my failure to follow through on my extant moral commitment to animals kept as pets. Why, they would ask, did I not recognize my implicit commitment to equal moral status among animals more generally? (I ask myself such questions, but never quite answer them.) But if future generations do come to regard eating animals as obviously morally wrong in this way, perhaps none the less they might withhold blame from people like me, on the grounds that what they regard as my moral failing is sufficiently within the bounds of contemporary routine moral judgement. I think that identifying forms of moral resentment that fall short of blame but which are still agent-directed is the key to achieving appropriate moral response across historical and cultural distance. More generally, distinguishing routine from exceptional moral judgements helps us honour the universalist trajectory of moral psychology and language, but without doing violence to historical contingency.

In this chapter I have characterized the virtue for which the phenomenon of testimonial injustice creates the need—the virtue of testimonial justice; and I have explored the historical contingency of its possession conditions. The picture we have arrived at is of a virtue which may, at a given point in history, be unavailable in respect of some prejudices. Having characterized the virtue in this historically situated manner, however, let us now place it in a maximally ahistorical setting—the setting of the State of Nature. Doing so will reveal how far the virtue of testimonial justice is a fundamental epistemic virtue—that is, an epistemic virtue serving a purpose which transcends history in that it arises out of an epistemic need that is present in any human society.

5

The Genealogy of Testimonial Justice

5.1 A THIRD FUNDAMENTAL VIRTUE OF TRUTH

In *Truth and Truthfulness* Bernard Williams makes use of a philosophical method that is traditionally employed only in political philosophy.[1] The method is to construct a fictional State of Nature scenario as the basis from which to draw philosophical conclusions about a given concept or institution. He constructs the State of Nature, however, not with a view to characterizing our most basic political needs but rather our most basic epistemic needs, with a view to illuminating the concepts of truth and truthfulness. His construction echoes that of Edward Craig in *Knowledge and the State of Nature*,[2] though his purpose is different. Craig's project (which I shall discuss more fully in the next chapter) is to illuminate the concept of knowledge by way of a practical explication of why we have that concept. Williams's chief purpose is to illuminate the concept of truthfulness through a practical explication of why it is a virtue, and how it comes to be an intrinsic value.

The State of Nature is to be considered as a minimal human society—a society of minimal social organization—in which people live in groups and therefore share some basic needs. Naturally, given the project, the focus is on epistemic needs, with other needs entering into the story only in so far as they are bound up with epistemic concerns. The construction of epistemic life in the State of Nature has three stages relating to three collective epistemic needs:

(1) the need to possess enough truths (and not too many falsehoods) to facilitate survival: that is, sufficient practically relevant information

---

[1] Bernard Williams, *Truth and Truthfulness: An Essay in Genealogy* (Princeton: Princeton University Press, 2002).
[2] Edward Craig, *Knowledge and the State of Nature: An Essay in Conceptual Synthesis* (Oxford: Clarendon Press, 1990).

regarding, say, which foods are good to eat, which are poisonous, and so on.

Obviously, it will be profoundly advantageous to have at one's disposal not only one's own eyes and ears, so to speak, but the eyes and ears of others too. An individualistic policy of self-reliance would be a bad survival strategy. Thus the first need immediately generates a second:

(2) the need to participate in an epistemic practice whereby information is shared or pooled.

The pooling of epistemic resources exploits whatever divisions of epistemic labour arise out of divisions of other sorts of labour. At the most basic level there will be a simple, unfixed division of epistemic labour arising from the fact that people will be in different places at different times, so that fellow inquirers can make use of the 'purely positional advantage' someone may have *vis-à-vis* a question on which the answer is sought. Such a positional advantage might be 'being up a tree', so as to be able to observe whether a predator is coming, or 'having been there at the time' and thus having occupied the requisite spatio-temporal positioning for observing what happened.

So far the construction is as Craig's and, like Craig, Williams observes that situations of scarcity and other types of competition, not to mention plain malevolence, can create motives for deception and concealment—an interest that Williams casts in terms of the advantage of being a selfish free-rider on an otherwise trustful and co-operative epistemic practice. But this is a problem that Craig and Williams handle slightly differently, so that the third stage of the State of Nature story marks a point of divergence between the two accounts. Craig's third stage involves an emphatic change of perspective from that of speaker to that of hearer or inquirer, and we shall discuss the significance of this below. By contrast, Williams's third stage retains the speaker perspective, for his concern is with speakers' truthfulness—something which does not depend on recognition by a hearer. He observes that the collective—whose members all have an interest in using the pool of information—has a basic need to generate a pressure to counter the interest in being a selfish free-rider on an existing trustful practice. Some action-guiding pressure must be created to encourage people to be truthful or trustworthy informants to their fellow inquirers even on those occasions when it does not suit their individual interests. Thus Williams's third stage registers:

(3) the need to encourage dispositions in individuals that will stabilize relations of trust.

The requisite dispositions naturally fall into two kinds, as Williams explains:

Since we are considering people, who have beliefs and desires and intentions, and who may or may not express their beliefs, it is already natural to think of these dispositions as falling into two different kinds. One kind of disposition applies to their acquiring a correct belief in the first place, and their [competence for] transporting that belief in a reliable form to the pool. The other desirable dispositions—desirable, that is to say, from the social point of view of those using the pooled information—are necessary because reflective creatures will have the opportunity within this structure for deceit and concealment; they will also have the motives for them, as when a hunter has found a prey which he would rather keep for himself and his immediate family. (This is the force of Voltaire's famous remark to the effect that men have language in order to conceal their thoughts.)[3]

Thus the virtues of Accuracy and Sincerity are born (the capitals acknowledge that these are somewhat abstracted versions of accuracy and sincerity), where each relates respectively to a certain set of dispositions that shore up the relations of epistemic trust that are needed for the practice of pooling information. Accuracy and Sincerity are indeed genuine virtues and not just skills, since both lie under the remit of the will. This is obviously so of Sincerity, but it is also true of Accuracy, as Williams notes, since whether or not one is Accurate in what one reports to fellow inquirers depends, for instance, upon how hard one tries, how tenacious one is in getting past mere appearances, how much care one takes, and on many other aspects of epistemic conduct.[4]

It is an interesting question how much the emergence of the virtues of Accuracy and Sincerity achieves. I believe it achieves rather more than Williams seems to give it credit for. To show that two cardinal intellectual

---

[3] Williams, *Truth and Truthfulness*, 44.

[4] For a broader discussion of the ways in which belief comes under the will, see Linda Zagzebski, *Virtues of the Mind: An Inquiry into the Nature of Virtue and the Ethical Foundations of Knowledge* (Cambridge: Cambridge University Press, 1996), P. I, sect. 4.2. For a contrasting perspective, defending the view that all virtues are skills, see Paul Bloomfield, 'Virtue Epistemology and the Epistemology of Virtue', *Philosophy and Phenomenological Research*, V 60, no. 1 (Jan. 2000), 23–43.

virtues come into being by springing directly from absolutely basic epistemic needs is to show that these two virtues *must* arise in human society. Not only naturalism, then, when it comes to Accuracy and Sincerity, but universalism too. This much is surely Williams's point. But what he seems to underestimate is the extent to which the advent of these two virtues comprising truthfulness already illustrates the emergence of truthfulness as a *non-instrumental or intrinsic* value, albeit from decidedly instrumental origins.[5] I think therefore that Williams concedes too much when says that a limitation of the story so far is 'that the values of Accuracy and Sincerity alike are *instrumental*: they are entirely explained in terms of other goods, and in particular the value of getting what one wants, avoiding danger, mastering the environment, and so on';[6] for this is not true. Part of their explanation has been that these values emerge as the response to the need for social pressure on individuals to be truthful *even when there are strong countervailing instrumental considerations*, so that those whose testimony is indeed accurate and sincere are revealed as moved by virtue and not merely by instrumental reasons.[7]

Considered as virtues, then, Accuracy and Sincerity contribute their own action-guiding power to the stabilization of relations of trust, and so their emergence already signals the transformation of truthfulness from a value that influences people's epistemic conduct only in so far as it is a useful means to their ends to a value whose influence is non-instrumental. That is to say, the action-guiding power of these virtues of truth is already enough to at least initiate the transformation of truthfulness from an instrumental value to an intrinsic one. Another way of putting it would be to say that the person who has the virtue of Accuracy, say, is distinguished by the fact that she is motivated to accuracy for its own sake: she is moved by the value of accuracy independently of whether it will serve her purposes on any particular

[5] Williams treats 'non-instrumental' and 'intrinsic' as broadly equivalent. What distinguishes non-instrumental/intrinsic values from merely instrumental ones is that while intrinsic values are explained by reference to instrumental interests, the explanation is not reductive; see *Truth and Truthfulness*, 90.

[6] Ibid. 58.

[7] There is an interestingly parallel debate relating to the pursuit and, so to speak, pooling of scientific knowledge in the real world, which turns on how far purely 'strategic' or instrumental trust (along with various institutional constraints such as replication of results and peer review) is sufficient for the sort of co-operation required to eliminate error and fraud. See Michael Blais, 'Epistemic Tit for Tat', *Journal of Philosophy*, 84 (July 1987), 363–75, for the view that it is sufficient, and John Hardwig, 'The Role of Trust in Knowledge', *Journal of Philosophy*, 88 (Dec. 1991), 693–708, for the view that it is not.

occasion (we shall return to this feature of virtue below). Williams, however, seems to give little weight to this aspect of the virtues, for he goes on to offer an independent argument specifically in favour of the idea that truthfulness is an intrinsic value.[8] Such an argument obviously has independent interest, but I doubt whether it is needed to bolster the virtues of Accuracy and Sincerity already established. Moreover, if these virtues as they stand cannot stabilize relations of trust sufficiently, it is doubtful that giving social articulation to the idea that the two virtues compose an intrinsic value would really help. Someone who remains unmoved by the idea that truthfulness is a value enshrined in certain virtues is unlikely to be much reformed by the moral emphasis afforded by its status as an intrinsic value. I suggest, therefore, that we take Williams's independent argument for truthfulness being an intrinsic value as detachable from concerns about stabilizing trust, and that we allow that relations of epistemic trust in the State of Nature are already stabilized, so far as it is socially realistic to try to do so, by the emergence of Accuracy and Sincerity as virtues. Or, putting the point differently, we might say that the pressure which these virtues put on people to be truthful for its own sake is already a significant pressure in the direction of regarding truthfulness as intrinsically valuable.

We are now in a position to inquire whether there is another virtue of truth that emerges alongside Accuracy and Sincerity in the State of Nature. To see that there is, it will help to switch over to Craig's third stage in the story, so that we can make explicit the requisite transfer from the point of view of the speaker to that of the hearer or inquirer.[9]

---

[8] Williams, *Truth and Truthfulness*, 92.

[9] Epistemology's undue preference for the former was something which, as Craig notes, Williams had flagged up as important to epistemology in *Problems of the Self*, where he presents the distinction by observing that there is

a rather deep prejudice in philosophy, that knowledge must be at least as grand as belief, that what knowledge is, is belief plus quite a lot; in particular, belief together with truth and good reasons. This approach seems to me largely mistaken. It is encouraged by concentrating on a very particular situation which academic writings about knowledge are notably fond of, that which might be called the *examiner* situation: the situation in which I know that *p* is true, this other man has asserted that *p* is true, and I ask the question whether this other man really knows it, or merely believes it. I am represented as checking on someone else's credentials for something about which I know already. ... But this is far from our standard situation with regard to knowledge; our standard situation with regard to knowledge (in relation to other persons) is rather that of trying to find somebody who knows what we don't know; that is, to find somebody who is a source of reliable information about something .... Our standard question is not 'Does Jones know that *p*?' Our standard question is

The materials supplied by the State of Nature story, so far told from the speaker's point of view, do not include the materials needed for gathering truths from others. We have seen that the need to pool information makes certain demands on speakers—that they possess the virtues of Accuracy and Sincerity—but equally it makes demands on hearers, and we have not yet addressed the question as to what they might be. Clearly, hearers or inquirers in the State of Nature will need to be open to truths offered to them by their peers, and to be open without being credulous of testimony that is in fact false. Inquirers in the State of Nature, then, need to be able to distinguish trustworthy from non-trustworthy informants so that they can be responsibly discriminating in what propositions they accept as true. Now, if there were no residual inaccuracy or insincerity left in the State of Nature once the virtues of Accuracy and Sincerity had emerged, then clearly our hearer-inquirers would not be vulnerable to accepting non-truths as truths, and there would be no cost attached to being gullible (or rather, there would be no such thing as gullibility). But that would be to introduce mere fantasy into the State of Nature construction, rendering it too far from human nature to serve any explanatory function. The idea that Accuracy and Sincerity are virtues can only bring so much pressure to bear to ensure that pooled apparent information is genuine information, and so we confront the need for hearers to be discriminating as to whom they acquire information from. This collective epistemic need is as basic as any other we have mentioned, and it arises directly from the second. Thus the third stage in Craig's construction relates to the need to distinguish good from bad informants. It registers:

(3′) the need for potential informants to bear 'indicator properties': that is, properties which, by definition, reliably indicate that they are conveying the truth.

For Craig, an indicator property might be many things, from a property such as 'looking in the right direction at the time', to something that

rather 'Who knows whether *p*?' (Bernard Williams, 'Deciding to Believe' in *Problems of the Self: Philosophical Papers 1956–1972* (Cambridge: Cambridge University Press, 1973), 146)

Williams believed that the State of Nature account of the concept of knowledge indicated that knowledge was prior to belief; though Craig engineers his own account carefully to leave room for the traditional analytical commitment to the view that, at least in humans, knowledge involves a true belief plus (let us call it) warrant. For an independent case for the view that knowledge is prior to belief, see Timothy Williamson, *Knowledge and its Limits* (Oxford: Oxford University Press, 2000), chs. 1 and 2.

relates to individual expertise such as 'having a good track record of getting such things right'. In the State of Nature, indicator properties will naturally be fewer and simpler than indicators of authority might be in any actual, more institutionalized society; but we can add without distortion to Craig's conception such possible indicator properties as 'replying with confidence' or even 'seeming to know what she was talking about', given that such things as these are basic features of human discursive socialization, and that, for a range of quotidian subject matters not fraught by competitive interests and so on, such properties would indeed be reliable as indicators of epistemic trustworthiness.

We can say, then, that in the State of Nature the hearer must be appropriately responsive to indicator properties so that she can participate in the pooling of information and so share in knowledge. Hearers need dispositions that lead them reliably to accept truths and reject falsehoods. In other words, hearers in the State of Nature need dispositions that help ensure that their credibility judgements are not too wide of the mark. In earlier chapters I urged that real historical social settings throw up many pressures that are likely to distort our credibility judgements, and I focused on identity prejudice in particular. Our present focus on the State of Nature invites us to ask what sorts of original countervailing pressures exist there to distort the forming of proper credibility judgements. We already have it that people in the State of Nature live in groups, and these groups are characterized by divisions of labour that lead to divisions of specifically epistemic labour. But now we should push the conception a little further by envisaging the relations of insider and outsider that human groups generate, and the relations of allegiance and enmity that naturally spring from them. (Almost this much is implicit in Williams's and Craig's talk of competition, scarcity, and plain malevolence as motivations to deceive or conceal.) The human groups in the State of Nature, then, will consequently have among their concepts some equivalents of 'outsider' and 'insider', 'allies', 'enemies', and 'competitors', at the very least. And this means that social perception and judgement in the State of Nature will involve social categorization, which means that in the making of credibility judgements there will be some reliance on stereotypes. Once we consider that there must be some significant division of labour (without committing ourselves to any division in particular), it becomes even clearer that stereotypical social perceptions will inform credibility judgements in the State of Nature. Indeed, given my account of testimony, this is a proper part of how people in the State of Nature succeed in meeting the need stated as stage (3′) of Craig's construction—the need to discriminate good from bad informants.

Thus the State of Nature, minimally social though it remains, contains both sufficient social identity concepts and sufficient practical pressures to produce some basic identity-prejudicial stereotypes (ignorant outsiders, rivals out to trick one, and so on). There will be some reliable stereotypes here, of course, but to insist that the State of Nature is a place where there is no pressure in the direction of prejudicial stereotyping would be to insist that people in the State of Nature were so psychologically well balanced that the normal basic human impulses that drive prejudice are entirely absent.[10] But this would simply be another way of introducing mere fantasy into our careful abstraction. Rather, we must allow that some restricted class of identity-prejudicial stereotypes will tend to be present in the State of Nature. This being so, it follows that hearers' powers to discriminate genuine from false information will need to include a certain anti-prejudicial sensitivity even in the State of Nature ('Just because he's not one of us doesn't mean he's a liar/a fool'). The complex of virtues that make for critical openness to the word of others in the State of Nature needs to include a specifically anti-prejudicial virtue such that the hearer reliably corrects for any counter-rational influence that identity power would otherwise have on his credibility judgements. This corrective anti-prejudicial virtue is already familiar to us from our previous discussion as the virtue of testimonial justice, but since here it relates only to those basic prejudices at work in the State of Nature, and is thus an abstraction of the real historical virtue, let us flag this (to harmonize with Williams's account) with capitals: Testimonial Justice. What the genealogical setting allows us to see is that from the point of view of pooling knowledge, this virtue in the hearer is the essential counterpart to the virtues of Accuracy and Sincerity in the speaker. Accuracy and Sincerity sustain trust as regards *contributing* knowledge to the pool; Testimonial Justice helps sustain trust as regards *acquiring* knowledge from the pool.

It seems, then, that the virtue that prevents hearers from doing speakers a testimonial injustice is revealed to be a third basic virtue of truth, for the reason that it frees hearers in the State of Nature

[10] This conception of prejudices as a normal feature of human psychology is supported by Elisabeth Young-Bruehl's argument that prejudices are not pathological (*The Anatomy of Prejudices* (Cambridge, Mass.: Harvard University Press, 1996), see e.g. pp. 32 and 209).

from the prejudice that would cause them to miss out on truths they may need. The collective's need to stabilize relations of epistemic trust, then, is revealed as requiring pressures to be brought not only in the direction of Accuracy and Sincerity in speakers, but also in the direction of Testimonial Justice in hearers. For this anti-prejudicial virtue emerges, just as Accuracy and Sincerity do, from the basic need to pool information in a minimal social environment where there are none the less native human tendencies towards not only deception and concealment but also prejudice. We should note that the State of Nature as I have now depicted it marks a departure not only from Williams but also from Craig, for my story leaves little room for indicator properties *per se*. Indicator properties are guaranteed by definition to be reliable, and the presence of prejudice in the State of Nature encourages a conception on which there are no indicator properties as such, but only their defeasible counterparts—'markers' of authority, let us call them. (Let signs of trustworthiness be 'positive markers', and signs of non-trustworthiness 'negative markers'.) The practical-conceptual point behind Craig's indicator properties is that truthfulness is prior to deceit, trust prior to distrust—there must be *some* reliable markers of authority, or else the whole practice of pooling information will simply not get going. Quite so; but we can honour this point without insisting on indicator properties as such, simply by stipulating that markers in the State of Nature are reliable in the main. Any more than this would be a step too far in the direction of rational idealization, for it would obscure our very subject matter. The relevant picture of the State of Nature for the present project must not obscure the fact that human nature is such that, however simple the human groupings or societies, prejudice within and between groups is inevitably in the offing. If so, then even in the State of Nature, the human tendency to prejudice is present, alongside motivations to deception and concealment, as a significant counter-veridical pressure.

To recap, we took the point from Williams that, since human beings in the State of Nature will have motivations for deception and concealment, there is a need to encourage two kinds of disposition in speakers, one relating to Accuracy and the other to Sincerity; and these dispositions constitute two basic virtues of truth. What we have now discovered is that there is another disposition that is equally fundamental to the control of wayward motivations that would otherwise disrupt the sharing of knowledge in the State of Nature: the disposition in hearers to avoid prejudice in their judgements of credibility. Without this disposition among users of the information pool, the epistemic community would be vulnerable to another systematic epistemic dysfunction, the risk of which is as profoundly built into structures of human motivation as is the dysfunction that arises from self-interested motivations to conceal or deceive. The risk of the dysfunction of testimonial injustice arises from the fundamental human proneness to prejudice, especially identity prejudice; the risk of the dysfunction of concealment or deception arises from the fundamental human proneness to act from self-interest. Given the plausible assumption that many identity prejudices are at root some sort of psychological defence mechanism, there is room to argue that the prejudices that occur in the State of Nature *are* a form of self-interest. But there is no need to insist that prejudice is every bit as basic in human nature as (other forms of) self-interest. All we need for the present argument is the idea that people in the State of Nature display a tendency not only to self-interest *per se* but also to those forms of identity prejudice most basic in human nature. Both represent natural patterns of human motivation that need controlling if the practice of pooling knowledge is to get going. Testimonial Justice is revealed as a third fundamental virtue of truth.

All this concerns the virtue of Testimonial Justice—the abstracted virtue proper to the State of Nature scenario. But of course the real historical virtue of testimonial justice has the very same structure. It grows out of the original basic version into some more layered historical form, where the precise form it takes—the place it has in moral and epistemic discourse, the importance and meaning attributed to it, indeed the degree to which it is distinguished or named at all—will vary depending on the historical-cultural moment. Perhaps in our time the nearest approximation we have is a notion of 'fair-mindedness', or else we employ negative formulations in terms of a hearer's not being biased or prejudiced. But neither approximation captures the essentially corrective nature of the virtue; and certainly we do not generally distinguish any such virtue as the antidote to the widespread and sometimes profound discrimination that testimonial injustice really is. History has not yet done very much for the virtue of testimonial justice.

Just as real historical virtues are usually more layered than their State of Nature counterparts, so are the stereotypes of epistemic authority more layered and potentially more unreliable than anything found in the State of Nature. Looking to history, Steven Shapin gives us a compelling example of a prejudicial stereotype of epistemic authority that was operative in seventeenth-century England. It seems that *being a gentleman* constituted a positive marker of epistemic trustworthiness in both its aspects—competence and sincerity. Shapin tells us that the gentleman was, quite literally, accorded privileged competence, even in matters of perception:

The first consideration implicated in the culture of gentlemanly veracity was rarely given explicit treatment in the practical ethical literature of early modern Europe. Nevertheless, it was an absolutely fundamental feature of the practical assessment of testimony, and one which might assist in discriminating the worth of testimony from gentle and nongentle sources. This was the ascription to gentlemen of *perceptual competence*.[11]

From Shapin's account we may also surmise that being a gentleman effectively functioned as a marker of sincerity too. The gentleman enjoyed the economic and social independence brought by social advantage, and this elevated social position meant that he was seen to be generally free from the sorts of beholdenness that might be thought to, and might actually, provide motivations for deceiving others. Further, the question of non-deception was shored up by a code of gentlemanly honour. Not only did his social privilege mean that he was seen to have little to gain from deception; it meant that he stood to lose a great deal if he were seen to flout the code—a noble track record was worth protecting.

If Shapin is right, it seems that there was a historical moment in England when being a gentleman was a key marker of epistemic trustworthiness, not with respect to any particular question or range of questions, but generally. If being a gentleman was a positive marker of authority, being non-gentle and/or female was a negative marker. Seventeenth-century women's economic and social dependence meant that their supposed lack of rational authority—like that of non-gentle men—went for the most part without saying:

There were powerful institutions of exclusion that affected the cultural and political role of women, as well as of nongentle men. But precisely because those institutional systems were so effective, and because the justifications overwhelmingly picked out dependence as a disqualifying circumstance, the *literate culture* of early modern England was not nearly so significantly marked by identifications of gender disabilities as it was by commentary on 'ignobility,' 'servility,' and 'baseness'.[12]

---

[11] Steven Shapin, *A Social History of Truth: Civility and Science in Seventeenth-Century England* (Chicago and London: University of Chicago Press, 1994), 75; italics original.
[12] Ibid. 88.

Not that Elizabethan versifiers were exactly silent on the subject:

> A woman's face is full of wiles,
> Her tears are like the crocadill ...
> Her tongue still chats of this and that,
> Than aspen leaf it wags more fast;
> And as she talks she knows not what,
> There issues many a truthless blast.[13]

Whatever form the prejudicial stereotypes of authority may take in history, the power of prejudice to corrupt discursive relations is markedly increased in the transition from the State of Nature to historical society, if only because any real society contains so much more social complexity to provide new motivations for prejudice. This means that the virtue of Testimonial Justice becomes an even more important feature of epistemic life in the transition. It may also become a more admirable virtue to possess in the context of the real-world social mêlée, since it is bound to become harder to achieve. I have been focusing on Testimonial Justice primarily as an *intellectual* virtue. But we must not forget that this virtue serves not one but two ultimate values: it simultaneously protects both truth and justice. The person who possesses the virtue reliably avoids epistemically undermining others, and she avoids missing out on truths offered too. But now this raises the question as to how we should categorize the virtue. Is testimonial justice to be considered primarily as an ethical defence against injustice or an intellectual defence against error?

5.2 A HYBRID VIRTUE: INTELLECTUAL-ETHICAL

Someone might wish to press the question whether testimonial justice is an intellectual or a moral virtue. If intellectual virtues generally have truth as their ultimate end,[14] and moral virtues have some form of the good as theirs, then it may legitimately be asked which value figures as

---

[13] Humfrey Gifford, in Norman Ault (ed.), *Elizabethan Lyrics* (New York: Capricorn Books, 1960); quoted in Shapin, *Social History of Truth*, 89.

[14] I take this idea to be relatively uncontroversial, but note the exception of Montmarquet. He argues for a conception of intellectual virtues such that they need not be truth-conducive, but rather are 'qualities that a truth-desiring person would *want* to have' (James A. Montmarquet, *Epistemic Virtue and Doxastic Responsibility* (Lanham, Md.: Rowman and Littlefield, 1993), p. x). See also his 'Epistemic Virtue', *Mind*, 96 (1986), 482–97.

the ultimate end of testimonial justice. Let us try to anchor the matter by reminding ourselves that the disposition at the heart of the virtue is such that the subject is motivated to neutralize the impact of prejudice in her credibility judgements, and that this serves equally both justice and truth. Maybe this shows that we should resist the dichotomous question of whether testimonial justice is an intellectual or a moral virtue. We should bring to mind the fact that the answer to this superficially weighty question simply hangs on whether truth or justice is featured as the ultimate end of the virtue. This surely lightens the burden of our question somewhat, in so far as it seems to leave room for the possibility that there is no definitive answer independent of context.

But let us go more slowly. We need to consider how virtues are individuated, and to look more closely at how intellectual and ethical virtues compare in structure. A passage from Linda Zagzebski is helpful in both connections:

> A *virtue* ... is a deep and enduring acquired excellence of the human person that includes both a motivational component and a component of reliable success in bringing about the end of the motivational component. A motivation is an emotion-disposition that initiates and directs action towards an end. The motivational component is distinctive of the particular virtue, but a complete taxonomy of the virtues will probably reveal that the immediate ends of the particular virtues are not ultimate, but that several virtues have the same ultimate end. For example, generosity, compassion, kindness and charity ultimately aim at the well-being of others, even though each of them has a more immediate end—in the case of compassion it is relief of the suffering of others; in the case of generosity it is increasing our neighbors' possession of the goods of life. Intellectual virtues ultimately aim at the truth, but each also has a more immediate end such as distinguishing reliable from unreliable authority, or gathering a sufficient amount of relevant evidence.[15]

Particularly helpful in the present context is the idea that individual virtues have a distinctive motivational component. Compassion, for instance, is distinguished by the immediate end of relieving the suffering of others, even while it may share with certain other virtues the ultimate end of the well-being of others. The view of how to individuate virtues that we may take from this (though Zagzebski is not explicitly proposing it) strikes me as obviously right. Given that clusters of virtues may share the same ultimate end—the ultimate end of truth is common to many

---

[15] Linda Zagzebski, Précis of *Virtues of the Mind, Philosophy and Phenomenological Research*, 60, no. 1 (Jan. 2000), 169–77, at 172.

intellectual virtues—the ultimate end cannot be what distinguishes one virtue from another. Only the more immediate end can do that, or, which comes to the same thing, the motive to the immediate end. This insight helps further lighten our superficially weighty question of whether the virtue of testimonial justice is intellectual or ethical. If we ask what is the immediate end of testimonial justice considered as an intellectual virtue, the answer is 'neutralizing prejudice in one's credibility judgements', and its ultimate end will be truth. For neutralizing prejudice is necessary for achieving the appropriate openness to truth that the subject is ultimately aiming at—if the hearer allows prejudice to influence her credibility judgement, she is liable to miss out on a truth. If we now ask what is the immediate end of testimonial justice considered as an ethical virtue, the answer is, once again, 'neutralizing prejudice in one's credibility judgements', and its ultimate end will be justice. For neutralizing prejudice is the necessary means to avoiding doing one's interlocutor a testimonial injustice. Thus testimonial justice considered either as an intellectual virtue or as an ethical virtue contains the very same individuating motivation: to neutralize prejudice in one's credibility judgement. I conclude that they are one and the same virtue, even while the ultimate end that is most appropriately attached (truth or justice) will change according to the context.[16] In contexts where the practical predicament is such that openness to the truth is paramount, it will be appropriate to consider the virtue under the aspect of an intellectual virtue. In contexts where ethical considerations are paramount, it will be most appropriate to consider it under the aspect of an ethical virtue.

Consider the following examples. If, for instance, the hearer is a detective who displays the virtue of testimonial justice as she tries to ascertain from a teenager with a track record of petty crime exactly what happened at the scene of some incident, then, although ethical considerations never lose their force, the main *point* of the detective's motivation to be unprejudicially open to whatever truths this teenager may convey is, clearly, to discover the facts. In such a discursive situation, epistemic considerations are paramount, because the hearer's chief practical purpose is to get at the truth. Consequently, it is most appropriate to consider the ultimate end of the virtue being exercised by the detective to be truth, and so the virtue she displays in neutralizing

---

[16] I am indebted to Andrew Chitty for a provocative emailed question and to Anne Kelleher for a helpful subsequent discussion of the issues raised, which together helped me see my way through these issues.

her prejudice against the teenager is testimonial justice as an intellectual virtue. By contrast, we might imagine an example in which it is a counsellor talking to the teenager. While she may care a great deal about how far he may or may not be telling her the truth, the reason she cares about this relates not to any interest in the facts *per se* but to a different practical purpose that she has in hearing what he has to say: she is trying to develop a relationship of (among other things) epistemic trust between them, in so far as his exclusion from that sort of trust, with all the alienation and resentment that goes with it, is a contributing cause of his anti-social behaviour. Above all, she must endeavour to neutralize any prejudice against him in her own credibility judgements in order that at least she, of all people, should avoid enacting prejudice against him by failing to believe him when he tells her the truth. She must distinguish herself from all those other adults in authority who don't believe a word he says. In such a case, it is most appropriate to regard justice as the ultimate end of the virtue displayed by the counsellor, and so what she exhibits is the virtue of testimonial justice considered as an ethical virtue.

These two examples illustrate the contextualist answer that I have proposed to the question of how to categorize the virtue of testimonial justice. But we should add that there may also be contexts in which the practical circumstances are indeterminate as to whether intellectual or ethical concerns are paramount, so that we simply cannot say under which aspect the virtue of testimonial justice figures—we cannot say whether its ultimate end is truth or justice. Consider, for instance, the scenario in which our teenager is talking this time to his social worker. She is engaged in an ongoing project of trying to encourage him to include himself and be included in the ordinary relations of trust (ethical and epistemic) that make for social inclusion and social functionality quite generally. This means that a paramount aim in her exchanges with him is to let him know that he is being given credit where credit is due, and that includes the credit of epistemic credibility. However, an equally important aspect of her particular purpose is that he should not be allowed to see her as a pushover, so she must show him that if he lies to her, she will know. He needs to learn that she will respect him, respect his word, so long as he merits it, and only so long as he merits it. This feature of her purpose reveals considerations of truth to be equally as important in the context as considerations of justice. Both ultimate ends have equal title, and so we should conclude that in such contexts truth and justice feature as a joint ultimate end, and that the virtue displayed by the social worker is at once intellectual and ethical. The possibility of such contexts strongly encourages the more general thought that in testimonial justice we have discovered something of a novelty: a virtue that is genuinely hybrid in that it aims at both truth and justice. While this may be a philosophically intriguing idea, there is nothing suspiciously mysterious about it. The hybridity of the virtue stems from the fact that negative identity prejudice—the thing whose impact on judgement the virtue neutralizes—is both an intellectual and an ethical offence. With this in mind, it seems entirely fitting that the virtue which guards against it should turn out to be both ethical and intellectual in character, at once a virtue of truth and a virtue of justice.

One assumption, however, that might lead someone to find my claim to hybridity for the virtue of testimonial justice suspiciously mysterious is the Aristotelian assumption that ethical and intellectual virtues are different in kind. The considerations that lead Aristotle to this view, however, are far from persuasive.[17] One of them is that while ethical virtues are acquired through practice and habituation, intellectual virtues are taught.[18] But this seems an over-statement at best. While intellectual instruction may help someone to acquire intellectual virtue, and may be crucial to the development of skills required for intellectual virtue (the skill, for instance, of doing long multiplication, of employing correct grammar, of formalizing an argument), none the less the business of cultivating the virtues themselves cannot fail crucially to involve learning by example, practice, and habituation, just as the moral virtues do. How else could one hope to learn and internalize how to resist the temptation to jump to a conclusion, or how to attain the non-egoism required for openness to challenge from alternative points of view, or how to persevere so far and no further in finding evidence for a controversial hypothesis? Such things are matters of judgement, and the honing of a person's judgement takes time and practice and habituation, in intellectual matters as in moral. Furthermore, the motivational component in many intellectual virtues will need to be firmly entrenched in the agent's psychology, as jumping to attractive conclusions on insufficient evidence, for instance, may sometimes be a very tempting prospect. It does not seem possible that teaching or instruction alone could entrench our motivations in this way; not unless

---

[17] See Zagzebski, *Virtues of the Mind*, Prt. II, sect. 3.2.

[18] Aristotle, *The Ethics of Aristotle: The Nicomachean Ethics*, trans. J. A. K. Thomson (London: Penguin, 1976), 91; II.1; 1103ª14–ᵇ1.

the teaching incorporated the requisite practice and habituation that is really doing the educational work.

This leads us to the second reason for scepticism that intellectual virtues can be taught: their acquisition clearly involves the training of the emotions. The point is therefore closely connected with Aristotle's other main claim in favour of intellectual and ethical virtues being of different kinds: namely, that the two sorts of virtue pertain to the two different parts of the soul, where one part concerns reason and the other emotion, most fundamentally feelings of pleasure and pain. He asserts that intellectual virtues 'belong to the part that has reason and prescribes to the soul in so far as it possesses reason, whereas the virtues of character belong to the part that is non-rational'.[19] But this conception seriously underestimates the involvement of emotions in the intellectual virtues. Emotional performance is a proper part of intellectual performance, so assessments of a person's emotions can be a proper part of an assessment of them *qua* knower. As Nancy Sherman and Heath White have argued:

If diffidence or caution stands in the way of exploring new frontiers, of asking bold questions, of submitting one's work to public scrutiny or acclaim, then it is an emotional defect in a knower. Similarly, if love of self turns into a grandiosity that makes listening to competing viewpoints difficult, if it squashes collaborative effort and makes teamwork a matter of hierarchical command, then such narcissism is, again, an emotional defect in a knower.[20]

More generally, the motivation in an intellectual virtue may often be an emotion or have some emotional content. Consider the virtue of intellectual courage, or perseverance. It is hard to imagine these as containing a motivation that has no emotional content. For these reasons, then, Aristotle's conception of the difference between intellectual and moral virtues need not trouble us.

---

[19] *Eudemian Ethics*, II.1; 1220ª5–13; quoted in Zagzebski, *Virtues of the Mind*, 142. But note that Sarah Broadie argues, in *Ethics with Aristotle* (Oxford: Oxford University Press, 1991), that Aristotle's distinction between the non-rational desiderative and the rational parts of the soul does *not* in fact coincide with his distinction between virtues of character and virtues of intellect—although she acknowledges that he at one point writes as if they do and at no point states that they do not. She says that they are not coincident because the rational part of the soul prescribes to the other part and is 'desiderative in its own right'. Thus: 'The virtues of character are virtues of the desiderative: that is to say, they are virtues of the reason-responsive part of the soul, but also of the prescriptive part *qua* desiderative' (p. 71).

[20] Nancy Sherman and Heath White, 'Intellectual Virtue: Emotions, Luck, and the Ancients', in M. DePaul and L. Zagzebski (eds.), *Intellectual Virtue: Perspectives from Ethics and Epistemology* (Oxford: Clarendon Press, 2003), 42.

Aristotle's particular conception could have made it difficult to suggest that testimonial justice was a hybrid virtue because he held that they were so fundamentally different in kind. But in itself the idea that ethical and intellectual virtues are two different sorts of virtue, permitting some non-trivial categorical differences, is no obstacle to the idea that there might be some exceptional hybrid cases. Julia Driver, for instance, has, proposed that intellectual and ethical virtues can be distinguished by reference to the source of their primary value, so that intellectual virtues derive their primary value from the value of truth, whereas ethical virtues derive theirs from the value of the well-being of others.[21] This is a persuasive idea and fits well with our claim that testimonial justice functions in some contexts as an intellectual virtue and in others as an ethical one, having as an ultimate end now truth and now justice. It seems that there is no obstacle in principle to the claim that testimonial justice is a hybrid virtue.

Someone might, however, remain suspicious that our virtue should exhibit quite such a happy harmony between epistemic and ethical ends. Taken generally, after all, there is no guarantee that epistemic and ethical ends will harmonize.[22] If some down-trodden schoolteacher is told in no uncertain terms by the unscrupulous head teacher that when the school inspector visits the classroom, he must ask the pupils a question and make sure that he picks from among the sea of raised hands someone who will come out with the right answer, this epistemic aim might be best served by a policy that is not remotely just. It might be best served, for instance, by picking the pupil who, notoriously, always gets her big brother to text her the answers on her mobile. There is no general guaranteed harmony between epistemic ends and ethical ends, and my characterization of the virtue of testimonial justice does not rely on any such romanticism. My argument that the virtue of testimonial justice is a hybrid virtue depends simply on the fact that when we look and see, we find that correcting for prejudice is necessary for avoiding missing out on truths offered by an interlocutor *and* necessary for avoiding doing them an injustice in their capacity as a knower. Let me, finally, bring these claims home with a couple of illustrations. The illustrations isolate the different ends of truth and justice respectively in

[21] See Julia Driver, 'The Conflation of Moral and Epistemic Virtue', in Michael Brady and Duncan Pritchard (eds.), *Moral and Epistemic Virtues* (Oxford: Blackwell, 2003), 101–16.
[22] I thank Alex Voorhoeve for this point.

order to show as starkly as possible why the subject who is motivated to either of these ends will, other things being equal, be motivated to neutralize prejudice in her credibility judgement.

First, the epistemic end. The claim is that the purely epistemic end of not missing out on truths offered by an interlocutor requires one to neutralize prejudice in one's credibility judgements. To illustrate the point, let us imagine a character we might call the *ruthless truth-seeker*: someone who (in the local context) is highly motivated to the truth, but not at all to justice. As the tyrannical boss of a large advertising company, she cares not at all about the well-being as such of her employees; yet she is wholly committed to being unprejudiced in her judgements of their credibility, because she recognizes that this is what is required for an efficient harvest of their knowledge and creative ideas. Second, let us isolate the ethical end. Here the claim is that the purely ethical end of avoiding doing an injustice to an interlocutor requires one to neutralize prejudice in one's credibility judgement. For example, we might stretch our imaginations a little further to envisage the character of the *fair-minded conversationalist*: an anxious host whose sole aim is to avoid causing offence to any of his guests, which he may do if he greets their word with prejudice. He may have no interest whatever in the truth or falsity *per se* of what he is told in the course of dinner party chat, but he is very concerned to avoid doing an injustice to any guest. This solitary motive requires him to neutralize any prejudice in his credibility judgements. The purely ethical motive to justice, then, just like the purely epistemic motive to truth, is on its own sufficient to require the subject to neutralize prejudice in his credibility judgements.

Before we take leave of these two peculiar characters, we ought briefly to inquire whether either of them possesses the virtue of testimonial justice. I take it that if any virtue were displayed, then the ruthless truth-seeker would display testimonial justice as an intellectual virtue, and the fair-minded conversationalist would display it as an ethical virtue. Certainly what they *do* seems all right (they both neutralize any prejudice in their credibility judgements, as is required by their ultimate ends of truth and justice respectively); yet one would certainly be very reluctant to attribute the *virtue* to either of them. What agents do is important, but virtue is equally concerned with the motivational states that lie behind actions. As Aristotle says:

Virtuous acts are not done in a just or temperate way merely because *they* have a certain quality, but only if the agent also acts in a certain state, viz. (1) if he knows what he is doing, (2) if he chooses it, and chooses it for its own sake, and (3) if he does it from a fixed and permanent disposition.[23]

Neither of our characters is such that we could safely attribute either the second or the third requirement to them, and so neither has the proper commitment to neutralizing prejudice in their credibility judgements. The ruthless truth-seeker cares only about harvesting information and ideas, so that the slightest shift of context is likely to reveal her as not remotely concerned to eradicate her prejudices as such. One senses, for instance, that were the profit motive not served by non-prejudice in her credibility judgements, she would readily dispense with her anti-prejudicial self-discipline. The fair-minded conversationalist is depicted principally as an anxious host whose primary concern is to avoid insulting his guests in any way, detectable by them or not, so that a shift of context might once again reveal quite a different attitude to his prejudices. One senses that once the evening has passed over without incident, he might be relieved to free himself of his anti-prejudicial self-discipline along with the other burdens associated with the role of host. Even though our obviously artificial characters' actions are perfectly in tune with the dictates of the virtue of testimonial justice (considered now as an intellectual virtue, now as an ethical one), none the less our ruthless truth-seeker certainly does not exhibit the virtue, and probably nor does the fair-minded conversationalist, for the requirements of choosing the action for its own sake and of stability of disposition are not fulfilled, or not fulfilled clearly enough.

I hope it is now evident that the virtue of testimonial justice is indeed a hybrid, and that its hybridity depends on no over-optimism about general harmony among epistemic and ethical values. Its hybridity depends only on the demonstrated harmony of epistemic and ethical ends in the specific case of neutralizing prejudice.

[23] Aristotle, *Ethics of Aristotle: The Nicomachean Ethics*, 97; II. 4; 1105^{a}9–^{b}2.

6

Original Significances: The Wrong Revisited

Having mined the State of Nature for the original counterpart of the virtue of testimonial justice, let us now look to see what the State of Nature scenario might add to our understanding of the wrong that is done to the speaker in any case of testimonial injustice.

6.1 TWO KINDS OF SILENCE

While Craig's State of Nature story furnishes the starting point for Williams's own construction, their different projects mean that their stories diverge at stage (3), as we have seen. In sum, Williams's story moves to Accuracy and Sincerity, whereas Craig's moves to indicator properties. In Williams's genealogy the guiding question is about the status of truthfulness in our lives, so that the State of Nature construction moves from the need to pool information to the need for social pressures upon speakers to be truthful even when it is not in their interests. By contrast, in Craig's genealogy the guiding question concerns why we have the concept of knowledge—why, over and above the idea that people can possess and convey true beliefs, do we have an added concept such that we can talk about people *knowing* things and conveying *knowledge*? In order to answer this question, Craig uses the State of Nature conceit to construct not only a scenario but, moreover, a *concept*—namely that of the 'good informant'. This is a concept which is shown, as it emerges from the State of Nature construction, to arise naturally from the most basic human epistemic needs. Any human society will develop such a concept. He then develops the hypothesis that this constructed concept constitutes the 'core' of our concept of a knower, and thus bears a practical explanatory relation to the concept of knowledge. Roughly, the explanation of why we have the concept of knowledge is that it arises from our fundamental need to distinguish good informants: originally, knowledge is what good informants can be relied on to share with us. Stages (1)–(3) in his construction represent the three different components of the good informant: someone who (1) is likely enough in the context to be right about what you want to know, (2) is communicatively open (principally, sincere) in what he tells you, and (3) bears indicator properties so that you can recognize that (1) and (2) are satisfied.

This third condition—the bearing of indicator properties—is what leads an inquirer to identify this or that person as a good informant in the first place. We have already observed that even in the State of Nature this mechanism can be subject to basic prejudices, so that we must expect to find there an original counterpart to the real-life phenomenon of testimonial injustice. Craig's scenario now allows us to add to this the related point that a significant form of the injustice in the State of Nature (as I have elaborated it) occurs when prejudice, manifested in what I have called markers of trustworthiness, leads to a tendency for some groups simply not to be asked for information in the first place. Now this most straightforward of epistemic exclusions—barred entry to the community of informants—is obviously also a crucial feature of the politics of epistemic real life. The exclusion in fact marks a commonplace form of testimonial injustice: those social groups who are subject to identity prejudice and are thereby susceptible to unjust credibility deficit will, by the same token, also tend simply not to be asked to share their thoughts, their judgements, their opinions. (If the word of people like you is generally not taken seriously, people will tend not to ask for it.) This kind of testimonial injustice takes place in silence. It occurs when hearer prejudice does its work in advance of a potential informational exchange: it pre-empts any such exchange. Let us call it *pre-emptive* testimonial injustice. The credibility of such a person on a given subject matter is already sufficiently in prejudicial deficit that their potential testimony is never solicited; so the speaker is silenced by the identity prejudice that undermines her credibility in advance. Thus purely structural operations of identity power can control whose would-be contributions become public, and whose do not.

The silencing of those who are subject to pre-emptive testimonial injustice is, like other forms of testimonial injustice, highly context-dependent: it would be stretching the pessimistic social imagination too far to imagine a society (original or historical) that contained social groups whose members' knowledge or opinions were *never* solicited on *any* subject matter. For a start, even in the most severely oppressive societies, members of the most subordinated groups will rely on and co-operate epistemically *with each other*, and this will remain so even if they have internalized the oppressive ideology to a significant degree. But, more than this, it is clear that, for instance, Tom Robinson might have been relied on and trusted epistemically on certain matters even by the more thoroughly racist white citizens of Maycomb County—matters relating to his daily work, no doubt, and indeed many everyday matters of practical import, so long as there was no challenge to a white person's word, no perceived implication of non-inferiority of intellect, nothing about the subject matter that might be seen to imply that this Negro was getting above himself. The tendency for incoherence in human prejudice, sustained through mechanisms of psychological compartmentalization, is such that significant pockets of epistemic trust can remain relatively untouched, even by a powerful racist ideology that corrupts that same trust in countless other contexts.

The fundamental importance of indicator properties in the State of Nature, then, directs our attention to the pre-emptive form of testimonial injustice, and it is perhaps worth remarking that this form of the injustice may be especially hard to detect from the outside, for it is by definition literally passed over in silence. If we turn our imagination to the real social world and place the phenomenon of pre-emptive testimonial injustice in relations of social power, we readily see how it could function as a mechanism of silencing: not being asked is one way in which powerless social groups might be deprived of opportunities to contribute their points of view to the pool of collective understanding. (We shall explore this general theme in the next chapter.) Testimonial injustice, then, can silence you by prejudicially pre-empting your word.

To reveal the second way in which testimonial injustice might silence you, let us examine a different aspect of Craig's story, an explicitly ethical aspect of epistemic practice in the State of Nature. Craig makes the suggestion that the practice of pooling information gives rise to a distinctively *co-operative* ethos within the practice. Something about the epistemic co-operation that fellow poolers of information are inevitably involved in generates a distinctively ethical attitude among them. Craig acknowledges that this ethical attitude is hard to capture, and he talks of the 'special psychology of team-work in a community'.[1] He also

---

[1] Edward Craig, *Knowledge and the State of Nature: An Essay in Conceptual Synthesis* (Oxford: Clarendon Press, 1990), 36.

makes the pregnant suggestion that this special psychology is implicit in the distinction between someone's being treated as an 'informant' and their being treated as a 'source of information', and I think this is the key to understanding not only the positive ethical attitude shared by participants in the practice but also something about the wrong done to someone who is prejudicially excluded from that practice. Broadly speaking, informants are epistemic agents who convey information, whereas sources of information are states of affairs from which the inquirer may be in a position to glean information. Thus, while objects can only be sources of information, people can be either informants (as when someone tells one something one wants to know) or sources of information (as when the fact that one's guest arrives bedraggled and shaking her umbrella may allow one to infer that it has been raining).

What, then, is the ethically distinctive character of an inquirer's attitude to an informant? 'What I have in mind is the special flavour of situations in which human beings treat each other as subjects with a common purpose, rather than as objects from which services, in this case true belief, can be extracted.'[2] And Craig notes that this idea of common purpose surfaces in the fact that informants, unlike mere sources of information, have some sympathetic grasp of the inquirer's predicament that allows them to be actively helpful. But testimonial injustice—especially when it is systematic—also wrongfully deprives the subject of a certain fundamental sort of respect, and the distinction between a source of information and an informant helps reveal this deprivation as also a form of *objectification*. The subject is wrongfully excluded from the community of trusted informants, and this means that he is unable to be a participant in the sharing of knowledge (except in so far as he might be made use of as an object of knowledge through others using him as a source of information). He is thus demoted from subject to object, relegated from the role of active epistemic agent, and confined to the role of passive state of affairs from which knowledge might be gleaned. He is ousted from the role of participant in the co-operative exercise of the capacity for knowledge and recast in the role of passive bystander—a role in which, like objects, he is able to exercise no greater epistemic capacity than that of featuring in potentially informative states of affairs. The moment of testimonial injustice wrongfully denies someone their capacity as an informant, and in confining them to their entirely passive capacity as a source of information, it relegates

---

[2] Craig, *Knowledge and the State of Nature*, 36.

them to the same epistemic status as a felled tree whose age one might glean from the number of rings. In short, testimonial injustice demotes the speaker from informant to source of information, from subject to object. This reveals the intrinsic harm of testimonial injustice as *epistemic objectification*: when a hearer undermines a speaker in her capacity as a giver of knowledge, the speaker is epistemically objectified.

In order to explore this idea of epistemic objectification, we will do well to compare it to that highly resonant model for objectification that comes to us from feminism in the form of the critical concept 'sexual objectification'. The notion of sexual objectification is sometimes used as a necessarily pejorative idea (to indicate women's being represented and/or treated as mere objects for men's sexual gratification), or it can be understood as covering not only that pejorative idea but also an attitude and behaviour towards another person that is ethically perfectly all right and, as Martha Nussbaum has suggested, might even be 'a wonderful part of sexual life'.[3] Nussbaum characterizes the objectifier as 'treating one thing as another: One is treating as an object what is really not an object, what is in fact, a human being.'[4] This formulation does not, however, quite capture the view that she herself is to arrive at. Nussbaum argues for the view that treating a person as an object is not always inappropriate, let alone ethically bad, and that context is all when it comes to the question of whether or not a given case amounts to an ethically bad sort of objectification. This seems to me exactly right. In itself, being treated as an object is not the problem, since we are all objects *inter alia*. The morally crucial distinction is perhaps best captured in terms of the difference between, on the one hand, someone's being treated as an object in a context or a manner that does not deny that they are *also a subject* and, on the other hand, someone's being treated as a *mere* object—where the 'mere' signifies a more general denial of their subjectivity. Since humans are essentially more than mere objects, this latter treatment amounts to a sort of dehumanization. Indeed, I think we would do well to adopt the ready-made Kantian formulation and say that the question of whether a certain treatment of a person amounts to a morally acceptable or morally bad sort of objectification depends on whether it involves them being treated as a

---

[3] Nussbaum is quoting the legal theorist Cass Sunstein: Martha Nussbaum, *Sex and Social Justice* (New York and Oxford: Oxford University Press, 1999), 214.
[4] Ibid. 218.

means, compatibly with their also being at the same time an end in themselves,[5] or, alternatively, as a *mere* means. Since this captures such a common ethical idea about what it is to treat fellow human beings as full human beings, I think we can lift this bit of Kant's terminology without dragging the rest of his considerable philosophical apparatus along with it.

It is part of normal co-operative social life to make use of others, and be made use of oneself, as a means. We, for instance, make perfectly ethical use of the postman to get our letters sent. Nussbaum effectively points to a sexual example of a similarly ethically innocuous instrumentalization of another person:

If I am lying around with my lover on the bed and use his stomach as a pillow, there seems to be nothing at all baneful about this, provided ... I do so with his consent ... and without causing him unwanted pain, provided, as well, that I do so in the context of a relationship in which he is generally treated as more than a pillow. This suggests that what is problematic is not instrumentalization per se but treating someone primarily or merely as an instrument. The overall context of the relationship thus becomes fundamental.[6]

I think the Kantian way of putting the distinction is apposite in the present context, not least because it can help further reveal the ethical import of the distinction that brought us to the notion of epistemic objectification: namely, the distinction between someone's being treated as an informant and their being treated as a source of information. With the Kantian distinction in the background, we can see how there might be a crucial moral difference between treating someone as a source of information and treating them, as we may now put it, as a *mere* source of information. Making use of someone as a source of information is ethically perfectly all right (recall what one may benignly glean from the bedraggled, umbrella-shaking guest considered simply as a feature of a state of affairs), provided there is nothing about the context which means that you are doing so in a way that denies their epistemic subjectivity more generally—provided, that is, that there is nothing about your treatment of them, and nothing about your broader relationship and attitude to them, that undermines their general status as a subject of knowledge.

Now of course there will be few contexts in which a hearer's prejudice is so insanely thoroughgoing that he fails to regard his interlocutor as a

---

[5] Nussbaum herself uses this particular Kantian term; see Ibid. 223.   [6] Ibid.

subject of knowledge *at all*. We have already remarked on the context dependence of the sort of prejudice that leads to testimonial injustice: the jurors of Maycomb County would have trusted Tom Robinson on many an issue relating to the harvest he was working on, and Herbert Greenleaf would have been ready to trust Marge on many a matter less apparently susceptible to distortion by her female intuitiveness than the question of her lover's disappearance. So the mark of epistemic objectification of the bad kind must be that there is something about the broader relationship between hearer and speaker—the attitudes held by the hearer about the speaker, for instance—that undermines the speaker's epistemic subjectivity. That there is something generally undermining to the speaker's epistemic subjectivity in the relationship between the jurors of Maycomb County and Tom Robinson is obvious. The prejudices that Atticus Finch catalogues in his summing-up speech are, we suppose, exactly those that shape the jurors' perception of Tom, and together they radically undermine his general status as an epistemic subject, more than enough to constitute the jurors' epistemic objectification of him as morally bad. The presence of any significantly identity-prejudicial attitudes against the speaker will always undermine their general status as a subject of knowledge, and so cannot fail to render any resultant epistemic objectification morally bad. We may conclude, then, that such central cases of testimonial injustice always involve a morally bad kind of epistemic objectification.

Both of our main examples are cases where the epistemic objectification results from testimonial injustice. But what about cases where the hearer is right to judge her interlocutor as epistemically untrustworthy on the matter in hand, so that there is no injustice? Even if, in such cases, there is nothing about the overall relationship between speaker and hearer to impugn the humanity of the speaker, is it not still the case that in judging one's interlocutor to be untrustworthy, one epistemically excludes him and thereby, in some sense at least, denies his epistemic subjectivity? Well, Yes; but this cannot be epistemic objectification of the bad kind, for there is neither epistemic nor ethical fault in judging someone, without prejudice, to be untrustworthy if they are indeed untrustworthy—on the contrary, there is epistemic merit in it. No doubt we should give some ethical weight to the fact that judging someone untrustworthy does *pro tem* strip them of their function as an informant and confine them to functioning merely as a source of information—perhaps, for instance, we have an ethical obligation not to over-react to a one-off moment of untrustworthiness, never trusting them again about anything—but other things being equal, there is no wrong done here. Some forms of epistemic objectification, then, are ethically acceptable, not to mention epistemically meritorious. Once again, the crucial factor is that there should be nothing about the context that casts the token negative credibility judgement made by the hearer as an instance of any general tendency on the hearer's part to unfairly downgrade the speaker's epistemic subjectivity; nothing to undermine them more generally in their capacity as a knower.

Our use of Kant's distinction between treating someone as a means and as a *mere* means prompts a general comparison between our newly elaborated conception of the wrong that is involved in epistemic injustice—morally bad epistemic objectification—and the general Kantian conception of moral wrong. The sort of epistemic objectification that we are concerned with is the cognitive counterpart to Kant's practical rationality conception of what constitutes immoral treatment of another person—treating them in a way that denies or undermines their status as a rational agent. In testimonial injustice, one person undermines another's status as a subject of knowledge; in Kant's conception of immorality, one person undermines another's status as rational agent. Obviously the two sorts of wrong are closely intertwined. At the very least, they are both instances of the undermining of a dimension of a person's rationality, where that rational capacity is conceived as essential to human value. They both also involve an idea of the wrongdoer treating another as if she were a lesser rational being. We might say that both picture the wrongdoer as engaged in an ontological violation of another person—the violation involved in treating them as if they were not (or not fully) a rational being, practically or cognitively conceived.

The two sorts of insult to a person's rationality may tend to come together. In cases of systematic testimonial injustice, an identity prejudice against a social type's epistemic trustworthiness is likely to be accompanied by a parallel identity prejudice against their practical rationality. Near the end of *To Kill a Mockingbird*, Scout, our child-narrator, reports Maycomb County's attitude to Tom's death (recall that he was shot by the prison guards), and we are given an especially poisonous reminder of how racial prejudice can attack the black subject's practical rationality:

Maycomb was interested by the news of Tom's death for perhaps two days; two days was enough for the information to spread through the county. 'Did you hear about? ... No? Well, they say he was runnin' fit to beat lightnin' ... '
To Maycomb, Tom's death was Typical. Typical of a nigger to cut and run.

Typical of a nigger's mentality to have no plan, no thought for the future, just run blind first chance he saw. Funny thing, Atticus Finch might've got him off scot free, but wait—? Hell no. You know how they are. Easy come, easy go. Just shows you, that Robinson was legally married, they say he kept himself clean, went to church and all that, but when it comes down to the line the veneer's mighty thin. Nigger always comes out in 'em.[7]

The undermining of someone as a knower is, conceptually and historically, closely related to their being undermined as a practical reasoner. The two sorts of insult to their humanity are importantly distinct, however, relating as they do to two different functions of rationality, and it seems to me that moral philosophy should concern itself with both.

We have taken sexual objectification as a model to help us develop the idea of epistemic objectification, and this invites us to consider how these different sorts of objectification might be related to one another. In particular, there is a well-known radical feminist view according to which a social climate in which women are sexually objectified creates a certain phenomenon of silencing such that women are given so little credibility in sexual discursive contexts that their word is as noise—canonically, when they say 'No' to a man's sexual advances, or bring a legal charge of sexual assault. The view in question is put forward in relentlessly polemical style by the feminist legal theorist Catharine MacKinnon. MacKinnon casts pornography as the essence of women's subordination to men, on the grounds that pornography not only represents women as enjoying being used, sometimes violently, as sexual objects by men, but also thereby socially constructs women as being men's sexual instrument, so that the sexual ideology encapsulated in mainstream hard-core pornography is a powerful force in making actual men and women relate sexually to each other according to eroticized dominance and submission. (The kind of construction at stake here is best interpreted as what we have called constitutive construction.[8]) Thus a certain sort of sexual reality is created, but it is a sexual reality in which women are not themselves—it is just that the falsification involved in the pornographic construction has become so naturalized that it tends to invisibility, even to women. (This, at any rate, is how I synthesize the sometimes apparently conflicting messages of MacKinnon's text, which

---

[7] Harper Lee, *To Kill a Mockingbird* (London: William Heinemann, 1960), 244.

[8] For a sympathetic reworking of MacKinnon's view, see Sally Haslanger, 'On Being Objective and Being Objectified', in Louise M. Antony and Charlotte E. Witt (eds.), *A Mind of One's Own: Feminist Essays on Reason and Objectivity* (Boulder, Colo.: Westview Press, 1993/2002).

seems at some points to say that women can only be as pornography constructs them to be, even while the overriding critical point turns on claiming that pornography effects an abusive falsification of women and heterosexual sexuality.[9])

That a lot of pornography eroticizes male dominance and female submission is in itself an entirely familiar feminist idea that may well strike one as right. But let me also sound a note of qualification about MacKinnon's uncompromising view. Her totalizing vision of the impact of such pornography on heterosexual relations, and gender relations more generally, is in my view luridly overstated in various respects. It essentializes the multifarious nature of women's historical subordination to men as foundationally a matter of sexual subordination; it attributes to pornography too powerful an influence on the social construction of heterosexuality when many other cultural practices and institutions also have a powerful, and sometimes countervailing, influence; and, simply, it is excessively pessimistic in its portrayal of sexual and other social relations between men and women—a pessimism which here and there rings unpleasantly anti-men. None the less, the grim vision of relations between women and men does surely contain real insight into the effects that a corrupt sexual ideology, undoubtedly peddled in much pornography, can have not only on sexual but also on epistemic and discursive relations between men and women. Before we leave the concept of epistemic objectification, then, its connection with sexual objectification and the concept of silencing seems worth a closer look.

---

[9] Compare, for instance, the following two quotations:

[Pornography] institutionalises the sexuality of male supremacy, fusing the erotization [*sic*] of dominance and submission with the social construction of male and female. ... Men treat women as who they see women as being. Pornography constructs who that is. *Men's power over women means that the way men see women defines who women can be ... Pornography is not imagery in some relation to a reality elsewhere constructed. It is not a distortion, reflection, projection, expression, fantasy, representation, or symbol either. It is a sexual reality.* (Catharine MacKinnon, 'Francis Biddle's Sister', in *Feminism Unmodified: Discourses on Life and Law* (Cambridge, Mass. and London: Harvard University Press, 1987), 172–3; italics added.)

Speaking socially, the beliefs of the powerful become proof, in part because the world actually arranges itself to affirm what the powerful want to see. ... *Beneath this, though, the world is not entirely the way the powerful say it is or want to believe it is. If it appears to be, it is because power constructs the appearance of reality by silencing the voices of the powerless, by excluding them from access to authoritative discourse.* Powerlessness means that when you say 'This is how it is,' it is *not* taken as being that way. (Ibid. 164; extended italics added.)

A first connection to bring out is that if we put MacKinnon's view together with our account of epistemic objectification, we greet the possibility that one sort of objectification can be causally related to another sort of objectification. If women suffer sexual objectification owing to a complex identity prejudice that denies them status as full human subjects, it becomes more likely that they will suffer epistemic objectification too. And vice versa—different forms of objectification suffered by a given social group will be connected via a common tracker prejudice, so there is no particular reason to regard sexual objectification as the first cause of other forms of objectification to which women might be subject. One is not obliged to represent any particular form of objectification as causally fundamental, for different forms of objectification may be mutually supportive. But, in any case, our main interest in the connection between sexual and epistemic objectification lies not in the general idea that they might be causally related via a common prejudice, but more specifically in the possibility that a climate of sexual objectification might give rise to cases of testimonial injustice so extreme that the epistemic injustice crosses over into a fundamental communicative dysfunction.

MacKinnon's view is that women's powerlessness in the pornographic society leads to their being given so little credibility by their male interlocutors that their speech is effectively silenced. This is a different sort of silencing from that which we have already countenanced in the form of pre-emptive testimonial injustice. MacKinnon's central conception of silencing (there is a range of distinct phenomena she alludes to as silencing[10]) involves an intriguingly different kind of credibility deficit, and one which makes helpfully explicit the dimension of epistemic objectification that we have been exploring: 'Pornography makes women into objects. Objects do not speak. When they do, they are by then regarded as objects, not as humans, which is what it means to have no credibility.'[11] In such a climate of sexual objectification, women's extreme lack of credibility would give rise to an especially acute form of testimonial injustice. In such a situation, women's testimony is not quite pre-empted (they do say things to men), but it might as well be, since it is not heard as genuine testimony at all.

[10] These span many different ways in which women are forced to engage in sexual fakery. See ibid. 194–5.
[11] Ibid. 182. I thank Rae Langton for directing my attention to this aspect of MacKinnon's view.

Like pre-emptive testimonial injustice, such cases of silencing involve a massive advance credibility deficit, but here it is in advance of an utterance that *is* forthcoming. What is not forthcoming is any genuine credibility judgement in respect of the speaker's utterance, for the dehumanizing sexual ideology is such that the man never really *hears* the woman at all—her utterance simply fails to register with his testimonial sensibility. This is one construal of the silencing that concerns MacKinnon: an extreme kind of testimonial injustice, characterized by a radical communicative dysfunction.

That testimonial injustice might, in some social contexts, take the form of silencing of this radical sort is a possibility that comes into view only on a construal of silencing that begins from women's lack of credibility. But there is more than one way to flesh out the idea of silencing, and the suggestion that it is an extreme form of testimonial injustice is of course just one. In entertaining the testimonial injustice account, then, we should bear in mind an alternative account, given by Jennifer Hornsby and Rae Langton, which is worked out not in an epistemological frame but rather in the framework of speech act theory in the philosophy of language.[12] They both draw on J. L. Austin's theory, and in particular his idea of illocutionary acts as requiring 'uptake' from the interlocutor to secure the communication. (A hearer's uptake is constituted by his grasping that the speaker is indeed communicating the content of her locution—for instance, grasping that in saying 'Look out!' she is warning him, or in saying 'No' she is refusing him.) Hornsby introduces an idea of 'reciprocity'—a primitive relational stance that fellow communicators have towards one another *as* communicators. Relations of reciprocity furnish the communicative climate that provides for uptake, and if it is eroded here or there by a pornographic sexual ideology, then these patches of erosion can cause the failure of uptake that silences women's would-be illocutions. The result might be that, in sexual contexts at least, a woman's 'No' does

---

[12] See Jennifer Hornsby and Rae Langton, 'Free Speech and Illocution', *Legal Theory*, 4 (1998), 21–37. Other relevant papers are Hornsby 'Speech Acts and Pornography', in Susan Dwyer (ed.), *The Problem of Pornography* (Belmont, Calif.: Wadsworth Publishing Company, 1995), 220–32; and Rae Langton, 'Subordination, Silence, and Pornography's Authority', in Robert Post (ed.), *Censorship and Silencing: Practices of Cultural Regulation* (Los Angeles: Getty Research Institute for the History of Art and the Humanities, 1998), 261–84. Langton's paper is in dialogue with a paper by Leslie Green in the same volume, which challenges Langton's claim that pornography is authoritative speech and questions under what circumstances the absence of felicity conditions amounts to silencing—see L. Green, 'Pornographizing, Subordinating, and Silencing', ibid. 285–311.

not receive its required uptake from a man, with the result that her would-be illocution thereby fails to communicate—it fails even to *be* the illocutionary act it would have been. (None the less, it perhaps remains more than noise; in a co-written paper the authors allow that a would-be illocution that lacks uptake might be cast as a less than 'fully successful' illocution.[13] This seems the right move, and a move that is important from the point of view of vindicating what women *do* achieve in saying 'No' in such contexts. It may be legally important, for instance, that a less than fully successful illocution of 'No' can be sufficient for withholding sexual consent, lest failure of uptake on the part of an attacker be construed as exculpating him from a charge of sexual assault.[14])

Hornsby and Langton, then, present a purely communicative conception of silencing, slightly different from MacKinnon's in emphasis, perhaps, in that they present the communicative failure as basically caused by failure of reciprocity, which is more fundamental than the failure of credibility that MacKinnon seems to emphasize. On Hornsby and Langton's account, silencing occurs prior to the moment at which a speaker's credibility is at issue, for the silenced woman's problem is not that her interlocutor regards her word as so worthless that when she says 'No' he doesn't hear her; rather, his stance towards her in the context is such that she is prevented from (fully successfully) performing the illocutionary act of refusal in the first place. His silencing her does not turn on any epistemic attitude he might have towards her, for the whole question of her credibility simply does not arise. On their account, then, silencing does not feature as a form of testimonial injustice. By contrast, on the construal I have put forward, according to which there might be social climates in which women lack credibility so drastically for certain subject matters that their word fails altogether to register in male hearers' testimonial sensibility, we can see how silencing might take the form of an extreme testimonial injustice. Either conception of silencing presents a coherent social possibility, but I tend to think that the epistemic model describes the more empirically likely possibility,

---

[13] See Hornsby and Langton, 'Free Speech and Illocution', esp. 26–27. The idea of an illocutionary act that does not 'fully succeed' is, as they note, taken from J. R. Searle, *Speech Acts: An Essay in the Philosophy of Language* (Cambridge: Cambridge University Press, 1969).

[14] For criticism on this score, see Daniel Jacobson, 'Freedom of Speech Acts? A Response to Langton', *Philosophy and Public Affairs*, 24 (1995), 64–79. Langton and Hornsby give a robust joint response in 'Free Speech and Illocution'.

simply because it requires less erosion of women's human status before the silencing effect kicks in.

6.2 THE VERY IDEA OF A KNOWER

Attention to Craig's 'practical explication' of knowledge has added two new dimensions to our understanding of the wrong involved in testimonial injustice. His emphasis on the importance in the State of Nature of indicator properties that distinguish good informants led us to identify the pre-emptive form of testimonial injustice—our first kind of silence. And his quasi-ethical distinction between a source of information and an informant led us to the notion of epistemic objectification, a climate of which can lead to the second kind of silencing associated with testimonial injustice. Finally, let us consider the main message of Craig's project in order to see what it may furnish as regards the more epistemological dimension of the wrong of testimonial injustice.

Craig's project has two main aspects: to relate the constructed concept of the good informant to our actual concept of knowledge so as to render a practical explication of that latter concept; and to relate this practical explication of knowledge to traditional analytic epistemology so that the familiar contours of the debates in that tradition get explained, perhaps explained away, by the practical account. The task facing us, however, concerns only the first aspect of his project. We saw, in Chapter 3, how testimonial injustice fits into the epistemology of testimony; now Craig's account of knowledge will help us further explore the phenomenon by providing a different, highly original epistemological framework within which it may be placed.[15]

The epistemological upshot of the State of Nature scenario for Craig is that the constructed concept of the good informant is seen to arise from no more than the most basic epistemic needs, and this shows that the concept arises in any human society. But this must now be related to the real concept of knowledge. There is a job of work here, since 'good

[15] Craig's project has a close affinity with that of Michael Welbourne, who has argued that we have the concept of knowledge in order to refer reflectively to that which is shared or 'commoned' in a successful piece of testimony. See his *Knowledge* (Chesham, Bucks: Acumen, 2001), esp. ch. 6; and *The Community of Knowledge* (Aberdeen: Aberdeen University Press, 1986).

informant' and 'knower' manifestly have different extensions. Craig's succinct illustrations of this point are the Mafioso Luigi, who knows but is no kind of informant, since he isn't telling; and Matilda (from the eponymous cautionary tale by Hillaire Belloc), whose appalling track record of lying means that nobody can believe a word she says, even when she has knowledge that there is a fire and is yelling so from the window. These are not counter-examples, since Craig is not presenting any analysis to which they could be counter-examples. Rather, they are illustrations of the acknowledged gap between the constructed concept of the good informant and our actual concept of knowledge. This gap is then bridged by a general thesis—itself a mini State of Nature genealogy—about the nature of concepts. The thesis is that there is a quite general tendency among concepts such that, however subjective their original core content, they become 'objectivized', in that they take on layers of content that conceal and override their original dependence on subjective powers of recognition. The thesis is called the *objectivization* of concepts. Take the example 'chair':

I may well be interested in 'something which I can now sit on' (only close and accessible objects need apply). But in due course I shall be interested, since I anticipate wanting to sit down at future times, in objects which I could sit on if I wanted to, or in whether there will be something which I can sit on when I want to (at the end of the walk). This interest will naturally lead to an interest in hearing the opinions of others as to where there are objects which I can sit on if I want to, irrespective of whether they want to sit on them or not; so I shall want them to operate an objectivised concept too. And if I grow a little more altruistic in my outlook I may even be interested in whether there is something which Fred can sit on if he wants to, irrespective of whether I shall want to sit on anything or not. Hence the concept of something which is, in abstraction from what any particular person wants at any particular time or place, or even from whether anyone ever wants to sit down, simply suitable for sitting on.[16]

This is intended as an everyday example of a general tendency towards objectivization displayed by concepts as such—a tendency for concepts to come to be concepts of something objective, of something independent of the subject's needs and capabilities. This tendency is explained by the presence of various basic practical pressures. In the case of 'chair', the practical pressures are one's interest in having something to sit on at times and places other than the here and now, one's interest in others being able to let one know about them in

---

[16] Craig, *Knowledge and the State of Nature*, 84.

circumstances where one is ignorant, and one's possible interest in finding something for others to sit on. In the case of the concept 'good informant', the practical pressures propelling it towards its objectivized form (bearer of knowledge) are three. First, the inquirer may not always need an informant right here right now, but may rather need to store up awareness of whom to go to for information as and when the need arises. (Consider the tourist's interest in knowing where the local hospital is, just in case.) Secondly, the inquirer may often be in a position of needing others to recommend informants to her, since they may be better placed to recognize properties relevant to the requisite reliability, and/or they may know better which properties correlate well with such reliability. (Consider the efforts one might make to get a recommendation for a good lawyer.) Finally, she may not care at all about getting hold of the information herself, but care very much that some relevant party in the community has it. (Consider the importance of someone in the community knowing what the right medical treatment is for any given likely malady.) These pressures, Craig argues, force the concept of the good informant into increasingly objectivized form, so that there might be a good informant who cannot be recognized as such by the inquirer, and, further, who cannot be recognized as such by anyone around here, and, further still, cannot be so recognized by anyone anywhere—yet she knows. Such is our actual concept of knowledge, and the basic practical pressures towards it from the starting core of the good informant bridge the gap between the two concepts, so that the resultant concept of a knower maintains the true belief requirement plus the presence of some property that correlates well with true belief,[17] but the requirement that the property be detectable (by way of indicator properties) has completely eroded away.

---

[17] Craig tends to describe the good informant as someone recognizable as having a true belief, which formulation puts belief at the core of what it is to know, and therefore depicts belief as prior to knowledge, so that knowledge is conceived as true belief plus a bit. Tim Williamson criticizes the State of Nature account on this score (*Knowledge and its Limits* (Oxford: Oxford University Press, 2000), 31 n. 3). But it is in principle entirely open to Craig to stick more strictly to a conception of the good informant as someone who is likely enough in the context to be right about *p* (a formulation he also uses), and therefore to allow that knowledge is prior to belief (belief not featuring at the core of what it is to know). I regard it as a virtue of the State of Nature approach that it can in principle remain agnostic on this score even while it can also give an explanation of our much rehearsed intuitions to the effect that knowing that *p* entails believing that *p* by reference to the fact that an informant who believes that *p* is more likely to come out with *p* when you ask him, and with enough conviction to convince you (see Craig, *Knowledge and the State of Nature*, 13–14).

With the presentation of objectivization completed, we can now ask what light the explanatory relation between 'good informant' and 'knower' may shed on the phenomenon of testimonial injustice. If the core of our concept of knowledge is captured in the concept of the good informant, because (as the State of Nature story shows) essentially what it is to be a knower is to participate in the sharing of information, then another dimension to the harm of testimonial injustice now comes into view. When someone is excluded from the relations of epistemic trust that are at work in a co-operative practice of pooling information, they are wrongfully excluded from participation in the practice that defines the core of the very concept of knowledge.

Previously (in Chapter 2) we saw various ways in which testimonial injustice cuts ethically deep. When we first homed in on the wrong of testimonial injustice, the intrinsic injustice emerged as a matter of the subject's being wronged in their capacity as a giver of knowledge, and thus in a capacity essential to human value. When we inquired further into the nature of this intrinsic harm, I suggested that it can inhibit the very formation of subjectivity (recall our pre-suffrage politically inclined woman). And in the present chapter I have revealed it as a distinctive form of objectification. But now, finally, Craig's practical explication of knowledge places us in a position to venture a specifically epistemological suggestion about how the injustice cuts deep: given Craig's account, what the recipient of a prejudicial credibility deficit is excluded from is the single practice that dramatizes the origin of what it is to be a knower at all. Testimonial injustice denies one access to what originally furnishes status as a knower. No wonder, then, that even relatively inconsequential testimonial injustices can carry a symbolic weight to the effect that the speaker is less than a full epistemic subject: the injustice sends the message that they are not fit for participation in the practice that originally generates the very idea of a knower.

This completes our exploration of testimonial injustice. It is a form of injustice that can cause deep and wide harm to a person's psychology and practical life, and it is too often passed over in silence. My discussion has been driven by the hope that we might become more socially articulate about this somewhat hidden dimension of discrimination, and thereby be in a better position to identify it, protest it when it happens to us and, at least sometimes, avoid doing it to others.

We can now move on to our second kind of epistemic injustice. Our knowledge of the social world is basically interpretive, and it is put at risk if the hermeneutical tools that we have to make sense of things are unevenly informed by the experiences of different social groups. In the next and final chapter, I shall try to develop the idea that some groups can suffer an unfair disadvantage in making sense of their own social experience. Thus we encounter our second distinctive form of epistemic injustice: *hermeneutical injustice.*

7

Hermeneutical Injustice

7.1 THE CENTRAL CASE OF HERMENEUTICAL INJUSTICE

Feminism has long been concerned with the way in which relations of power can constrain women's ability to understand their own experience. This feminist concern found its early expression in Marxist terms, so we see an articulation of it in the original and explicitly historical materialist form of feminist standpoint theory: 'The dominated live in a world structured by others for their purposes—purposes that at the very least are not our own and that are in various degrees inimical to our development and even existence.'[1] In this quotation from Nancy Hartsock, the word 'structured' has three significances. All three are pertinent to the historical materialist context, though only one is centrally relevant here. Hartsock's remark may be read materially, so as to imply that social institutions and practices favour the powerful; or it may be read ontologically, so as to imply that the powerful somehow constitute the social world; or again it may be read from an epistemological point of view, as the suggestion that the powerful have an unfair advantage in structuring collective social understandings. Our interest in forms of epistemic injustice naturally directs us to the epistemological reading. However, we shall never be far from related material and ontological questions, for it is obvious that certain material advantages will generate the envisaged epistemological advantage—if you have material power, then you will tend to have an influence in those practices by which social meanings are generated. And in the hermeneutical context of social understanding, it is also clear that, at least sometimes, if understandings are structured a certain way, then so are the social facts—we have already encountered cases of causal

[1] Nancy Hartsock, *The Feminist Standpoint Revisited and Other Essays* (Boulder, Colo.: Westview Press, 1998), 241.

and constitutive construction of social identity in the discussion of testimonial injustice, and we shall meet similar cases in connection with hermeneutical injustice. In hermeneutical contexts such as our knowledge of the social world, material and ontological questions naturally cluster around the epistemology, but it is our epistemic practices and their ethics that will remain our primary focus.

One way of taking the epistemological suggestion that social power has an unfair impact on collective forms of social understanding is to think of our shared understandings as reflecting the perspectives of different social groups, and to entertain the idea that relations of unequal power can skew shared hermeneutical resources so that the powerful tend to have appropriate understandings of their experiences ready to draw on as they make sense of their social experiences, whereas the powerless are more likely to find themselves having some social experiences through a glass darkly, with at best ill-fitting meanings to draw on in the effort to render them intelligible. If we look at the history of the women's movement, we see that the method of consciousness raising through 'speak-outs' and the sharing of scantly understood, barely articulate experiences was a direct response to the fact that so much of women's experience was obscure, even unspeakable, for the isolated individual, whereas the process of sharing these half-formed understandings awakened hitherto dormant resources for social meaning that brought clarity, cognitive confidence, and increased communicative facility. To put it in the terms introduced in relation to ethical relativism in Chapter 4, we can say that women were collectively able to overcome extant *routine* social interpretive habits and arrive at *exceptional* interpretations of some of their formerly occluded experiences; together they were able to realize resources for meaning that were as yet only implicit in the social interpretive practices of the time. From a hermeneutical position of relative comfort, one can forget quite how astonishing and life-changing a cognitive achievement of this sort can be; so let us first briefly revisit one woman's account in the late Sixties of a university workshop on women's medical and sexual issues, as relayed by Susan Brownmiller in her memoir of the US women's liberation movement:

Wendy Sanford, born into an upper-class Republican family, was battling depression after the birth of her son. Her friend Esther Rome, a follower of Jewish Orthodox traditions, dragged her to the second MIT session. Wendy had kept her distance from political groups. 'I walked into the lounge,' she recalls, 'and they were talking about masturbation. I didn't say a word. I was shocked, I was fascinated. At a later session someone gave a breast-feeding demonstration.

That didn't shock me, but then we broke down into small groups. I had never 'broken down into a small group' in my life. In my group people started talking about postpartum depression. In that one forty-five-minute period I realized that what I'd been blaming myself for, and what my husband had blamed me for, wasn't my personal deficiency. It was a combination of physiological things and a real societal thing, isolation. That realization was one of those moments that makes you a feminist forever.[2]

Here is a story of revelation concerning an experience of female depression, previously ill-understood by the subject herself, because collectively ill-understood. No doubt there is a range of historical-cultural factors that might help explain this particular lack of understanding—a general lack of frankness about the normality of depression, for instance—but in so far as significant among these explanatory factors is some sort of social unfairness, such as a structural inequality of power between men and women, then Wendy Sanford's moment of truth seems to be not simply a hermeneutical breakthrough for her and for the other women present, but also a moment in which some kind of epistemic injustice is overcome. The guiding intuition here is that as these women groped for a proper understanding of what we may now so easily name as post-natal depression, the hermeneutical darkness that suddenly lifted from Wendy Sandford's mind had been wrongfully preventing her from understanding a significant area of her social experience, thus depriving her of an important patch of self-understanding. If we can substantiate this intuition, then we shall see that the area of hermeneutical gloom with which she had lived up until that life-changing forty-five minutes constituted a wrong done to her in her capacity as a knower, and was thus a specific sort of epistemic injustice—a *hermeneutical injustice*.

Let us pursue the intuition. To see better what the contours of such an injustice might be, let us look at another example drawn from Brownmiller's memoir, which concerns the experience of what we are these days in a position to name sexual harassment:

One afternoon a former university employee sought out Lin Farley to ask for her help. Carmita Wood, age forty-four, born and raised in the apple orchard region of Lake Cayuga, and the sole support of two of her children, had worked for eight years in Cornell's department of nuclear physics, advancing from lab assistant to a desk job handling administrative chores. Wood did not know

---

[2] Susan Brownmiller, *In Our Time: Memoir of a Revolution* (New York: Dial Press, 1990), 182.

why she had been singled out, or indeed if she had been singled out, but a distinguished professor seemed unable to keep his hands off her.

As Wood told the story, the eminent man would jiggle his crotch when he stood near her desk and looked at his mail, or he'd deliberately brush against her breasts while reaching for some papers. One night as the lab workers were leaving their annual Christmas party, he cornered her in the elevator and planted some unwanted kisses on her mouth. After the Christmas party incident, Carmita Wood went out of her way to use the stairs in the lab building in order to avoid a repeat encounter, but the stress of the furtive molestations and her efforts to keep the scientist at a distance while maintaining cordial relations with his wife, whom she liked, brought on a host of physical symptoms. Wood developed chronic back and neck pains. Her right thumb tingled and grew numb. She requested a transfer to another department, and when it didn't come through, she quit. She walked out the door and went to Florida for some rest and recuperation. Upon her return she applied for unemployment insurance. When the claims investigator asked why she had left her job after eight years, Wood was at a loss to describe the hateful episodes. She was ashamed and embarrassed. Under prodding—the blank on the form needed to be filled in—she answered that her reasons had been personal. Her claim for unemployment benefits was denied.

'Lin's students had been talking in her seminar about the unwanted sexual advances they'd encountered on their summer jobs,' Sauvigne relates. 'And then Carmita Wood comes in and tells Lin *her* story. We realized that to a person, every one of us—the women on staff, Carmita, the students—had had an experience like this at some point, you know? And none of us had ever told anyone before. It was one of those *click, aha!* moments, a profound revelation.'

The women had their issue. Meyer located two feminist lawyers in Syracuse, Susan Horn and Maurie Heins, to take on Carmita Wood's unemployment insurance appeal. 'And then ... ,' Sauvigne reports, 'we decided that we also had to hold a speak-out in order to break the silence about this.'

The 'this' they were going to break the silence about had no name. 'Eight of us were sitting in an office of Human Affairs,' Sauvigne remembers, 'brainstorming about what we were going to write on the posters for our speak-out. We were referring to it as "sexual intimidation," "sexual coercion," "sexual exploitation on the job." None of those names seemed quite right. We wanted something that embraced a whole range of subtle and unsubtle persistent behaviors. Somebody came up with "harassment." *Sexual harassment!* Instantly we agreed. That's what it was.'[3]

Here is a story about how extant collective hermeneutical resources can have a lacuna where the name of a distinctive social experience

[3] Brownmiller, *In Our Time*, 280–1.

should be. So described, we can see that women such as Carmita Wood suffered (among other things) an acute cognitive disadvantage from a gap in the collective hermeneutical resource. But this description does not quite capture it, for if the epistemic wrong done to Carmita Wood were construed simply as a matter of plain cognitive disadvantage, then it is unclear why the epistemic wrong is suffered only by her and not also by her harasser. For the lack of proper understanding of women's experience of sexual harassment was a collective disadvantage more or less shared by all. Prior to the collective appreciation of sexual harassment as such, the absence of a proper understanding of what men were doing to women when they treated them like that was *ex hypothesi* quite general. Different groups can be hermeneutically disadvantaged for all sorts of reasons, as the changing social world frequently generates new sorts of experience of which our understanding may dawn only gradually; but only some of these cognitive disadvantages will strike one as unjust. For something to be an injustice, it must be harmful but also wrongful, whether because discriminatory or because otherwise unfair. In the present example, harasser and harassee alike are cognitively handicapped by the hermeneutical lacuna—neither has a proper understanding of how he is treating her—but the harasser's cognitive disablement is not a significant disadvantage to him. Indeed, there is an obvious sense in which it suits his purpose. (Or at least it suits his immediate purpose, in that it leaves his conduct unchallenged. This is not to deny that if he is a decent person underneath, so that a better understanding of the seriousness of his bad behaviour would have led him to refrain, then the hermeneutical lacuna is for him a source of epistemic and moral bad luck.) By contrast, the harassee's cognitive disablement is seriously disadvantageous to her. The cognitive disablement prevents her from understanding a significant patch of her own experience: that is, a patch of experience which it is strongly in her interests to understand, for without that understanding she is left deeply troubled, confused, and isolated, not to mention vulnerable to continued harassment. Her hermeneutical disadvantage renders her unable to make sense of her ongoing mistreatment, and this in turn prevents her from protesting it, let alone securing effective measures to stop it.

The fact that the hermeneutical lacuna creates such an asymmetrical disadvantage for the harassee already fuels the idea that there is something wrongful about her cognitive disadvantage in particular. We would not describe her as suffering an injustice if it were not significantly disadvantageous for *her in particular*. But there is more than this to be said about the wrong that she sustains. We need to find the deeper source of the intuition that she incurs an epistemic injustice. We can easily imagine, after all, similarly serious hermeneutical disadvantages that do not inflict any epistemic injustice. If, for instance, someone has a medical condition affecting their social behaviour at a historical moment at which that condition is still misunderstood and largely undiagnosed, then they may suffer a hermeneutical disadvantage that is, while collective, especially damaging to them in particular. They are unable to render their experiences intelligible by reference to the idea that they have a disorder, and so they are personally in the dark, and may also suffer seriously negative consequences from others' non-comprehension of their condition. But they are not subject to hermeneutical injustice; rather, theirs is a poignant case of circumstantial epistemic bad luck. In order to find the deeper source of the intuition that there is an epistemic injustice at stake in the examples from Brownmiller, we should focus on the background social conditions that were conducive to the relevant hermeneutical lacuna. Women's position at the time of second wave feminism was still one of marked social powerlessness in relation to men; and, specifically, the unequal relations of power prevented women from participating on equal terms with men in those practices by which collective social meanings are generated. Most obvious among such practices are those sustained by professions such as journalism, politics, academia, and law—it is no accident that Brownmiller's memoir recounts so much pioneering feminist activity in and around these professional spheres and their institutions. Women's powerlessness meant that their social position was one of unequal hermeneutical participation, and something like this sort of inequality provides the crucial background condition for hermeneutical injustice.

7.2 HERMENEUTICAL MARGINALIZATION

Hermeneutical inequality is inevitably hard to detect. Our interpretive efforts are naturally geared to interests, as we try hardest to understand those things it serves us to understand. Consequently, a group's unequal hermeneutical participation will tend to show up in a localized manner in hermeneutical hotspots—locations in social life where the powerful have no interest in achieving a proper interpretation, perhaps indeed where they have a positive interest in sustaining the extant misinterpretation (such as that repeated sexual propositions in the workplace are never anything more than a form of 'flirting', and their uneasy rejection by the recipient only ever a matter of her 'lacking a sense of humour'). But then in such a hotspot as this, the unequal hermeneutical participation remains positively disguised by the existing meaning attributed to the behaviour ('flirting'), and so it is all the more difficult to detect. No wonder that moments of its revelation can come as a life-changing flash of enlightenment. Unlike our example of a person with a condition that medical science cannot yet diagnose, what women like Carmita Wood had to contend with at work was no plain epistemic bad luck, for it was no accident that their experience had been falling down the hermeneutical cracks. As they struggled in isolation to make proper sense of their various experiences of harassment, the whole engine of collective social meaning was effectively geared to keeping these obscured experiences out of sight. Her unequal hermeneutical participation is the deeper reason why Carmita Wood's cognitive disablement constitutes an injustice.

Let us say that when there is unequal hermeneutical participation with respect to some significant area(s) of social experience, members of the disadvantaged group are *hermeneutically marginalized*. The notion of marginalization is a moral-political one indicating subordination and exclusion from some practice that would have value for the participant. Obviously there can be more and less persistent and/or wide-ranging cases of hermeneutical marginalization. Although the term will be most at home in cases where the subject is persistently denied full hermeneutical participation in respect of a wide range of social experiences, none the less we can apply the term in slighter cases. Thus someone might be hermeneutically marginalized only fleetingly, and/or only in respect of a highly localized patch of their social experience. But hermeneutical marginalization is always socially coerced. If you simply opt out of full participation in hermeneutical practices as a matter of choice (perhaps, fed up with it all, you become a modern hermit), then you do not count as hermeneutically marginalized—you've opted out, but you could have opted in. Hermeneutical marginalization is always a form of powerlessness, whether structural or one-off.

Social subjects of course have more or less complex social identities, and so one might be marginalized in a context where one aspect of one's identity is to the fore ('woman') but not in other contexts where other aspects of one's identity are determining one's level of participation ('middle-class'). The net result is that while a hermeneutically marginal-ized subject is prevented from generating meanings pertaining to some areas of the social world, she might well maintain a fuller participation as regards others. If she has a well-paid job in a large corporation with a macho work ethic, she may be entirely unable to frame meanings, even to herself, relating to the need for family-friendly working conditions (such sentiments can only signal a lack of professionalism, a failure of ambition, a half-hearted commitment to the job), and yet she may be in a hermeneutically luxurious position as regards her ability to make sense of other, less gendered areas of her work experience. Thus the complexity of social identity means that hermeneutical marginalization afflicts individuals in a differentiated manner; that is, it may afflict them *qua* one social type, but not another.

Sometimes a person's marginalization will be an effect of material power, so that their socio-economic background has put the kinds of job that make for full hermeneutical participation largely out of their reach. Sometimes it will be an effect of identity power, so that part of the explanation why they do not have those jobs is that there are prejudicial stereotypes in the social atmosphere that represent them as unsuitable, and which negatively influence the judgements of employers. Or, most likely, it may be a mixture of the two. If identity power is at work, it may be working purely structurally, in so far as there may be no social agent (individual or institutional) identifiable as responsible for the marginalization. Alternatively, it may make sense to hold some party responsible, as when, for example, ageist stereotypes of the slow senior worker who lacks ambition are irresponsibly peddled by employers to explain why they do not employ people over 50. In an example such as this, identity power is being used by employers against the older population in a way that threatens (among other things) to hermeneutically marginalize them by excluding them from the sorts of jobs that make for fuller hermeneutical participation. Hermeneutical marginalization need not be the result of identity power as well as plain material power, but it often will be.

We can now define hermeneutical injustice of the sort suffered by women like Carmita Wood. It is:

the injustice of having some significant area of one's social experience obscured from collective understanding owing to persistent and wide-ranging hermeneutical marginalization.

But the latter notion is cumbersome, and we would do well to make our definition slightly more explicit in terms of what is bad about hermeneutical marginalization of the persistent and wide-ranging sort. From the epistemic point of view, what is bad about this sort of hermeneutical marginalization is that it renders the collective hermeneutical resource *structurally prejudiced*, for it will tend to issue interpretations of that group's social experiences that are biased because insufficiently influenced by the subject group, and therefore unduly influenced by more hermeneutically powerful groups (thus, for instance, sexual harassment as flirting, rape in marriage as non-rape, post-natal depression as hysteria, reluctance to work family-unfriendly hours as unprofessionalism, and so on). Further, it is generally socially powerless groups that suffer hermeneutical marginalization, and so we can say that, from the moral point of view, what is bad about this sort of hermeneutical marginalization is that the structural prejudice it causes in the collective hermeneutical resource is essentially discriminatory: the prejudice affects people in virtue of their membership of a socially powerless group, and thus in virtue of an aspect of their social identity. It is, then, akin to identity prejudice. Let us call it *structural identity prejudice*. With this notion in place, we can now colour our definition slightly differently so that it better conveys the discriminatory nature of hermeneutical injustice. Hermeneutical injustice is:

the injustice of having some significant area of one's social experience obscured from collective understanding owing to a structural identity prejudice in the collective hermeneutical resource.

In bringing out its discriminatory character, this definition highlights the family resemblance to testimonial injustice. In both sorts of epistemic injustice, the subject suffers from one or another sort of prejudice against them *qua* social type.

Our definition has grown out of the effort to identify the sort of hermeneutical injustice suffered by Carmita Wood, and as a result, the definition is not generic. Rather, it specifically captures the central or systematic case of hermeneutical injustice—the case that is most relevant from the general point of view of social justice. Now what exactly does 'systematic' mean in the hermeneutical context? In the context of testimonial injustice, an injustice was systematic only if the identity prejudice causing it tracked the subject through different spheres of social activity, rendering them susceptible to other forms of injustice besides testimonial. Just as identity prejudice may track the subject in this way, so may marginalization. Indeed, for systematic cases, the hermeneutical marginalization *entails* marginalization of a socio-economic sort, since it entails non-participation in professions that make for significant hermeneutical participation (journalism, politics, law, and so on). Let us say, then, that if marginalization tracks the subject through a range of different social activities besides the hermeneutical, then the hermeneutical injustices to which it gives rise are systematic. Systematic hermeneutical injustices are part of the broad pattern of a social group's general susceptibility to different sorts of injustice. Like systematic testimonial injustices, they bear the aspect of oppression. At root, both kinds of systematic epistemic injustice stem from structural inequalities of power.

We have concentrated so far on the central case of hermeneutical injustice. By contrast, there can be cases of hermeneutical injustice that are not part of the general pattern of social power, and are more of a one-off. They are not systematic but *incidental*. Whereas systematic cases will tend to involve persistent, wide-ranging hermeneutical marginalization, incidental cases will tend to involve hermeneutical marginalization only fleetingly and/or in respect of a highly localized patch of the subject's experience. Incidental hermeneutical injustices, then, stem not from any structural inequality of power, but rather from a more one-off moment of powerlessness. What might an incidental case of hermeneutical injustice look like? In Ian McEwan's novel *Enduring Love* the main protagonist, Joe, is stalked by a young man called Jed Parry, a religious fanatic with delusions of love between him and Joe. When Joe tells his partner, Clarissa, about it, he meets first affectionate derision and then, later—although she accepts the basics of what he is telling her—her reaction is more one of concerned reserve about his state of mind. When, subsequently, he calls the police, Joe finds that the form of stalking he is enduring does not make the legal grade and is represented as trivial:

'Are you the person being harassed?'
    'Yes. I've been ... '
    'And is the person causing the nuisance with you now?'
    'He's standing outside my place this very minute.'
    Has he inflicted any physical harm on you?
    'No, but he ... '
    'Has he threatened you with harm?'
    'No.' I understood that my grievance would have to be poured into the available bureaucratic mould. There was no facility refined enough to process every private narrative. Denied the release of complaint, I tried to take comfort in having my story assimilated into a recognisable public form. Parry's behaviour had to be generalised into a crime.
    'Has he made threats against your property?'

'No.'

'Or against third parties?'

'No.'

'Is he trying to blackmail you?'

'No.'

'Do you think you could prove that he intends to cause you distress?'

'Er, no.'

... 'Can you tell me what he's doing then?'

'He phones me at all hours. He talks to me in the ... '

The voice was quick to move back to his default position, the interrogative flow chart. 'Is he using obscene or insulting behaviour?'

'No. Look, officer. Why don't you let me explain. He's a crank. He won't let me alone.'

'Are you aware of what he actually wants?' ...

'He wants to save me.'

'Save you?'

'You know, convert me. He's obsessed. He simply won't leave me alone.'

The voice cut in, impatience taking hold at last. 'I'm sorry caller. This is not a police matter. Unless he harms you, or your property, or threatens the same he's committing no offence. Trying to convert you is not against the law.' Then he terminated our emergency conversation with his own little stricture. 'We do have religious freedom in this country.'[4]

Joe's own understanding of his experience of being stalked is only slightly hindered by the lack of hermeneutical reciprocation by partner and police, but still a collective hermeneutical lacuna is preventing him from rendering his experience communicatively intelligible. It is very much in his interests to share his experience with certain others from the start; but he cannot, for the true nature of his experience of being stalked by Jed Parry is obscured by two misfit interpretations that trivialize it in different ways. According to one, he seems to be failing to see the funny side and becoming worryingly obsessed; according to another he is exaggerating the level of threat and even cramping someone else's religious freedom into the bargain. But if the obscurity of Joe's experience constitutes a kind of hermeneutical injustice, this has nothing to do with any general social powerlessness or any general subordination as a generator of social meaning, for his social identity is that of the proverbial white, educated, straight man. Still, he is none the less up against a one-off moment of hermeneutical marginalization. The competing and trivializing interpretations coming from Clarissa

---

[4] Ian McEwan, *Enduring Love* (London: Vintage, 1998), 73–4.

and the police respectively mean that Joe's hermeneutical participation is hindered in respect of a significant, if highly localized, patch of his social experience, and for this reason his case qualifies as a hermeneutical injustice. The injustice does not stem from any structural identity prejudice—on the contrary, he suffers the injustice not because of, but rather in spite of, the social type he is. Clearly Joe's hermeneutical injustice is not a systematic case; it is incidental.

Awareness of such cases motivates a more generic definition of hermeneutical injustice than those so far given, which were designed to capture what we can now more clearly see to be the distinctively systematic case. The generic definition now called for captures hermeneutical injustice *per se* as

the injustice of having some significant area of one's social experience obscured from collective understanding owing to hermeneutical marginalization.

This definition simply omits what is special to the systematic case: namely, that the hermeneutical marginalization is 'persistent and wide-ranging', or, equivalently, that there is a 'structural prejudice in the collective hermeneutical resource'. This generic definition, then, covers both the systematic case and the incidental case. As ever, the systematic case is central from our point of view. But in parallel with our discussion of systematic versus incidental cases of testimonial injustice, the fact that a hermeneutical injustice is incidental does not mean that it is not ethically serious. Indeed, it is life-shattering for Joe that his experience is not better understood from the start, since this allows Jed Parry's stalking to escalate to ultimately mortally threatening levels, and it contributes too to the eventual collapse of his long relationship with Clarissa. Incidental hermeneutical injustices, then, can be disastrous in someone's life. What distinguishes systematic cases is, as ever, not the seriousness of the token harm, but something more general: they help reveal the place of hermeneutical injustice in the complex of social injustices.

We have encountered, then, two sorts of hermeneutical injustice: systematic and incidental. If someone is disadvantaged, as for instance Joe is, from having their experience left obscure owing to a lacuna in the collective hermeneutical resource, then that is broadly sufficient for a claim of incidental hermeneutical injustice, even though the hermeneutical marginalization is localized and one-off. By contrast, if someone is disadvantaged, as for instance Carmita Wood is, by having their experience left obscure owing to a lacuna in the collective hermeneutical resource, where the lacuna is caused and maintained by a wide-ranging and persistent hermeneutical marginalization, then the hermeneutical injustice is systematic. For in such cases the hermeneutical marginalization is part of a more general susceptibility to different forms of social marginalization, so that any given hermeneutical injustice incurred is likewise part of a more general susceptibility to different kinds of injustice. There is, then, a certain structural parallel with the forms of testimonial injustice. In contrast, however, to the case of testimonial injustice, hermeneutical injustice, whether incidental or systematic, involves no culprit. No agent *perpetrates* hermeneutical injustice—it is a purely structural notion. The background condition for hermeneutical injustice is the subject's hermeneutical marginalization. But the moment of hermeneutical injustice comes only when the background condition is realized in a more or less doomed attempt on the part of the subject to render an experience intelligible, either to herself or to an interlocutor. The hermeneutical inequality that exists, dormant, in a situation of hermeneutical marginalization erupts in injustice only when some actual attempt at intelligibility is handicapped by it.

That hermeneutical injustice most typically manifests itself in the speaker struggling to make herself intelligible in a testimonial exchange raises a grim possibility: that hermeneutical injustice might often be compounded by testimonial injustice. This will indeed tend to be the case wherever the hermeneutical injustice is systematic, because members of multiple marginalized groups will tend to be subject to identity prejudice. If they try to articulate a scantly understood experience to an interlocutor, their word already warrants a low prima facie credibility judgement owing to its low intelligibility. But if the speaker is also subject to an identity prejudice, then there will be a further deflation. In such a case, the speaker is doubly wronged: once by the structural prejudice in the shared hermeneutical resource, and once by the hearer in making an identify-prejudiced credibility judgement.

Imagine someone in Carmita Wood's position trying to tell her employer about the professor's behaviour. The hermeneutical lacuna where the words 'sexual harassment' should be means that there is already a serious problem about the plausibility of whatever it is she manages to articulate by way of telling her story (perhaps she succeeds in saying that she is 'made uncomfortable' by his persistent 'flirtation'). But then if we add to this some risk of identity prejudice in respect of gender, and/or ethnicity, and/or class, we see that she is also susceptible to suffering a testimonial injustice. People in her position, then, are susceptible to a double epistemic injustice. Worse still, what we see here are the perfect conditions conducive to a runaway credibility deflation, as the implausibility of what is said creates a lens through which the personal credibility of the speaker may become unduly deflated, which in turn creates a lens through which the credibility of what is said may come to be even more deflated ... and so on.[5] From Brownmiller's story it is plausible that Carmita Wood's attempts to communicate the nature of her experience is likely to have met with just such a runaway deflation of credibility. Such a predicament identifies a worst case scenario for a speaker as regards epistemic injustice.

The observation that hermeneutical injustice will tend to manifest itself in attempts at communication directs our attention to a rather different version of the injustice. We have considered hermeneutical gaps or lacunas only as absences of proper interpretations, blanks where there should be a name for an experience which it is in the interests of the subject to be able to render communicatively intelligible. But we must recognize that a hermeneutical gap might equally concern not (or not only) the content but rather the form of what can be said. Thus the characteristic expressive style of a given social group may be rendered just as much of an unfair hindrance to their communicative efforts as an interpretive absence can be. If, for instance, as has been famously argued by Carol Gilligan, women (at least at one point in history) have 'a different voice' when it comes to ethical judgement, and a voice that is not recognized as rational but is rather marginalized as morally immature, then women's attempts at communicative intelligibility when it comes to moral matters are hindered by a hermeneutical gap of this kind.[6] And the hindrance to their expressive efforts is unjust in so far as it derives from hermeneutical marginalization—that is, in so far as it derives from the fact that their powerlessness bars them from full participation in those practices whereby social meanings are generated, for these are also the practices whereby certain expressive styles come

[5] I echo Karen Jones's way of explaining the phenomenon of runaway reductions of credibility; see 'The Politics of Credibility', in Louise M. Antony and Charlotte E. Witt (eds.), *A Mind of One's Own: Feminist Essays on Reason and Objectivity*, 2nd edn. (Boulder, Colo.: Westview Press, 2002).

[6] Carol Gilligan, *In A Different Voice: Psychological Theory and Women's Development* (Cambridge, Mass.: Harvard University Press, 1982); see also Sara Ruddick, *Maternal Thinking: Towards a Politics of Peace* (London: The Women's Press, 1990).

to be recognized as rational and contextually appropriate. Recall the reception that Herbert Greenleaf gives to Marge Sherwood's attempts to render her suspicions of Ripley communicatively intelligible: 'Marge, there's female intuition, and then there are facts—'. If one lives in a society or a subculture in which the mere fact of an intuitive or an emotional expressive style means that one cannot be heard as fully rational, then one is thereby unjustly afflicted by a hermeneutical gap—one is subject to a hermeneutical injustice.

7.3 THE WRONG OF HERMENEUTICAL INJUSTICE

I have talked in terms of hermeneutical injustice involving an asymmetrical cognitive disadvantage. The general point here is that collective hermeneutical impoverishment impacts on members of different groups in different ways. It did not harm the interests of Carmita Wood's harasser that he (as the example goes) did not have a proper grasp of the nature of his treatment of her; but it harmed Carmita Wood a great deal that she could not make adequate sense of it to herself, let alone to others. The asymmetry arises from the concrete social and practical context in which the collective hermeneutical impoverishment impinges. It is only when the collective impoverishment is concretely situated in specific social situations that it comes to be especially and unjustly disadvantageous to some groups but not others. Hermeneutical lacunas are like holes in the ozone—it's the people who live under them that get burned. Fundamentally, then, hermeneutical injustice is a kind of structural discrimination. Compare a society that has a welfare state providing free healthcare at the point of delivery, but where there is a gap in state provision: no free dental care. Formally speaking, there is nothing intrinsically unjust about there being a general lack of free dental care, for it is the same for everyone—there is, so to speak, a collective lacuna in the welfare system. There is a formal equality, then; but as soon as one looks at how this formal equality plays out in practice in the lived social world, a *situated* inequality quickly reveals itself: people who cannot afford private dental care suffer from the lack of general provision, and people who can afford it do not. In such cases of formal equality but lived inequality, the injustice is a matter of some group(s) being asymmetrically disadvantaged by a blanket collective lack; and so it is, I suggest, in the case of hermeneutical injustice. A hermeneutical injustice is done when a collective hermeneutical gap impinges so as to significantly disadvantage some group(s) and not others, so that the way in which the collective impoverishment plays out in practice is effectively discriminatory.

Let us say, then, that the primary harm of hermeneutical injustice consists in a *situated hermeneutical inequality*: the concrete situation is such that the subject is rendered unable to make communicatively intelligible something which it is particularly in his or her interests to be able to render intelligible. This reveals another deep connection with the wrong of testimonial injustice. The primary harm of (the central case of) testimonial injustice concerns exclusion from the pooling of knowledge owing to identity prejudice on the part of the hearer; the primary harm of (the central case of) hermeneutical injustice concerns exclusion from the pooling of knowledge owing to structural identity prejudice in the collective hermeneutical resource. The first prejudicial exclusion is made in relation to the speaker, the second in relation to what they are trying to say and/or how they are saying it. The wrongs involved in the two sorts of epistemic injustice, then, have a common epistemic significance running through them—prejudicial exclusion from participation in the spread of knowledge.

Such is the primary harm. Is there also a secondary kind of harm (caused by the primary one) that may be usefully distinguished? Yes, for the primary harm of situated hermeneutical inequality must, by definition, issue in further practical harms—those harms which render the collective hermeneutical impoverishment asymmetrically disadvantageous to the wronged party. To illustrate, let us simply remind ourselves of Carmita Wood's story. The primary epistemic harm done to her was that a patch of her social experience which it was very much in her interests to understand was not collectively understood and so remained barely intelligible, even to her. From the story we can see that among the secondary harms caused by this were that she developed physical symptoms of stress, could not apply successfully for a transfer owing to the fact that she had no nameable reason to cite, and eventually simply had to quit her job. Further, when she came to apply for unemployment benefits, the lack of a name for the cause of all this again guaranteed that she lost out—she was refused the benefits. A little imagination allows one to see how far-reaching the ramifications of such a case of hermeneutical injustice can be. If Carmita Wood, and other women like her, had never gone to consciousness-raising meetings, the experience of sexual harassment would have remained under wraps for much longer, and would have done more to ruin the professional advancement, the personal self-confidence, and, most relevantly here, the general epistemic confidence of women than it was in fact allowed to do, thanks to second wave feminism.

When you find yourself in a situation in which you seem to be the only one to feel the dissonance between received understanding and your own intimated sense of a given experience, it tends to knock your faith in your own ability to make sense of the world, or at least the relevant region of the world. We can see, then, that, like testimonial injustice, hermeneutical injustice not only brings secondary practical disadvantages, it also brings secondary epistemic disadvantages. Indeed, the sorts of epistemic disadvantages at stake are the very same as those we discussed at some length in respect of testimonial injustice, for they once again stem most basically from the subject's loss of epistemic confidence. The various ways in which loss of epistemic confidence might hinder one's epistemic career are, to reiterate, that it can cause literal loss of knowledge, that it may prevent one from gaining new knowledge, and more generally, that it is likely to stop one gaining certain important epistemic virtues, such as intellectual courage.

With the primary and secondary aspects of the harm of hermeneutical injustice set out, perhaps we can now dig a little deeper into the nature of the primary aspect—the situated hermeneutical inequality—to see whether it might sometimes extend to influence the construction of the individual subject, rather as we saw in the case of testimonial injustice. Is hermeneutical injustice sometimes so damaging that it cramps the very development of self? Consider a new example. In Edmund White's autobiographical novel *A Boy's Own Story*, which tells the story of his growing up in 1950s America, we are presented with many different ways in which the hermeneutical resources of the day burden his sexual experience with layers of falsifying meaning. Here he is staying at the family home of his beloved Tom, a new friend from school. This passage gives us a series of contemporary constructions of homosexuality that partly condition, yet remain crucially dissonant with, the boy's actual experience of his own desire and sexual identity:

'You know,' Tom said one day, 'you can stay over any time you like. Harold'—the minister's son, my old partner at Squirrel—'warned me you'd jump me in my sleep. You gotta forgive me. It's just I don't go in for that weird stuff.'

I swallowed painfully and whispered, 'Nor—' I cleared my throat and said too primly, 'Nor do I.'

The medical smell, that Lysol smell of homosexuality, was staining the air again as the rubber-wheeled metal cart of drugs and disinfectants rolled silently by. I longed to open the window, to go away for an hour and come back to a room free of that odor, the smell of shame.

I never doubted that homosexuality was a sickness; in fact, I took it as a measure of how unsparingly objective I was that I could contemplate this very sickness. But in some other part of my mind I couldn't believe that the Lysol smell must bathe me, too, that its smell of stale coal fumes must penetrate my love for Tom. Perhaps I became so vague, so exhilarated with vagueness, precisely in order to forestall a recognition of the final term of the syllogism that begins: If one man loves another he is a homosexual; I love a man ...

I'd heard that boys passed through a stage of homosexuality, that this stage was normal, nearly universal—then that must be what was happening to me. A stage. A prolonged stage. Soon enough this stage would revolve, and after Tom's bedroom vanished, on would trundle white organdy, blue ribbons, a smiling girl opening her arms. ... But that would come later. As for now, I could continue to look as long as I liked into Tom's eyes the color of faded lapis beneath brows so blond they were visible only at the roots just to each side of his nose—a faint smudge turning gold as it thinned and sped out toward the temples.[7]

In this series of constructions we move swiftly from the schoolboy propaganda that our boy would 'jump' Tom in his sleep, through the idea that homosexuality is a sickness, to the falsely normalizing idea that homosexual desire is just 'a stage' on the road to the normality that is heterosexual life. The passage ends, however, with such tender attention to Tom's features that the younger narrator's desire for Tom is at last conveyed simply, unburdened, as a form of sexual love. The natural truth of his desire makes the hermeneutical burlesque of jumpings and sicknesses and developmental stages seem poignantly ridiculous.

But the narrator's younger self is being formed through the lens of all these constructions, so that his longed-for experience of simple reciprocated desire for men is not an option when it comes to subject positions available for him to occupy. As he grows up, he has to contend with various powerful bogeymen constructions of The Homosexual. None of them fits, but these collective understandings are so powerful, and the personal experiential promise of an alternative understanding so lonely and inarticulate, that they have some significant power to construct not only the subject's experience (his desire becomes shameful and so on) but also his very self. Not without a fight, for sure, and this

---

[7] Edmund White, *A Boy's Own Story* (London: Picador, 1983), 117–18.

autobiographical story presents us above all with a young person who wrestles these bullying would-be selves with courage and wit, now giving in to their bid to claim his identity, now resisting. This is more explicit in another passage that recounts a visit to a psychoanalyst, Dr O'Reilly. In this passage we see how one version of the unnatural homosexual—as a vampire-like version of a man—leads our adolescent subject to fear the name, and to experience his own nascent identity as a homosexual as a terrifying prospect, something to be pre-empted at all costs and, in so far as it already exists, disguised:

> Just as years before, when I was seven, I had presented myself to a minister and had sought for his understanding, in the same way now I was turning to a psychoanalyst for help. I wanted to overcome this thing I was becoming and was in danger soon of being, the homosexual, as though that designation were the mold in which the water was freezing, the first crystals already forming a fragile membrane. The confusion and fear and pain that beset me ... had translated me into a code no one could read, I least of all, a code perhaps designed to defeat even the best cryptographer. ...
>   I see now that what I wanted was to be loved by men and to love them back but not to be a homosexual. For I was possessed with a yearning for the company of men, for their look, touch and smell, and nothing transfixed me more than the sight of a man shaving and dressing, sumptuous rites. It was men, not women, who struck me as foreign and desirable and I disguised myself as a child or a man or whatever was necessary in order to enter their hushed, hieratic company, my disguise so perfect I never stopped to question my identity. Nor did I want to study the face beneath my mask, lest it turn out to have the pursed lips, dead pallor and shaped eyebrows by which one can always recognize the Homosexual. What I required was a sleight of hand, an alibi or a convincing act of bad faith to persuade myself I was not that vampire.[8]

At some level his personal sexual experience was of a simple love of men; yet this aspect of his experience being inarticulable, the only psychological rebellion he could hope to pull off against what this meant about his identity was denial. Denial is the first stage of the double-think (the sleight of hand, the act of bad faith) that is required in order to rebel against internalized yet falsifying hermeneutical constructions of one's social identity. For authoritative constructions can, as we have seen, effect a constitutive construction of one's identity, so that one comes to count socially as a vampire-like creature, even while it remains the case that one is not. Recall (from Chapter 2) that constitutive

---

[8] Ibid. 169–70.

construction falls short of causal construction, for while the former is a matter of what one counts as socially, the latter is a matter of actually coming to be what one is constructed as being. White's autobiographical story gives us no particular reason to think of him as subject to causal construction, though it is entirely plausible that being constitutively constructed as an unnatural vampire-like creature with shameful desires might encourage one to live out a familiar motif of inverted rebellion by behaving more and more like such a creature in defiant embrace of one's sins. One may be able to pull this off ironically, but then again one may not. In any case, it is enough to notice that so much of what the younger narrator is grappling with as he grows up and his social identity congeals around him can be thought of as authoritative—collectively endorsed meanings attaching to homosexuality that have the power not just to haunt him with bogeyman would-be selves but actually to constitute his social being. His sometimes playful resistance to these constructions of his identity is, as regards his social being, a matter of life and death.

To the extent that resistance is possible, part of what makes it possible is historical contingency. Our narrator had history on his side inasmuch as the Sixties were on the horizon, when all sorts of sexual liberations were to be articulated, indeed demanded. But something else that allows for resistance is that other aspects of one's identity (being educated and middle-class, perhaps) might equip one with resources for rebellion, as will certain personal characteristics (our narrator was surely fiercely intelligent, psychologically tough, and socially resourceful). Authoritative constructions in the shared hermeneutical resource, then, impinge on us collectively but not uniformly, and the non-uniformity of their hold over us can create a sense of dissonance between an experience and the various constructions that are ganging up to overpower its nascent proper meaning. As individuals, some authoritative voices have special power over us, while others, for whatever reason, do not. Our narrator, for instance, is wholly untroubled by negative Christian constructions of homosexuality, for he simply does not believe in the ropes and pulleys of heaven above and eternal damnation below, and his plain anti-authoritarian impulse renders him gloriously immune to whatever remaining visceral hold religious censure might have had over him. When he spends Thanksgiving with the Scotts—the housemaster Latin teacher and his wife, both fervent Christians ambitious to convert him (and equally ambitious to seduce him, their fear of being bourgeois outstripping their fear of being sinners)—they introduce him to Father Burke, 'their "confessor" and spiritual guardian'[9]:

'Well, yes,' I said, 'I am seeing a psychiatrist because I have conflicts over certain homosexual tendencies I'm feeling.'

At these words Father Burke's face lurched up out of his hands. Not the nervous little confession he had expected. He recovered his poise and decided to laugh boisterously, the laugh of Catholic centuries. '*Conflicts?*' he whooped, in tears of laughter by now. Then, sobering for a second, the priest added in a low, casual voice, 'But you see, my son, homosexuality isn't just a *conflict* that needs to be *resolved*'—his voice picked up these words as though they were nasty bits of refuse—'homosexuality is also a sin.'

I think he had no notion how little an effect the word *sin* had on me. He might just as well have said, 'Homosexuality is bad *juju*.'[10]

By contrast, however, this immunity to the idea of sin is no enduring defence, for it takes almost nothing from the priest—only his identity as a priest, or perhaps simply as a straight male confessor—to conjure up a conspiracy of truly mortifying stereotypes that instantly produce an unstoppable operation of identity power, controlling and constricting our young narrator's discursive behaviour and sense of self. The passage continues:

'But I feel very drawn to other men,' I said. Although something defiant in me forced these words out, I felt myself becoming a freak the moment I spoke. My hair went bleach-blond, my wrist went limp, my rep tie became a lace jabot: I was the simpering queen at the grand piano playing concert versions of last year's pop tunes for his mother and her bridge club. There was no way to defend what I was. All I could fight for was my right to choose my exile, my destruction.[11]

A person's bold sense of dissonance, then, is a fragile thing, for a construction that one is able simply to find absurd may swiftly be followed by one that holds sway over one's psyche. But at least a sense of dissonance is possible. What makes it possible is that if one finds one or more of the common constructions of one's sexuality as shameful to be manifestly false, even ridiculous, then this raises the question as to whether other discourses in league with it are suspect too. Finding something potentially authoritative to be absurd gives one critical courage; one hermeneutical rebellion inspires another. The sense

[9] White, *A Boy's Own Story*, 199.
[10] Ibid. 204.   [11] Ibid.

of dissonance, then, is the starting point for both the critical thinking and the moral-intellectual courage that rebellion requires. That, I take it, is part of the mechanism of consciousness raising. Put a number of people together who have felt a certain dissonance about an area of social experience, and factor in that each of them will have a different profile of immunity and susceptibility to different authoritative discourses, and it is not surprising that the sense of dissonance can increase and become critically emboldened.

The primary harm of hermeneutical injustice, then, is to be understood not only in terms of the subject's being unfairly disadvantaged by some collective hermeneutical lacuna, but also in terms of the very construction (constitutive and/or causal) of selfhood. In certain social contexts, hermeneutical injustice can mean that someone is socially constituted as, and perhaps even caused to be, something they are not, and which it is against their interests to be seen to be. Thus, as I put the point previously in our discussion of the wrong of testimonial justice, they may be prevented from becoming who they are. Testimonial and hermeneutical injustice have this identity-constructive power in common, then, as a possible feature of their primary harm. But in other respects their primary harms are utterly different. The wrong of testimonial injustice is inflicted individual to individual, so that there are immediate questions to be answered concerning the hearer's culpability or non-culpability and, more generally, concerning what virtue it is desirable to cultivate in ourselves as hearers. By contrast, hermeneutical injustice is not inflicted by any agent, but rather is caused by a feature of the collective hermeneutical resource—a one-off blind spot (in incidental cases), or (in systematic cases) a lacuna generated by a structural identity prejudice in the hermeneutical repertoire. Consequently, questions of culpability do not arise in the same way. None the less, they do arise, for the phenomenon should inspire us to ask what sorts of hearers we should try to be in a society in which there are likely to be speakers whose attempts to make communicative sense of their experiences are unjustly hindered. It will not be enough to exercise the virtue of testimonial justice, for that counteracts only the risk of testimonial injustice—it ensures only that one reliably receives the word of others without prejudice. What is needed in respect of hermeneutical injustice is a virtue such that we receive the word of others in a manner that counteracts the prejudicial impact that their hermeneutical marginalization has already had upon the hermeneutical tools at their disposal. Let us, finally, turn to this question.

7.4 THE VIRTUE OF HERMENEUTICAL JUSTICE

The virtue in question is like the virtue of testimonial justice, in that it will be corrective in structure. But whereas, as I argued, testimonial justice can take naïve form with respect to this or that prejudice, so that the hearer is simply free of the prejudice in the first place and does not have to monitor (reflectively or unreflectively) its influence on her judgement; by contrast, the virtue of hermeneutical justice is always corrective. In all cases of this sort of injustice, the relevant gap in hermeneutical resources has genuinely reduced the communicative intelligibility of the speaker in one or another way (in respect of content or form), so their relative unintelligibility is not something to which the virtuous hearer could be naïvely immune. On the contrary, if a hearer simply failed to register the fact that their interlocutor's efforts at intelligibility were hampered, this could only be a failing on the part of the hearer. The form the virtue of hermeneutical justice must take, then, is an alertness or sensitivity to the possibility that the difficulty one's interlocutor is having as she tries to render something communicatively intelligible is due not to its being a nonsense or her being a fool, but rather to some sort of gap in collective hermeneutical resources. The point is to realize that the speaker is struggling with an objective difficulty and not a subjective failing.

Such a sensitivity involves, once again, a certain reflexive awareness on the part of the hearer, for a speaker whose communicative efforts are hampered by hermeneutical injustice may seem to be making no sense at all to one hearer (as when Marge expresses her suspicions to Herbert Greenleaf in an emotional or intuitive style), while to another hearer (perhaps another woman) she may seem to be making a manifestly reasonable point. The virtuous hearer, then, must be reflexively aware of how the relation between his social identity and that of the speaker is impacting on the intelligibility to him of what she is saying and how she is saying it. What Greenleaf needed to be aware of was that Marge's intuitive style of expression struck him as less than rational largely because he is a man and has been taught to use and to rationally respect a different style. The virtue of hermeneutical justice naturally shares this demand for reflexive awareness with the virtue of testimonial justice, for both virtues explicitly govern epistemic conduct in the socially situated context—they both guard against forms of identity prejudice, and so they are both, apart from anything else, virtues of reflexive social awareness.

What this sort of reflexive sensitivity allows for is some sort of correction to the initial credibility judgement, where the incomplete intelligibility of what the speaker said will have led to a judgement of low credibility. In discursive exchanges relating to social understanding, the hearer's credibility judgement is perhaps best described not simply in terms of an assessment of the likelihood that the speaker's utterance is true, but rather in terms of an assessment of the truthfulness of the interpretation offered. This redescription simply allows for the fact that in hermeneutical contexts the orientation to truth needs to allow for the possibility that there is more than one interpretation with equal title to truth, in the sense that there can sometimes simply be no answer to the question of whether speaker A's or speaker B's interpretation is *the* true one. In hermeneutical contexts, then, the responsible hearer's credibility judgement is an assessment of the degree to which what is said *makes good sense*—the degree to which it is a truthful interpretation. Now, in cases where the speaker's efforts are hindered by a hermeneutical injustice, the virtuous hearer will register this and make allowances, so that her initially low credibility judgement is revised upwards to compensate for the hindrance. Where possible, the virtuous hearer will achieve a credibility judgement that reflects the degree to which the interpretation the speaker is struggling to articulate *would make good sense if the attempt to articulate it were being made in a more inclusive hermeneutical climate—one without structural identity prejudice.* In such a credibility judgement, the prejudicial impact of the speaker's hermeneutical marginalization is corrected for. The guiding ideal is that the degree of credibility is adjusted upwards to compensate for the cognitive and expressive handicap imposed on the hermeneutically marginalized speaker by the non-inclusive hermeneutical climate, by structural identity prejudice. As ever, this will be an imprecise business in practice, but I think the ideal makes enough intuitive sense to genuinely guide our practice as hearers.

Louise Antony makes a brief proposal that is related to our guiding ideal. She suggests that it might be rational for men to adopt 'a kind of epistemic affirmative action: to adopt the *working hypothesis* that when a woman, or any member of a stereotyped group, says something anomalous, they should assume that it's *they* who don't understand, not that it is the woman who is nuts'.[12] Such a working hypothesis is obviously closely related to the virtue of hermeneutical justice, for they both spring from the idea that speakers put at an objective interpretive and expressive disadvantage should have judgements of their discursive performance appropriately compensated. However, I think that there would be difficulties in developing the working hypothesis model, for the hearer needs to be indefinitely context sensitive in how he applies the hypothesis. A policy of affirmative action across all subject matters would not be justified, because, as I have already argued, the complexity of social identity means that hermeneutical marginalization affects individual speakers in a differentiated manner: a white middle-class woman might, as a woman, be unable to frame certain meanings in a given context, while as white and middle-class she is not remotely disadvantaged in her capacity to frame meanings required in other contexts. (In the first sort of context, her seeming nuts should prompt reflection on the possibility of hermeneutical injustice; in the second sort of context, if she seems nuts, well, maybe she is.) By the same token, a policy applied to speakers simply in virtue of their membership of some negatively stereotyped or powerless group would not be justified: the speaker may be a woman, but the fact that she is white and middle-class may mean that there is no hermeneutical gap depriving her of the expressive resources she needs, in the context, to render herself intelligible. I therefore suggest that the best way to honour the compensatory idea is in the form of a capacity for indefinitely context-sensitive judgement—in the form, then, of a virtue.

Let us now envisage what the virtuous hearer actually does. In practical contexts where there is enough time and the matter is sufficiently important, the virtuous hearer may effectively be able to help generate a more inclusive hermeneutical micro-climate through the appropriate kind of dialogue with the speaker. In particular, such dialogue involves a more pro-active and more socially aware kind of listening than is usually required in more straightforward communicative exchanges. This sort of listening involves listening as much to what is *not* said as

[12] Louise Antony, 'Sisters, Please, I'd Rather Do It Myself: A Defense of Individualism in Feminist Epistemology', in Sally Haslanger (ed.), *Philosophical Topics: Feminist Perspectives on Language, Knowledge, and Reality*, 23, no. 2 (Fall 1995), 89.

to what is said. Such virtuous behaviour by a hearer will be more or less difficult to achieve depending on the circumstances, and in particular, depending on how much or how little is shared with the speaker in terms of relevant social experience. Virtuous hearers' performance is constrained by their own social identity *vis-à-vis* that of the speaker. Alternatively (again, practical context permitting), the virtuous hearer may seek out extra corroborating evidence; for instance, by consulting other relevantly placed people—people with a similar social identity and experience to the speaker. I agree with Karen Jones's suggestion, in the course of her illuminating discussion of astonishing reports, that where there is a reason for the hearer to doubt the reliability of his own patterns of trust—as there is in cases of hermeneutical injustice—it is rational for him to drop the presumption against acceptance, and also to assume some increased burden of seeking corroborating evidence.[13] These two norms are clearly part and parcel of the context-sensitive judgements made by the hermeneutically just hearer.

In practical contexts where there is not sufficient time, or where the particular hearer, however virtuous, cannot be expected to 'listen through' to the meaning that is immanent in what the speaker is saying, the virtue of hermeneutical justice may simply be a matter of *reserving* judgement, so that the hearer keeps an open mind as to credibility. What she brings to the discursive exchange is a background social 'theory' that is informed by the possibility of hermeneutical injustice, with the result that she may avoid resting content with an unduly low judgement of credibility, and such a 'theory' may often tell her little more than that she should be suspicious of her initial spontaneous credibility judgements when it comes to speakers like this on a subject matter like that. Ideally, a virtuous Herbert Greenleaf would have been able to perceive Marge as someone whose emotional and intuitive style fell into a hermeneutical gap, and he would have heard her in a way that at least made room for the possibility that she had a point. But, more realistically, a virtuous Greenleaf might merely have sensed the alienness to him as a man of her intuitive style as a woman, and reserved his judgement. This might have been virtue enough.

Interestingly, we can see from the profile we have drawn of the virtue that there are limits to the extent to which it can be possessed 'fully'—exercised spontaneously—for some of the responses it inspires

13 See Jones, 'Politics of Credibility', 164–5.

in the hearer do not look like the sort of thing that could possibly be done without reflection: actively seeking out extra corroborative evidence, for instance. Pro-active listening, by contrast, does seem the kind of thing that one's testimonial sensibility could be trained to trigger spontaneously; perhaps, indeed, it can only be done well if it is done with a good measure of spontaneity. It may only be in respect of some virtuous responses, then, that the virtue of hermeneutical justice can be possessed in spontaneous form. Where it is so possessed, our account of that spontaneity is as it was in the case of the virtue of testimonial justice: the hearer's testimonial sensibility has been sufficiently educated by individual and collective experience that she corrects or suspends her credibility judgement without reflection. In so far as the virtue may be possessed in spontaneous form, the social 'theory' that shapes the hearer's credibility judgements has (over some suitable social span of speakers) become second nature.

What of the question whether the virtue of hermeneutical justice is an intellectual or an ethical virtue? What exactly is the virtue's structure? As in our discussion of the virtue of testimonial justice, the virtue is to be individuated by its mediate end. The hermeneutically virtuous hearer is reliably successful in achieving the end of a psychologically entrenched motivation: namely, the motivation to make his credibility judgement reflect the fact that the speaker's efforts to make herself intelligible are objectively handicapped by structural identity prejudice in the collective hermeneutical resource. The mediate end of the virtue, then, is *to neutralize the impact of structural identity prejudice on one's credibility judgement*. And what of the virtue's ultimate end? Again, as per our discussion of testimonial justice, we can say that there will be practical contexts in which matters of social understanding are paramount, so that it will be appropriate to interpret hermeneutical justice as ultimately aimed at understanding, and thus as an intellectual virtue. But there will be other contexts in which the goal of understanding is less important than that of justice, so that we should interpret it as aiming ultimately at justice, and regard it as an ethical virtue. There again, there will be contexts in which understanding and justice are of equal practical importance, so that the most appropriate interpretation features the virtue as ultimately aiming at a joint intellectual and ethical end.

If Greenleaf is fundamentally the decent man who cares for Marge that I have interpreted him to be, then his exchanges with her concerning her suspicions of Ripley give us material with which to imagine the virtue of hermeneutical justice functioning with such a joint ultimate end. What Greenleaf needed to do was to appreciate Marge's hermeneutical marginalization (as regards expressive style) and somehow to reflect this in his credibility judgement. This would have served both ethical and epistemic ends, for a more virtuous credibility judgement would have helped him mitigate an injustice to someone he cared about, and it might even have allowed him to take in the important truth that she was struggling to render intelligible—it all points to Ripley. When it comes to determining whether the virtue of hermeneutical justice is functioning on any given occasion as an intellectual or an ethical virtue, then, the answer is the same as for the virtue of testimonial justice: only the practical context can decide. Sometimes it features under the aspect of an intellectual virtue, sometimes under the aspect of an ethical virtue, and sometimes both at once. Hermeneutical justice, like testimonial justice, is a hybrid virtue—as, I dare say, is any virtue that counteracts an epistemic injustice.

Finally, let us acknowledge a secondary ethically positive role for the virtue of hermeneutical justice, in which the virtue takes on a significance above and beyond the hearer's treatment of his interlocutor on a given occasion. Even though this virtue can only mitigate, rather than pre-empt, any given instance of hermeneutical injustice, none the less the collective exercise of the virtue could ultimately lead to the eradication of hermeneutical injustice. In so far as the exercise of the virtue at least sometimes involves the creation of a more inclusive hermeneutical micro-climate shared by hearer and speaker, its general exercise is obviously conducive to the generation of new meanings to fill in the offending hermeneutical gaps, and it is thereby conducive to reducing the effects of hermeneutical marginalization. In so far as this is so, the exercise of the virtue ultimately aims at the actual elimination of the very injustice it is designed only to correct for. This cheering reflection needs, however, to be tempered with the thought that hermeneutical marginalization is first and foremost the product of unequal relations of social power more generally, and as such is not the sort of thing that could itself be eradicated by what we do as virtuous hearers alone. Shifting the unequal relations of power that create the conditions of hermeneutical injustice (namely, hermeneutical marginalization) takes more than virtuous individual conduct of any kind; it takes group political action for social change. The primary ethical role for the virtue of hermeneutical justice, then, remains one of mitigating the negative impact of hermeneutical injustice on the speaker. From the point of view of social change, this may be but a drop in the ocean; still, from the point of view of the individual hearer's virtue, not to mention the individual speaker's experience of their exchange, it is justice enough.

Conclusion

I have painted a picture of two kinds of epistemic injustice, testimonial and hermeneutical, and two virtues that are such as to prevent or mitigate these injustices respectively: testimonial justice and hermeneutical justice. And I have argued that these virtues are hybrid virtues in that they can function as either intellectual virtues or ethical virtues or both. In the Introduction I suggested that a useful response to the demise of postmodernism is to develop new ways of discussing the ethics of power in our lives as knowers. This is one way of thinking about the contribution I have tried to make in elaborating the notions of testimonial and hermeneutical injustice. More importantly, by elaborating them in the idiom of virtue epistemology, I hope to have shown how theoretical work of a socially situated tenor can connect up with a historically rich and newly burgeoning philosophical approach to matters of value and knowledge, and I hope in particular to have shown that the virtue epistemological framework provides for an attractive non-inferentialist position in the epistemology of testimony. What has at any rate been explored here is an area of the first-order ethics of epistemic practice. I think the very idea that there *is* a first-order ethics of epistemic practice indicates one viable way in which our philosophical discussions of what it takes to be a knower could come more properly to reflect the fact that the human condition is, necessarily, a socially situated condition.

Part of the point of identifying virtues of epistemic justice on the part of hearers is to clarify and amplify our philosophical conception of what constitutes good epistemic conduct in the socially situated context. But, by implication, it is also to lay a foundation for a conception of correlative institutional virtues—virtues possessed, for instance, by the judiciary, the police, local government, and employers. Combating epistemic injustice clearly calls for virtues of epistemic justice to be possessed by institutions as well as by individuals. It would be nice to think that the virtues of testimonial and hermeneutical justice as I have constructed them might be more or less fit for purpose not only at the level of the individual but also at the level of the institutional. In exploring epistemic injustice as an ethical phenomenon, therefore, this book also points to the possibility of a different sort of treatment, one more directly concerned with institutional conduct, and so placed more squarely in the political frame. As I said at the outset, however, in terms of our philosophical understanding of epistemic injustice, the ethical is primary, and that, accordingly, has been my focus.

By exploring different forms of epistemic injustice, and by adopting the socially situated conception of epistemic subjects that is needed for such an exploration, we come to see that there is such a thing as epistemic justice, and that a philosophical framework that prescinds from matters of social identity and power could never give an account of it. I believe that the only way to fully understand the normative demands made on us in epistemic life is by changing the philosophical gaze so that we see through to the negative space that is epistemic injustice. That is what I have aimed to do in this book.

Bibliography

Alcoff, Linda Martín, 'On Judging Epistemic Credibility: Is Social Identity Relevant?', in Naomi Zack (ed.), *Women of Color and Philosophy* (Oxford: Blackwell, 2000).

Antony, Louise, 'Sisters, Please, I'd Rather Do It Myself: A Defense of Individualism in Feminist Epistemology', in Sally Haslanger (ed.), *Philosophical Topics: Feminist Perspectives on Language, Knowledge, and Reality*, 23, no. 2 (Fall 1995), 59–94.

Aristotle, *The Ethics of Aristotle: The Nicomachean Ethics*, trans. J. A. K. Thomson (London: Penguin, 1976).

Arpaly, Nomy, *Unprincipled Virtue: An Inquiry into Moral Agency* (Oxford: Oxford University Press, 2003).

Audi, Robert, *Epistemology: A Contemporary Introduction to the Theory of Knowledge* (London: Routledge, 1998).

Bartky, Sandra Lee, 'On Psychological Oppression', in her *Femininity and Domination: Studies in the Phenomenology of Oppression* (New York and London: Routledge, 1990).

Beauvoir, Simone de, *Memoirs of a Dutiful Daughter*, trans. James Kirkup (London: Penguin, 1959; originally published in French as *Mémoires d'une jeune fille rangée* (Paris: Librairie Gallimard, 1958).

Blais, Michael, 'Epistemic Tit for Tat', *Journal of Philosophy*, 84 (July 1987), 363–75.

Bloomfield, Paul, 'Virtue Epistemology and the Epistemology of Virtue', *Philosophy and Phenomenological Research*, 60 no. 1 (Jan. 2000), 23–43.

Blum, Lawrence, 'Stereotypes and Stereotyping: A Moral Analysis', in Ward E. Jones and Thomas Martin (eds.), *Immoral Believing*, Special Issue of *Philosophical Papers*, 33, no. 3 (Nov. 2004), 251–89.

Bovens, Luc, and Hartmann, Stephan, *Bayesian Epistemology* (Oxford: Clarendon Press, 2003).

Broadie, Sarah, *Ethics with Aristotle* (Oxford: Oxford University Press, 1991).

Brown, Rupert, *Prejudice: Its Social Psychology* (Oxford: Blackwell, 1995).

Brownmiller, Susan, *In Our Time: Memoir of a Revolution* (New York: Dial Press, 1990).

Burge, Tyler, 'Content Preservation', *Philosophical Review*, 102, no. 4 (Oct. 1992), 457–88.

——— 'Interlocution, Perception, and Memory', *Philosophical Studies*, 86 (1997), 21–47.

Castoriadis, Cornelius, *World in Fragments: Writings on Politics, Society, Psychoanalysis, and the Imagination*, ed. and trans. David Ames Curtis (Stanford, Calif.: Stanford University Press, 1997).

Coady, C. A. J., *Testimony: A Philosophical Study* (Oxford: Clarendon Press, 1992).

Craig, Edward, *Knowledge and the State of Nature: An Essay in Conceptual Synthesis* (Oxford: Clarendon Press, 1990).

Diamond, Cora, 'Wittgenstein, Mathematics and Ethics: Resisting the Attractions of Realism', in Hans Sluga and David Stern (eds.), *The Cambridge Companion to Wittgenstein* (Cambridge: Cambridge University Press, 1996).

Driver, Julia, 'The Conflation of Moral and Epistemic Virtue', in Michael Brady and Duncan Pritchard (eds.), *Moral and Epistemic Virtues* (Oxford: Blackwell, 2003).

Faulkner, Paul, 'David Hume's Reductionist Epistemology of Testimony', *Pacific Philosophical Quarterly*, 79 (1998), 302–13.

Fogelin, Robert, *A Defense of Hume On Miracles* (Princeton: Princeton University Press, 2003).

Foucault, Michel, *Discipline and Punish: The Birth of the Prison*, trans. Alan Sheridan, London: Penguin Books, 1977, 256. Originally published in French as *Naissance de la prison* (Paris: Editions Gallimard, 1975).

——— *Michel Foucault; Power/Knowledge; Selected Interviews and Other Writings 1972–1977*, ed. C. Gordon, trans. C. Gordon, L. Marshall, J. Mepham, and K. Soper (Hemel Hempstead: Harvester Wheatsheaf, 1980).

——— 'How Is Power Exercised?', trans. Leslie Sawyer from Afterword in H. L. Dreyfus and P. Rabinow, *Michel Foucault: Beyond Structuralism and Hermeneutics* (Hemel Hempstead: Harvester Press, 1982).

Fricker, Elizabeth, 'Against Gullibility', in B. K. Matilal and A. Chakrabarti (eds.), *Knowing from Words: Western and Indian Philosophical Analysis of Understanding and Testimony* (Dordrecht: Kluwer, 1994).

——— 'Second-hand Knowledge', forthcoming in *Philosophy and Phenomenological Research*.

Fricker, Miranda, 'Reason and Emotion', *Radical Philosophy*, 57 (1991), 14–19.

——— 'Why *Female* Intuition?', *Women: A Cultural Review*, 6, no. 2 (Autumn 1995), 234–48.

——— 'Intuition and Reason', *Philosophical Quarterly*, 45, no. 179 (Apr. 1995), 181–9.

——— 'Rational Authority and Social Power: Towards a Truly Social Epistemology', *Proceedings of the Aristotelian Society*, 98, no. 2 (1998), 159–77.

——— 'Confidence and Irony', in Edward Harcourt (ed.), *Morality, Reflection, and Ideology* (Oxford: Oxford University Press, 2000).

——— 'Pluralism without Postmodernism', in M. Fricker and J. Hornsby (eds.), *The Cambridge Companion to Feminism in Philosophy* (Cambridge: Cambridge University Press, 2000).

——— 'Life-Story in Beauvoir's Memoirs', in Claudia Card (ed.), *The Cambridge Companion to Simone de Beauvoir* (Cambridge: Cambridge University Press, 2003).

Fricker, Miranda, 'Powerlessness and Social Interpretation', *Episteme*, 3, nos. 1–2 (2006).

Gaita, Raimond, *Good and Evil: An Absolute Conception*, 2nd edn. (Abingdon, Oxon.: Routledge, 2004).

Gatens, Moira, *Imaginary Bodies: Ethics, Power and Corporeality* (London: Routledge, 1996).

Gelfert, Axel, 'Kant on Testimony', *British Journal for the History of Philosophy*, 14, no. 4 (2006), 627–52.

Gifford, Humfrey, in Norman Ault (ed.), *Elizabethan Lyrics*, (New York: Capricorn Books, 1960).

Gilligan, Carol, *In a Different Voice: Psychological Theory and Women's Development* (Cambridge, Mass.: Harvard University Press, 1982).

Goldie, Peter, *The Emotions: A Philosophical Exploration* (Oxford: Clarendon Press, 2000).

Goldman, Alvin, *Knowledge in a Social World* (Oxford: Clarendon Press, 1999).

Green, Leslie, 'Pornographizing, Subordinating, and Silencing', in Robert Post (ed.), *Censorship and Silencing: Practices of Cultural Regulation* (Los Angeles: Getty Research Institute for the History of Art and the Humanities, 1998).

Haraway, Donna, 'Situated Knowledges: The Science Question in Feminism and the Privilege of Partial Perspective', *Feminist Studies*, 14, no. 3 (1988), 575–99.

Hardwig, John, 'The Role of Trust in Knowledge', *Journal of Philosophy*, 88 (Dec. 1991), 693–708.

Hartsock, Nancy, *The Feminist Standpoint Revisited and Other Essays* (Boulder, Colo.: Westview Press, 1998).

Haslanger, Sally, 'On Being Objective and Being Objectified', in Louise M. Antony and Charlotte E. Witt (eds.), *A Mind of One's Own: Feminist Essays on Reason and Objectivity* (Boulder, Colo.: Westview Press, 1993/2002).

_____ 'Ontology and Social Construction', in S. Haslanger (ed.), *Philosophical Topics: Feminist Perspectives on Language, Knowledge, and Reality*, 23, no. 2 (1995), 95–125.

Hobbes, Thomas, *Leviathan*, ed. Richard Tuck (Cambridge: Cambridge University Press, 1991).

Hookway, Christopher, 'Epistemic *Akrasia* and Epistemic Virtue', in A. Fairweather and L. Zagzebski (eds.), *Virtue Epistemology: Essays on Epistemic Virtue and Responsibility* (Oxford: Oxford University Press, 2001).

Hornsby, Jennifer 'Speech Acts and Pornography', in Susan Dwyer (ed.), *The Problem of Pornography* (Belmont, Calif.: Wadsworth Publishing Company, 1995), 220–32.

_____ and Langton, Rae, 'Free Speech and Illocution', *Legal Theory*, 4 (1998), 21–37.

Hume, David, *An Enquiry Concerning Human Understanding*, ed. L A. Selby-Bigge, 3rd edn. (Oxford: Clarendon Press, 1975).

—— *A Treatise of Human Nature*, ed. L. A. Selby-Bigge, 3rd edn. (Oxford: Clarendon Press, 1975).

Jacobson, Daniel, 'Freedom of Speech Acts? A Response to Langton', *Philosophy and Public Affairs*, 24 (1995), 64–79.

Jaggar, Alison, 'Love and Knowledge: Emotion in Feminist Epistemology', in A. Garry and M. Pearsall (eds.), *Women, Knowledge, and Reality: Explorations in Feminist Philosophy* (Boston: Unwin Hyman, 1989).

James, Susan, 'Freedom and the Imaginary', in Susan James and Stephanie Palmer (eds.), *Visible Women: Essays on Feminist Legal Theory and Political Philosophy* (Oxford and Portland, Ore.: Hart Publishing, 2002).

Jones, Karen, 'Trust as an Affective Attitude', *Ethics*, 107, no. 1 (Oct. 1996), 4–25.

—— 'The Politics of Credibility', in Louise M. Antony and Charlotte E. Witt (eds.), *A Mind of One's Own: Feminist Essays on Reason and Objectivity*, 2nd edn. (Boulder, Colo.: Westview Press, 2002).

Jussim, Lee, and Fleming, Christopher, 'Self-fulfilling Prophecies and the Maintenance of Social Stereotypes: The Role of Dyadic Interactions and Social Forces', in C. Neil Macrae, Charles Stangor, and Miles Hewstone (eds.), *Stereotypes and Stereotyping* (New York and London: The Guilford Press, 1996), 161–92.

Kahneman, Daniel, and Tversky, Amos, 'On the Psychology of Predication', *Psychological Review*, 80 (1973), 237–51.

Keller, Evelyn Fox, and Longino, Helen (eds.), *Feminism and Science* (Oxford: Oxford University Press, 1996).

Kusch, Martin, *Knowledge by Agreement: The Programme of Communitarian Epistemology* (Oxford: Oxford University Press, 2002).

Langton, Rae, 'Subordination, Silence, and Pornography's Authority', in Robert Post (ed.), *Censorship and Silencing: Practices of Cultural Regulation* (Los Angeles: Getty Research Institute for the History of Art and the Humanities, 1998).

Lee, Harper, *To Kill a Mockingbird* (London: William Heinemann, 1960).

Lehrer, Keith, *Self-Trust: A Study of Reason, Knowledge, and Autonomy* (Oxford: Clarendon Press, 1997).

Leyens, Jacques-Philippe, Yzerbyt, Vincent Y., and Schadron, Georges, *Stereotypes and Social Cognition* (London: Sage Publications, 1994).

Lippmann, Walter, *Public Opinion* (New York: Free Press, 1965; first published 1922).

Lipton, Peter, 'The Epistemology of Testimony', *Studies in History and Philosophy of Science*, 29 (1998), 1–31.

Lovibond, Sabina, *Realism and Imagination in Ethics* (Oxford: Blackwell, 1983).

—— *Ethical Formation* (Cambridge, Mass., and London: Harvard University Press, 2002).

Lukes, Steven, *Power: A Radical View* (London: Macmillan, 1974).

Lyons, Jack, 'Testimony, Induction and Folk Psychology', *Australasian Journal of Philosophy*, 75, no. 2 (1997), 163–77.

MacIntyre, Alasdair, *After Virtue: A Study in Moral Theory* (London: Duckworth, 1981).

MacKinnon, Catharine, *Feminism Unmodified: Discourses on Life and Law* (Cambridge, Mass., and London: Harvard University Press, 1987).

Macrae, C. Neil, Stangor, Charles, and Hewstone, Miles (eds.), *Stereotypes and Stereotyping* (New York and London: The Guilford Press, 1996).

McDowell, John, *Mind and World* (Cambridge, Mass.: Harvard University Press, 1994).

—— 'Are Moral Requirements Hypothetical Imperatives?', in *Mind, Value and Reality* (Cambridge, Mass., and London: Harvard University Press, 1998), essay 4, p. 85; originally published in the *Proceedings of the Aristotelian Society*, supp. vol. 52 (1978), 13–29.

—— 'Virtue and Reason', in *Mind, Value, and Reality* (1998), essay 3; originally published in *The Monist*, 62 (1979), 331–50.

—— 'Knowledge by Hearsay' in *Meaning, Knowledge, and Reality* (Cambridge, Mass., and London: Harvard University Press, 1998), essay 19; originally published in B. K. Matilal and A. Chakrabarti (eds.), *Knowing from Words: Western and Indian Philosophical Analysis of Understanding and Testimony* (Dordrecht: Kluwer, 1994).

McEwan, Ian, *Enduring Love* (London: Vintage, 1998).

McGarty, Craig, Yzerbyt, Vincent Y., and Spears, Russell (eds.), *Sterotypes as Explanations: The Formation of Meaningful Beliefs about Social Groups* (Cambridge: Cambridge University Press, 2002).

Minghella, Anthony, *The Talented Mr Ripley—Based on Patricia Highsmith's Novel* (London: Methuen, 2000).

Montmarquet, James A., 'Epistemic Virtue', *Mind*, 96 (1986), 482–97.

—— *Epistemic Virtue and Doxastic Responsibility* (Lanham, Md.: Rowman and Littlefield, 1993)

Murdoch, Iris, *The Sovereignty of Good* (London: Routledge, 1970).

Nagel, Thomas, 'Moral Luck', in *Mortal Questions* (Cambridge: Cambridge University Press, 1979).

Nisbett, R., and Ross, L., *Human Inference: Strategies and Shortcomings of Social Judgement* (Englewood Cliffs, NJ: Prentice-Hall, 1980).

Nussbaum, Martha, 'The Discernment of Perception: An Aristotelian Conception of Private and Public Rationality', in *Love's Knowledge: Essays on Philosophy and Literature* (Oxford: Oxford University Press, 1990), 54–105.

—— *Sex and Social Justice* (New York and Oxford: Oxford University Press, 1999).

—— *Upheavals of Thought: The Intelligence of the Emotions* (Cambridge: Cambridge University Press, 2003).

O'Neill, Onora, *Constructions of Reason: Explorations of Kant's Practical Philosophy* (Cambridge: Cambridge University Press, 1989).

—— 'Vindicating Reason', in Paul Guyer (ed.), *The Cambridge Companion to Kant* (Cambridge: Cambridge University Press, 1992).

—— Reid, Thomas, *Inquiry into the Human Mind*, ed. Timothy Duggan (Chicago: University of Chicago Press, 1970); first published 1764.

Rosenthal, Robert, and Jacobson, Lenore, *Pygmalion in the Classroom: Teacher Expectation and Pupils' Intellectual Development* (New York: Holt, Rinehart and Winston Inc., 1968).

Ruddick, Sara, *Maternal Thinking: Towards a Politics of Peace* (London: The Women's Press, 1990).

Searle, J. R., *Speech Acts: An Essay in the Philosophy of Language* (Cambridge: Cambridge University Press, 1969).

Shapin, Steven, *A Social History of Truth: Civility and Science in Seventeenth-Century England* (Chicago and London: University of Chicago Press, 1994).

Sherman, Nancy, and White, Heath, 'Intellectual Virtue: Emotions, Luck, and the Ancients', in M. DePaul and L. Zagzebski (eds.), *Intellectual Virtue: Perspectives from Ethics and Epistemology* (Oxford: Clarendon Press, 2003).

Shklar, Judith, *The Faces of Injustice* (New Haven and London: Yale University Press, 1990).

Snyder, M., Tanke, E. D., and Berscheid, E., 'Social Perception and Interpersonal Behavior: On the Self-fulfilling Nature of Social Stereotypes', *Journal of Personality and Social Psychology*, 35, (1977), 656–66.

Spelman, Elizabeth, 'Anger and Insubordination', in A. Garry and M. Pearsall (eds.), *Women, Knowledge, and Reality: Explorations In Feminist Philosophy* (Boston: Unwin Hyman, 1989), 263–74.

Stangor, Charles (ed.), *Stereotypes and Prejudice: Essential Readings* (Philadelphia: Psychology Press, 2000).

Statman, Daniel, 'Moral and Epistemic Luck', *Ratio*, 4 (Dec. 1991), 146–56.

Steele, Claude M., and Aronson, Joshua, 'Stereotype Threat and the Intellectual Test Performance of African Americans', in Charles Stangor (ed.), *Stereotypes and Prejudice: Essential Readings* (Philadelphia: Psychology Press, 2000), 369–89.

Taylor, Shelley E., 'The Availability Bias in Social Perception and Interaction', in D. Kahneman, P. Slovic, and A. Tversky (eds.), *Judgement under Uncertainty: Heuristics and Biases* (Cambridge: Cambridge University Press, 1982), 190–200.

Tversky, Amos, and Kahneman, Daniel, 'Judgment under Uncertainty: Heuristic and Biases', *Science*, 185 (1974), 1124–31.

Wartenberg, Thomas E., 'Situated Social Power', in T. Wartenberg (ed.), *Rethinking Power* (Albany, NY: State University of New York Press, 1992).

Welbourne, Michael, *The Community of Knowledge* (Aberdeen: Aberdeen University Press, 1986).

—— *Knowledge* (Chesham, Bucks: Acumen, 2001).

White, Edmund, *A Boy's Own Story* (London: Picador, 1983).

Williams, Bernard, 'Interlude: Relativism', in *Morality: An Introduction to Ethics* (Cambridge: Cambridge University Press, 1972).

———'Deciding to Believe', in *Problems of the Self: Philosophical Papers 1956–1972* (Cambridge: Cambridge University Press, 1973).

———'Internal and External Reasons', in *Moral Luck: Philosophical Papers 1973–1980* (Cambridge: Cambridge University Press, 1981).

———'Moral Luck', in *Moral Luck: Philosophical Papers 1973–1980* (Cambridge: Cambridge University Press, 1981).

——— *Shame and Necessity* (Berkeley and Los Angeles: University of California Press, 1993).

———'Internal Reasons and the Obscurity of Blame,' in *Making Sense of Humanity and Other Philosophical Papers* (Cambridge: Cambridge University Press, 1995).

——— *Truth and Truthfulness: An Essay in Genealogy* (Princeton: Princeton University Press, 2002).

Williamson, Timothy, *Knowledge and its Limits* (Oxford: Oxford University Press, 2000).

Young, Iris Marion, 'Five Faces of Oppression', in Thomas E. Wartenberg (ed.), *Rethinking Power* (Albany, NY: State University of New York Press, 1992).

Young-Bruehl, Elisabeth, *The Anatomy of Prejudices* (Cambridge, Mass.: Harvard University Press, 1996).

Zagzebski, Linda, *Virtues of the Mind: An Inquiry into the Nature of Virtue and the Ethical Foundations of Knowledge* (Cambridge: Cambridge University Press, 1996).

——— Précis of *Virtues of the Mind, Philosophy and Phenomenological Research*, 60, no. 1 (Jan. 2000), 169–77.

Index